Death

Death in *Supernatural*

Critical Essays

Edited by AMANDA TAYLOR *and*
SUSAN NYLANDER

Foreword by Julian Richings
Afterword by Lynn S. Zubernis

McFarland & Company, Inc., Publishers
Jefferson, North Carolina

ISBN (print) 978-1-4766-6861-1
ISBN (ebook) 978-1-4766-3585-9

LIBRARY OF CONGRESS AND BRITISH LIBRARY
CATALOGUING DATA ARE AVAILABLE

Front cover image © 2019 lassedesignen/Shutterstock

Manufactured in the United States of America

*McFarland & Company, Inc., Publishers
Box 611, Jefferson, North Carolina 28640
www.mcfarlandpub.com*

Acknowledgments

We would like to thank the following individuals for their time and support of our project: Tamy Burnett, Layla Milholen, John Taylor, Julian Richings, Lynn S. Zubernis, the officers and organizers of the Southwest Popular/American Culture Association, Bonnie (the Bonnster) Nylander, and Stephanie Morris.

We are especially indebted to the creators, writers, cast, and crew of *Supernatural* for developing such a rich world that makes us think, laugh, and cry so often. We are proud to be part of the SPN Family.

Table of Contents

Resurrection

When Women Die

Grief and Grieving

Foreword

JULIAN RICHINGS

(AKA DEATH)

On the backlot set in Vancouver, I climbed into a 1959 Cadillac with the license plate "BUH BYE." It was cold, horribly early, and the big white beast of a vehicle handled like an oil tanker.

An assistant director pointed to a chalk mark on the pavement, barely visible amidst a confusion of cables, sandbags, and camera equipment. "That's your mark. Ready?" A stunned gasp from me. "You'll be fine," he said, banged on the roof, yelled "Rolling!" and said, "Welcome to the show!"

And, what a welcome it was! Footage of that early-morning drive was cut together with close-ups and wide shots of me walking along the sidewalk accompanied by Jen Titus' haunting rendition of "O, Death." The montage was to become one of the most celebrated character introductions in recent television history. What a gift for an actor.

And, it got better. My introduction was followed by an extended scene in a Chicago diner in which Death chastises Dean before handing over his ring. Everything is off-kilter. The diner looks ordinary enough, but there's a terrible storm raging outside, and the cubicles are full of dead bodies. "I invite you to contemplate how insignificant I find you," Death says, and that's just an opening salvo.

I had been given so much to play with. The dialogue harkened back to the formality of a previous age but was dripping with attitude. It put Dean squarely in his place, with relish (and mustard and a pickle). Death may be "old Dean, very old," but he's alive with a pulsing wit and a fascination with things human. Dean's "ridiculous bravado" is going to be taken down a peg. If Death's introduction had grand visual style, this second scene took it to another level verbally. So many colors, so many notes for me to play.

My role in the series evolved over the next few seasons, with Death dropping by for the odd visit. And, then my appearances expanded beyond the small screen. I began attending *Supernatural* conventions (cons), where I met in person thousands of people across the world.

I think this is where I first truly understood firsthand the full impact of *Supernatural* as a cultural force. I came to the realization that I was not merely playing a cool character; I was representative of something bigger, and the fanbase was engaging with Death on a deep sociological level.

Supernatural cons are unique and entirely different in tone to comic-cons. *Supernatural* fans are an interwoven international family. Fans celebrate their fictional heroes—Sam, Dean, Castiel—but also have a direct relationship with the actors who play them. Over the years, a happy confluence has evolved between the persona of each actor and the character they portray. The spontaneity and authenticity of Misha, Kim, Osric, and the boys in the band are greatly valued at cons and add resonance to the multifaceted *Supernatural* universe. Their appearances add to the mythology of the show itself.

The blurring of character/persona/actor is further celebrated in the widespread, gender-fluid cosplay of fans at these events, and continues in fan-based tributes like the Hillywood parodies, which are successful full-on productions in and of themselves.

Through my convention appearances, I came to realize the significance of Death, not only as a character in the show, but also as myself, Julian, the guy who plays Death, and a member of the *Supernatural* family.

For me, conventions are gatherings that celebrate not only the Winchester brothers but disparate members of the family, including Uncle Death, Cousin Kevin, and of course the Wayward Sisters, who so nearly generated their own spinoff series. In fact, an entire book could be written about the role of women in *Supernatural* and the fans' appetite for strong female leads, but that's for another volume of essays.

Photo-ops with Death are popular at cons. Hugs with Death, brushes with Death, and various scenarios are played out, such as someone offering Death a bribe of pizza to save their friend. Photo sessions are a mix of giddiness and nerves, always conducted with a great sense of fun, and with a knowledge of being part sacred, part profane.

One thing is certain; for *Supernatural* fans, death is not a taboo subject, but immediate and accessible, and as Death the character, I became the actor temporarily entrusted with the ring, the cane, and the suit. And, there's the thing: the role of Death is bigger than me. It goes beyond my work as an actor, my race, and gender. Appropriately, the Scythe was passed to Billie, played by Lisa Berry. And then, after Billie … who knows … we're only at Season Fourteen … and the show just keeps on rolling.

Since I stepped nervously into that white Cadillac back in Season Five, it's been a wonderful ride. *Supernatural* has impacted the lives of millions of fans worldwide. The show doesn't simply get old and hang in; it continues to connect with its audience in so many new and surprising ways. Yet, its very popularity puts it at risk of being considered somehow insubstantial. I disagree. The show and the *Supernatural* universe should be given serious consideration.

I'm delighted to introduce a book of in-depth essays exploring a subject that's close to me, and one that's pivotal in the show's continuing grip on our imagination—the matter of Death/death in *Supernatural*.

So welcome, dear reader. I know you will find this collection of essays to be a voyage as full of interest and enlightenment as life, and death, itself.

As the assistant director said as I climbed into my white chariot, "You'll be fine."

Enjoy.

Julian Richings is an actor who plays the role of Death on Supernatural. *He has played many similar roles; including the Ferryman in* Percy Jackson and the Lightning Thief, *plus an array of outsiders, misfits, doctors, and rock musicians over his forty year career. He has even been known to appear in the occasional comedy.*

"Oh, Hello Death!"

An Introduction

SUSAN NYLANDER *and*
AMANDA TAYLOR

In 2005, a young man arrives at his brother's apartment in the middle of the night saying, "Dad's on a hunting trip, and he hasn't been home in a few days." With that, our two heroes, Sam and Dean Winchester, begin an epic journey that would interfere with the social lives of fans and scholars alike. Thank Chuck for DVDs and streaming services, allowing fans and academics to pore over episodes again and again to glean each minor detail. The new discipline of *Supernatural* studies grows even as the series continues into a fourteenth season. This introduction serves to lay out the organization of this book, contextualize the various texts in the collection, and offer an overview and reminder of The Road So Far.

Supernatural made its debut in the fall of 2005 on a niche network, the WB, later CW. In the pilot episode, we see that Sam and Dean face early tragedy with the mysterious and violent death of their mother Mary, which leads their father John on a quest to find and kill the monster responsible. Being "raised as warriors," as Sam notes in the Pilot (1.01), to follow in John's footsteps, Sam and older brother Dean are bequeathed that quest as they assume the mantle of hunter. The nature of the show was at once both a familiar and novel concept. The show's creator, Eric Kripke, set his show on the road in the tradition of early television shows like *Route 66*, *The Fugitive*, and *Have Gun, Will Travel* but with a horror twist. In their black 1967 Chevrolet Impala, Sam and Dean follow two-lane blacktop in search of monsters, ghosts, ghouls, and even urban legends. The uncomplicated "Monster of the Week" format of Season One gives way to a greater story arc in Season Two and beyond.

Both the "Monster of the Week" procedural and the greater story arc formats have opened the door for scholars and academics to explore numerous themes and mythologies that *Supernatural* presents through thirteen seasons and counting. The "apocalyptic" story arc of Seasons Two through Five give way to seasonal arcs. Seasons Six and Seven deal with souls, identity, and power. In these seasons, Castiel tries to bring order to Heaven as the new God, inadvertently unleashing the Leviathans who come to embody and symbolize corporate power and greed in the series. After vanquishing the Leviathan leader Dick Roman at the end of Season Seven, Seasons Eight, Nine, and Ten, according to former showrunner Jeremy Carver, are a trilogy. In this trilogy, we learn about Purgatory (the monster afterlife), the Demon and Angel Tablets, and watch Sam come to terms with his identity as a hunter. As a whole, these three seasons are Sam's story, as he undergoes the Demon Tablet trials to shut the gates of Hell and rescue Dean from both demonhood and the Mark of Cain. The conclusion of Season Ten signals yet another arc shift as Death the Horseman (seemingly) dies at Dean's hands and the Darkness descends on the world. Season Eleven's arc traces the sibling rivalry of God (Chuck) and his sister, Amara, the Darkness, and introduces us to the British Men of Letters to take us into Season Twelve.

In Season Twelve, we learn that the British Men of Letters want to "make America safe" by re-training the American hunters. When American hunters prove intractable and unwilling to become mere tools, they are simply eliminated. In a move reminiscent of the American Revolution, Sam leads a band of American hunters against the British Men of Letters and comes out victorious against a better equipped army. That threat removed, Lucifer re-emerges as the birth of his son Jack draws near. The end of Season Twelve leaves us with an alternate universe, the birth of Lucifer's son, the deaths of Crowley and Castiel, and Mary trapped with an enraged Lucifer in the alternate universe.

Season Thirteen explores more than one alternate universe, the nature of the Nephilim through Jack, which also allows for a nature versus nurture study, and sees the return of many favorite characters, including the archangel Gabriel, AU versions of Bobby Singer, Kevin Tran, Charlie Bradbury, and a new, deadlier archangel Michael. Castiel's death at the end of Season Twelve did not leave fans grieving too long as we learn what happens to angels and demons when they die: they end in the Empty, where they are supposed to sleep forever. Castiel, somehow awakened by Jack, annoys the Empty's entity so much that Castiel is returned to Earth, though we are left to wonder if what is returned is fully and completely one hundred percent Castiel. At the time of writing, we eagerly anticipate the beginning of Season Fourteen.

We (the editors) came to *Supernatural* well after its premiere, and how we each came to the series has bearing both on how this collection came to be and for whom this collection is intended.

Susan's Road So Far

In September 2005, my father was put on hospice care, my mother was suffering from Alzheimer's disease, and I was caring for them both. At the same time, my sister was undergoing intensive chemotherapy. Oh, and I started graduate school. By May 2006, my parents and my sister were all deceased, and I was using grad school as a distraction from grief. Needless to say, a new television show on the WB network was not really on my radar that year. Fast forward a few years: I had written my master's thesis on Walt Whitman, his elegies, and the ways that Americans dealt with death throughout the nineteenth century. Yeah, I was working through some things.

Not long after that, I was finding my life on a more even keel, and that is when I came across episodes of *Supernatural* on the TNT network. What a revelation! This show had, to quote Calliope, "everything! Life, death, resurrection, redemption … all set to music you can really tap your toe to" ("Fan Fiction"). *Supernatural* became my new obsession.

Throughout the summer of 2012, I watched and re-watched the first seven seasons in preparation to watch Season Eight when it would begin, now on the CW, in the fall. The story arcs, the myriad themes, the fraternal relationship, and the music! It was the music that kept me enthralled. As a classic rock fan and radio disc jockey in my pre-academic life, the familiar tunes added to the love affair I was having with the boys and their constant road trip. The recaps or "Roads So Far" were intriguing. The video cuts that nailed the vocal and musical posts combined to create a visual and aural experience that enhanced the narrative the likes of which I had never seen. The ways in which the music furthers the story, the skillful blending of lyric as a form of added dialogue, and the endless insider rock music references captured my heart, and I had to marry this show. Did I say I was obsessed? Oh, yes, I was. Never one to keep things to myself, I had to share my obsession with my friend and grad school colleague, Mandy (Amanda) Taylor.

Mandy's Road So Far

I first came to *Supernatural* in the summer of 2012, between Season Seven and Season Eight. My friend and graduate school colleague Susan Nylander told me about a new show she had started watching. It was amazing, and I should start watching it *now* because she wanted, no, *needed*, someone to talk to about it. I spent two days at her house watching a carefully selected compilation of episodes—a few episodes from Season One, the opening episode and the last two episodes of Season Two—while Susan filled in the gaps with some judicious explication. At the end of Season Two's "All Hell Breaks Loose: Part 2," (2.22) I looked over at her with wide eyes and said the only thing that I could.

"Dude!"

Her smiling reply of, "I know, right?" sealed my fate.

So began my fanademic (fan + academic) relationship with *Supernatural.* I saw the narrative and academic possibilities within the first couple of episodes. With the guided tour through the first two seasons, I saw even more possibilities for inquiry and study. I accepted Susan's assignment to continue watching the series, keeping her updated as I went. As her time allowed, she would re-watch episodes with me. We texted frequently. I took notes and reported my observations; she added her observations. We had many discussions about what small details might mean; she expertly deflected my questions with you'll sees and just waits. Occasionally, she would ask me to tell her when I came to specific episodes.

One of these was "Two Minutes to Midnight" (5.21) in Season Five. At this point, Dean has rejected his destiny as archangel Michael's true vessel for the Apocalyptic showdown with Lucifer, whose true vessel is Sam. With time running out and the confrontation imminent, Sam and Dean have tracked down three of the four Horsemen of the Apocalypse and taken their rings in hopes to open a pathway to Hell and Lucifer's cage. Death's ring is the last one they need.

In a breakaway scene, Death arrives in Chicago driving a pearlesque 1959 Cadillac with Jen Titus' "O, Death" as a non-diegetic herald. Death is unhurried as he steps out of the car and walks along the city sidewalk. Most pedestrians moved aside for Death, although they didn't recognize him as such, except for one busy man talking on his cell phone. After the man collides with Death, Death casually brushes his shoulder and continues walking. As Death walks on and out of the camera's view, the man on the cell phone falls to his knees and collapses lifeless to the ground.

My text to Susan: Dude. I just love Death. Don't you?

Susan: Yeah. He's great, isn't he?

I hurried through the rest of the available seasons to prepare for Season Eight, both of us determined to find a way to make academic projects out of *Supernatural.* Eventually, we found a home for our *Supernatural* projects at the Southwest Popular Culture/American Culture Association (SWPACA) and its annual conference. Our first SWPACA presentation was in 2014—a collaborative paper on Death the Horseman, which became the impetus for this collection. Every year since, we have worked, and continue to work, with others to create a *Supernatural* studies segment of the conference. For us, it is not enough simply to watch the show. Every episode makes us think and rethink what has come before and speculate about what may come next. We are invested both as fans and scholars, two groups that think critically and deeply about the series in different and sometimes intersecting ways.

Supernatural *Scholarship*

Supernatural is a scholar's dream text, especially for English studies scholars, historians, cultural studies scholars, psychologists, musicologists, mythologists and folklorists, and others. The show draws on multiple belief systems, cultures, and mythoi to tell its stories, and the stories always have a particular twist. The scholarly conversations on *Supernatural* range from the mythology in the series to a study of the fandom, or "family" as *Supernatural* fans call themselves. One of the most thorough studies of the early seasons of the series is *TV Goes to Hell: An Unofficial Roadmap to Supernatural* edited by Stacey Abbott and David Lavery (2011). Covering Seasons One through Five, this collection dives into the apocalyptic nature of the series. *Supernatural and Philosophy: Metaphysics and Monsters … for Idjits*, edited by Galen A. Foresman (2013), investigates some of the philosophical issues the series raises, illustrating *Supernatural*'s uncanny ability to tackle hard and deep questions that may have multiple answers or no satisfactory answer at all.

Open-ended questions are one of *Supernatural*'s hallmarks—just when you think a question has been answered, or a plotline exhausted, they come up with a new twist, delighting and infuriating fans (and scholars) in the process. Books such as *Fan Phenomena: Supernatural* (Zubernis & Larsen), *Fangasm: Supernatural Fangirls* (Zubernis & Larsen), and *Family Don't End with Blood* (Zubernis) explore the fandom of *Supernatural* itself as well as the (at times troubled) relationships between the actors and fandom. The series has had a clear impact on actors, writers, and fans alike. For some fans, the series has helped them face and endure personal darkness they otherwise may not have survived.

This may be because, along with the hard and deep questions, *Supernatural* cannot help but explore darkness as well. Typically, monsters dwell in dark places, and killing them requires wading into this darkness. Arguably, the American cultural fascination with dark and monstrous things can be traced to the Gothic tradition. Melissa Edmundson's *The Gothic Tradition in Supernatural* explores this fascination, touching on several important themes and mythoi and serving as a touchstone for a few of the essays in this collection. *Television, Religion, and Supernatural: Hunting Monsters, Finding Gods* by Erika Engstrom and Joseph M. Valenzano III focuses on the relationship between religion and the series, specifically its relationship to Christianity and a general good vs. evil paradigm.

Our Project

Still missing in this body of scholarly work on *Supernatural* is a focused examination of death in the series. Our collection is the first step (of many others, we hope) in filling this gap. The collection offers a variety of ways to consider the importance and impact of death in the series, whether or not death is personified. Both Death the Horseman and reapers give viewers and the Winchesters someone/something to confront and resist, but death, the event, of course, may be harder for us to wrestle with.

Death is a subject most people shy away from. It has become one of the unmentionable topics; in fact, many people will discuss sex, religion, and politics before discussing the fate that awaits us all. Death is, of course, a fact of life and one that affects everyone in one way or another. Utilizing fiction to view, discuss, and understand difficult topics allows us a more comfortable space in which to confront the very realities we wish to avoid. Investigating this difficult topic through fiction then provides us a safe way to better make peace with the inevitable. This collection offers a way to do this, using *Supernatural* as an overall case study in death, dying, and grief.

While we would like this text to appeal to scholars who are interested in the ways that death is presented and represented in *Supernatural,* we would also like this text to be one that appeals to fans who would enjoy a deeper exploration of their favorite show and characters. It is with this in mind that we offer our collection of essays analyzing death in *Supernatural* with varied voices and styles.

The collection is split into various sections, allowing for essays on related topics to be grouped together. We begin with a section on *Supernatural*'s American pedigree; here you will find essays that tackle uniquely American ways of dealing with death.

In "Death American Style: Americana and a Cultural History of Death," Susan Nylander sets the stage for what is to come in a look at the ways that *Supernatural* reflects American pop culture, history, and death. Looking at the ways in which the show reflects ideals of American masculinity with regard to facing death, the so called "good death," and touching on the impact of the Civil War, Nylander offers a broad overview of *Supernatural*'s cultural identity. This essay grounds the series in its homage to Americana and opens the way for the next few essays that look at uniquely American death practices.

Rebecca Stone Gordon's "Got Salt? Human Remains and Haunting in *Supernatural*" explores the importance and use of human remains in the series. Focusing particularly on hauntings, those through ghosts or what Stone Gordon calls "material object remains," Stone Gordon argues that bodies are vital to *Supernatural.* Additionally, how those bodies are treated in the show offers insight into and reflects American cultural attitudes toward death and dying.

Sarah Elaine Neill's "A Familiar Soundscape: Existentialism, Winchester Exceptionalism and the Evolution of Death in *Supernatural*" argues that the musical soundscape of *Supernatural* is intimately tied with death and the past. The music signals important moments in the series, adds to the overall narrative, and creates associations for the viewers. Additionally, Neill explores the "philosophical nature" of the series, discussing existentialism and exceptionalism. Neill's essay adds a final touch to the more overt Americanist discussions of the series.

The next section of essays explores how folklore and specific myths contribute to attitudes toward and representations of death in the series. In "Blood, Death and 'Demonic Germ Warfare': Family and the Legend of Roanoke in *Supernatural*," Rebecca M. Lush examines how the series uses and repurposes the historical Lost Colony of Roanoke in the United States. Lush argues that *Supernatural* recontextualizes the myth in hopes of "solving" it but in reality, the show ends up repeating history instead. Lush claims that the use of this particular legend firmly casts *Supernatural* as both a symbol and reflection of American culture. As such, *Supernatural* can be read for its commentary on that culture at large by the way it (re)presents iconic American stories.

In "Wheelin' and Dealin: Crossroads Mythology, Deal-Making and Death in *Supernatural*," Racheal Harris employs folklore from the southern United States to examine the various types of deals made in the series. Harris argues that the deals the Winchester family makes shapes their attitudes toward death and dying. Of particular interest is the idea that death is not an end, but a beginning, or at least a transitional stage.

The next section of the collection builds on this idea of death as transition and avenue of transformation with a specific exploration of resurrection. Jessica George's "Death, Resurrection and the Monstrous Evolution of the Winchesters" investigates the problematic nature and consequences of resurrection, specifically the resurrections of Sam and Dean Winchester. George argues that each resurrection subtly and irrevocably changes each Winchester and brings them closer to monstrosity each time they rise from the dead. Drawing on monster theory and the Gothic tradition, George's essay helps us to see the consequences of defying the natural order.

Erin M. Giannini's essay "'When I come back, I'm gonna be pissed'": Signaling Narrative and Character Shifts Through Death in *Supernatural*" explores the ways death (and subsequent resurrection) refreshes both the narrative arcs and character development in the series. Giannini focuses on "significant" deaths of both Sam and Dean to show how both of them are able to take a different narrative direction or exhibit different characteristics after their death sojourn. Giannini argues that death does for *Supernatural* what regeneration does for *Doctor Who* and is a factor in *Supernatural's* longevity.

Moving on from resurrection, the collection next looks at the ways in which women are (mis)treated and shortchanged when it comes to death and dying in *Supernatural*, which has been and should be critiqued (and criticized) for its treatment of female characters. This is especially true with (at the time of writing) the CW's decision not to greenlight the coveted spinoff *Wayward Sisters*.

Anastasia Salter's "'The (Dead) Girl with the Dungeons and Dragons Tattoo': *Supernatural* and the Disposable Other" focuses on Charlie Bradbury. Salter examines the impact of Charlie's death on both the show and the fandom. Salter critiques the show for its general treatment of women and uses fan studies and fanfiction to show how the fandom has coped with and "fixed" Charlie's death. Salter argues that Charlie's death was both unnecessary and did not do justice to the "badassery" of the character. Instead of remaining the geekgirl icon and clear representative of the LGBTQ+ community, Charlie becomes just another female casualty because, it seems, the writers didn't quite know what to do with her.

In "'I prefer ladies with more experience': Virgins, Whores and Post-Feminine Death in *Supernatural*," Freddie Harris Ramsby explores the virgin/whore binary and how it influences the ways women die in the series, arguing that "virgins" get better, or at least somewhat less grisly, deaths than the "whores." Mary Winchester and Jessica Moore are held up as the "virgins" while demons Meg Masters and Ruby are held up as the "whores." Harris Ramsby argues that the "whores" exhibit post-feminist tendencies—particularly related to sex and sexuality—and that this contributes to their more violent deaths. Harris Ramsby couches all of this in a general critique of both the show's treatment of women overall and its tendency to privilege heteronormativity and masculinity.

The final section of the collection explores the ways *Supernatural* addresses grief and grieving, an often overlooked or underestimated aspect of death. In "Dean's Groundhog Day: Negotiating the Inevitability of Death via *Supernatural*," Michail-Chrysovalantis Markodimitrakis applies Freud's Uncanny and concepts of déjà vu and the death drive to an in-depth examination of Season Three's "Mystery Spot" (3.11). Markodimitrakis argues that "Mystery Spot" helps both Sam Winchester and the audience come to terms with the inevitability of death—at some point, no matter how many resurrections or divine interventions, Sam and Dean Winchester will die. So, too, will the viewers.

Finally, Amanda Taylor's essay "'In My Time of Dying': Lessons on Grief in *Supernatural*" investigates the series through the lens of grief scholars Elisabeth Kübler-Ross and Dorothy Becvar. Taylor analyzes the grief journeys of Bobby Singer, Sam Winchester, and Dean Winchester, showcasing each man's relationship with death (or Death, in Dean's case). Ultimately, Taylor argues that as we navigate these fictional grief journeys, we can more fully reconcile our own confrontations with mortality.

Though this collection is not comprehensive, we hope that it serves as the impetus for more *Supernatural* studies of the nature and character of Death/death, especially given that we have a new Horse(wo)man in Billie, who we learn has taken on the role and leadership as Death. So much to analyze in nearly 300 episodes.

What began as a niche show on a niche network has become much more. *Supernatural* has, in its thirteen seasons so far, surpassed all expectations. It has become the longest running show of its kind on the CW, created a legacy of charitable work through groups like Misha Collins' Random Acts and fundraising campaigns like Jared Padalecki's *Always Keep Fighting*, as well as his and Jensen Ackles' *You Are Not Alone, Love Yourself First,* and *You Are Enough* that have brought increased awareness to depression and suicide ideation. These campaigns and charities have raised millions of dollars, created an organization that trains fan volunteers to staff crisis hotlines—fans helping fans, and led the way to show what is possible when celebrities and fans work in tandem. This little show that could has done a lot of good in the world, brought joy to millions of viewers the world over, and has earned a place in academic scholarship that continues to grow. *Supernatural* studies is a growing field, and with this text, we offer our contribution to the canon.

American Traditions
and Attitudes

Death, American Style

Americana and a Cultural History of Death

SUSAN NYLANDER

"You don't know what you're a part of, Dean. You know, you had ancestors hacking the heads off vamps on the May-flower."—Samuel Campbell, "Exile on Main Street" (6.01)

At its foundation, *Supernatural* is an American show. Though *Supernatural* explores cultural myths and legends from around the world, the places and spaces the characters inhabit, the dialogue and story arcs, the very nature of the show itself is an American phenomenon, viewed through a lens that is uniquely American. From the classic muscle cars that traverse the two-lane blacktop arteries that weave their way through the heartland of the U.S., to the lead characters who take us on their journeys, the landscape, the language, and the locales are distinctly and distinctively American. It is no accident that Sam and Dean's birthplace is Lawrence, Kansas, a state that connects to so many others, the very heart of the country.

Supernatural's creator, Eric Kripke, Midwestern born himself, says that miles of two-lane blacktop and American metal in which to travel it is at the heart of the show. The Route 66 of it all, complete with funky motels and a classic rock soundtrack, screams Americana with a backward glance at what was and the wanderlust to see what is around the next bend. So, too, the boys' birthplace, Kansas, a state at war with its neighbor and the site of bloody massacres even before the Civil War broke out, is intentional. The border wars between Kansas and Missouri that would preface the bloodiest of American wars, the boys' surname Winchester, like the rifle that "won the West," as well as many other nods to American culture and history give the show its pedigree. The opening of *Supernatural* harkens to a not-too-distant past in American history when the nuclear family was the norm, American-made was the car to drive, Rock & Roll poured from every car radio, and the American way was the only way.

Supernatural's story opens in November 1983 when Ronald Reagan presents himself as the most American of presidents, complete with cowboy hat worn while astride a horse on his California ranch serving as the western White House, and his "Morning in America" optimism serves as a balm to the previous decades' cultural upheaval. The pilot episode's opening scene is indicative of this homey optimism as Mary brings Dean into baby Sam's nursery to kiss the infant goodnight. Before the title card, our idyllic scene gives way to horror as Mary burns on the ceiling, John is left a widower, and the children will become the ultimate latchkey kids.

Mary's death precipitates John's single-minded obsession to hunt down the creature that murdered his wife. Because of this "crusade," as adult Sam calls it in the pilot episode, John all but abandons the boys to their own devices, much as many other children in the 1980s were left on their own as women joined the workforce in record numbers, divorce rates skyrocketed, and economics required both parents to work, leaving them unable to stay home with their children. *Supernatural*, then, offers its audience a view of working and middle class American life with a side of horror and death.

Death the Horseman and death the event are given the American treatment in *Supernatural*. Sam and Dean offer us an American lens through which we view their experiences. Ultimately, this essay sets out to explore and demonstrate some of the ways in which *Supernatural* reflects how Americans have historically dealt with death as well as some of the ways it represents the American cultural history and traditions of death and mourning. Representing these traditions through fiction may help us not only understand historic traditions of death practices, but also offer us ways in which we may confront and deal with death in our own lives and in our own time.

Intimacy of Death

As a still fairly young country, the United States of America has a long history of war and struggle through 200-plus years of growth. It is in the nineteenth century that the American cultural identity begins to find its form, particularly during and after its seminal event, the Civil War. Death was a frequent visitor in the nineteenth century, and usually occurred at home, so people shared an intimacy with death that few today experience. With the prevalence of illness and accidents and the absence of antibiotics, a cold becomes fatal pneumonia and a cut finger becomes gangrenous, leading to infection, amputation, and possible death. Many women died in childbirth, and many infants never lived to see their second birthday. Death loomed everywhere in the most mundane of places and activities.

Because death was so frequent and so familiar, traditions were created, which brought order to the process of dying, death, and mourning. The *ars moriendi*, or rules for dying, were prescriptions for ensuring that those near death experienced what came to be called the "good death." What sounds like an oxymoron makes sense when we understand the belief systems that most Americans operated under in the eighteenth and nineteenth centuries. Overwhelmingly Christian in belief, many Americans looked to a heavenly reunion with their loved ones, and the "good death" gave them comfort and assurance of this belief.

This "good death" required witnesses, preferably loved ones who could see the last moments and hear the final words in order to be assured of the lost one's salvation. Witnessing the death of a loved one was followed by laying out the dead in the family parlor or other common room prior to burial. The community, therefore, had the opportunity to spend time with the corpse, contemplating mortality in a way we seldom do today. These intimate moments of peaceful passing among gathered family and friends were threatened with the start of the Civil War. From April of 1861 to April of 1865, Americans fought one another in the bloodiest conflict the nation had ever seen, and young men, both North and South, went far from home to do battle.

With Americans increasingly dying away from home, families could not be assured that their loved ones died a "good death," which included hearing their loved one's final words. Drew Gilpin Faust recounts the importance of this particular tradition of the *ars moriendi*. She states,

> Last words also imposed meaning on the life narrative they concluded and communicated invaluable lessons to those gathered around the deathbed. This didactic function provided a critical means through which the deceased could continue to exist in the lives of survivors. The teachings that last words imparted served as lingering exhortation and a persisting tie between the living and the dead [10–11].

John Winchester's last words to his son, Dean, at the end of "In My Time of Dying" (2.01) offer both hoped for closure and prophecy as he at once praises Dean for his steadfast role in the family and warns him to "watch out for Sammy." Faust goes on to say that "To be deprived of these lessons, and thus this connection seemed unbearable..." (11). In the episode that followed John's death, "Everybody Loves a Clown" (2.02), the brothers watch their father's corpse burn, and Dean denies Sam this connection when he tells Sam that their father had no last words. Thinking he is protecting his little brother, he is only delaying the inevitable and must later confess what their father said about Sam's potential future: that Dean must try to save Sam or kill him. The good death requires not merely witnessing a loved one's death or hearing their final words, but the disposition of the remains must occur. In previous times, this required a family's and community's efforts as well. Sam and Dean take it upon themselves to cremate John's body, which is another example of the intimacy and responsibility required of families and friends in an earlier time.

Changing Attitudes Regarding Death

Prior to the nineteenth century, overcrowded and unsanitary church graveyards held the dead, but things began to change as the living required more space in urban areas. Cities became increasingly populated, and planners looked for solutions that would alleviate the unsightly necropoli within and without the cities' limits. It would turn out to be a group of horticulturists who would find the answer. Rural cemeteries, large park-like burial spaces, began to create new and didactic relationships between the living and the dead.

The rural cemetery movement in the U.S. began in Boston with Mt. Auburn Cemetery in 1831, and the graveyard became a place for the living to commune with, and learn from, the dead. Families and even fraternal organizations bought plots of land to secure space for their members. Mt. Auburn became a must-see tourist destination. Carriages would tour the lush grounds, their inhabitants marveling at the well-designed spaces and landscaping. The dead, themselves, were seen in a new light, and the ways that people remembered and memorialized their dead changed.

Charles O. Jackson says that in the nineteenth century, Americans underwent a shift in how the dead were cared for, including presentation of the corpse, e.g., coffins began to be referred to as caskets, a repository for "something valuable" (303). He goes on to say,

> The dead had become precious. The attention to the burial receptacle and to the body constituted assurance that the deceased, properly reposed in an aesthetically pleasing setting, almost lifelike in appearance, would not really die for a long time to come. It was a natural corollary to the growing commitment to communion with the dead in the nineteenth century [304].

This view of, and communion with, the dead along with funerary accoutrements, in sentimental and tender displays, would continue into the twentieth century. Cemeteries became park-like settings to give mourners an opportunity to pay respects, grieve, and contemplate their own mortality surrounded by nature.

Rural cemeteries are commonplace today, and in *Supernatural*, most of the graveyards that Sam and Dean visit are those with lush landscaping, rolling hills, and artistic markers. A scene in "What is and What Should Never Be" (2.20) finds Dean visiting John's "grave" to talk with him, and in "Children

Shouldn't Play with Dead Things," (2.04) Sam goes to Mary's grave marker, even with no body buried there, to bring her John's dog tags. Though John's grave was merely a figment of Dean's fevered imagination thanks to Djinn poisoning, the representation of the space is indicative of Dean's experience in his waking life. While Dean finds Sam's visit to Mary's "grave" uncomfortable and unnecessary, Sam finds solace in having a place to visit. Dean says, "She doesn't even have a grave. There was no body left after the fire [...] You want to go pay your respects to a slab of granite put up by a stranger?" Sam reminds his brother that, "It's not about a body or a casket; it's about her memory, and after Dad, it just feels like the right thing to do." Dean replies, "It's irrational."

Dean's resistance to Sam's desire to visit Mary's grave is not an uncommon reaction as many modern people would rather ignore the thought of death and dying. It is much easier to do in our modern age when death has been professionalized and institutionalized. The lack of intimacy most Americans have with death allows us to avoid thinking about our own mortality. We send our sick and dying to hospitals to be cared for by disinterested others and allow professionals to prepare and bury the bodies of our loved ones. Care for the dying, post-mortem care for the dead, building a casket, and digging a grave were all once done by friends and family. What was once a community event has now become a paid profession thereby creating distance between the griever and the grieved.

Sam and Dean's intimacy with death and later Death the Horseman stems from their mother's violent murder, their predestined roles as angelic vessels, and of course, their jobs as hunters. This intimacy grows through the seasons (thirteen to date) as evidenced through their handling of human remains. While burning bones becomes routine, handling a victim's severed head in Season Two's "Bloodlust" (2.03) is an opportunity for Dean to tease Sam's grossed out reaction to having to open the mouth where they discover a set of retractable vampire teeth. Contrast this with later episodes like Season Five's "Sam, Interrupted," (5.11) in which Sam uses a bone saw to crack open a victim's skull to pull out his sucked-dry brain or Season Five's "My Bloody Valentine" (5.14) when the boys casually pick up and joke with human hearts. The routine handling of corpses creates an intimacy that most people, certainly most Americans, do not share.

Sam and Dean provide post-mortem care to their loved ones in the form of hunters' funerals. We see John's funeral pyre as the boys stand in silence watching their father's body burn. They burn the body of their newly-discovered brother Adam in similar fashion in Season Four's "Jump the Shark" (4.19). Sam and Dean assist Bobby in burning the body of Bobby's wife Karen, who had returned from the dead as a zombie in "Dead Men Don't Wear Plaid" (5.15). In Season Seven, we are told that Sam and Dean burned Bobby's remains, but Bobby's spirit manages to attach to an object that the boys later burn, which finally puts him to rest ("Survival of the Fittest"). The ritual of building a pyre, swaddling a corpse, and watching the body burn to ash seems to be common in the community of hunters as we see the same type of pyre and hunter's funeral in Season Ten's "The Prisoner" (10.22) when the boys burn Charlie Bradbury's body and in Season Twelve's "Celebrating the Life of Asa Fox" (12.06) when Asa and two other hunters killed at Asa's wake are set alight.

While hunters' funerals are not generally recommended in suburban backyards, most people cannot imagine having to so intimately perform any kind of post-mortem care for their loved ones as was the norm in past centuries. Yet, it is not merely the way we interact with the dead that is different today. New machines and innovations of the nineteenth century allowed for the dead to be displayed and disposed of in new fashion.

Bodies and New Technology

As the modern funerary industry rose out of the Civil War, new technology emerged, such as embalming, which allowed for preservation of the corpse so that those who died on a faraway battlefield would be able to be buried at home. Abraham Lincoln's son, Willie, died while his father was president. The child was embalmed, and three years later, Lincoln's embalmed body made the long journey from Washington to Illinois with multiple stops for viewings along the way. Embalming allowed a communion with the dead that eventual burial did not. In fact, newspaper accounts of Willie Lincoln's embalming mention how beautiful in death the child was: Thomas J. Craughwell writes, "The little boy looked so lovely that the Sunday Morning Chronicle reported, 'The embalming was a success and gave great satisfaction to all present'" (qtd. in Nylander 57). While in Washington, the boy's body was placed in a tomb, not buried. Not content with a photographic representation, Lincoln reportedly would sit with the boy's corpse in the mausoleum. When Lincoln's body made the journey to Springfield, Willie's body was brought home, too. After the Civil War, the funeral industry began to promote embalming as a means of sanitation and a way to respect the corpse for a better viewing. Sam and Dean seldom have to worry about embalming fluid as when they generally salt and burn a body, it is either skeletal remains, or as in the case of John, Bobby, Charlie, Asa Fox, or other hunters, the bodies are newly dead, and no embalming is necessary prior to being placed on the funeral pyre.[1]

While communion with the dead evolved through the years to include wakes and viewings, we see a number of instances in *Supernatural* when vigils are kept with dead or dying individuals. The episode "In My Time of Dying"

(2.01) finds John sitting with Dean, who is comatose and on life support, while Dean's spirit hovers nearby berating his father's seeming lack of concern for his son's imminent death. Dean lays out Sam's body and monologues his grief and regrets in "All Hell Breaks Loose: Part 2" (2.22), and Sam brings his brother's body back to Dean's room in the bunker at the end of Season Nine's finale, "Do You Believe in Miracles?" (9.23). As tears run down Sam's face, he contemplates his brother's battered body that Sam has obviously washed prior to laying him across his bed. This communion with a loved one's corpse harkens back to that earlier age when families cared for their dead without an intercessor. These moments in the show remind us that death will come for us and those we love, and no matter how well we believe we are prepared for it, the emotions of these losses always seem to catch us unawares.

Photographs and Memories

Another new technology of the nineteenth century is photography. For the first time in history, the average or common person could have a visual representation of their physical form. Before daguerreotypes and photographs, only royalty or nobles could afford to sit for a portrait, but many Civil War soldiers, both Northern and Southern, visited photographic studios to have their picture taken, which may have been a comfort to their loved ones if the soldier was later lost in battle. As I wrote in *Whitman, Elegy, and the Nineteenth Century Culture of Death and Mourning*, photographs remind those grieving of their lost loved ones, and viewing the likeness may recreate memories as well as allow them to "'re-place' the lost loved one within the context of past and present" (17).

> Roland Barthes sees in a photograph "the return of the dead." Barthes believes photography works to establish that the "referent" or object of the photograph has existed, was real at the time the photo was taken, and viewing a photograph allows the spectator to see for him/herself that reality better than any painting would. Barthes says that, "The Photograph does not necessarily say what is no longer, but only for certain what has been. This distinction is decisive." If, however the subject of a particular photograph is no longer living, the beholder may be able to "reanimate" the deceased in the mind [17–19].

We see this reanimation play out more than once in *Supernatural*. The importance of visual representation is evident for Sam and Dean right from the beginning of the series. In the pilot episode, Sam has a photograph of Mary and John, which sits on a bookshelf in the apartment he shares with Jessica. It is the same framed photo that adorned Mary's nightstand that we briefly see before her death. Sam later says, "If it weren't for pictures, I wouldn't even know what Mom looked like" (1.01). Dean's angry reaction to this may be because photographs are what allow his four-year old self to "reanimate" his mother, to hold onto the memories he has of Mary that Sam does not, and may explain why those photographs play such a vital role in later episodes. For many years, Dean keeps a photograph in his wallet. This photo of Mary and himself, as well as pictures of the family unit posed in front of the family home, show up in various episodes as reminders of what once was for the Winchesters.

The photo of Mary and the toddler Dean finds a place of honor when Dean finally gets his own room in the Men of Letters bunker in Season Eight's episode "Everybody Hates Hitler" (8.13). As Dean is decorating his room with the physical items that matter the most to him, such as his weapons and his vinyl record albums, he tenderly removes the photograph from his wallet and places it gently upon his desk where he can see it from many places in the room. By having this visual representation, Dean is able to keep Mary "alive" in some ways. It is not surprising, then, that Sam uses both of the photographs to try to reach Dean in the Season Ten finale, "Brother's Keeper" (10.23), as Dean has determined that he will never be free of the Mark of Cain and is convinced by Death the Horseman that Sam must die. These photographic touchstones keep Dean from killing his brother, using Death's scythe on its owner instead.

The power of photography is evident in Season Five's "Abandon All Hope" (5.10) when Bobby insists that Jo, Ellen, Sam, Dean, and Castiel all pose for a photograph with him the night before they will hunt Lucifer. At the end of the episode, after Jo and Ellen's sacrificial deaths, the photograph is laid on the fire to burn, a metaphoric hunters' funeral for the two women who gave their lives so that the Brothers Winchester would live to fight another day.

Heroic and Sacrificial Deaths

John, Sam, and Dean Winchester all represent the myth of the rugged individual associated with the building of American culture, especially the settling of the Western states following the Civil War. The up-by-his-bootstraps American hero is a staple of books, movies, and TV shows. Robert A. McDermott describes much of John's and Dean's characters when he states:

> In contemporary American culture, individualism is associated with anticommunity values, with the conventional male ideal of the solitary hero. The popular idea of individualism, like the prevalent idea of freedom, is tied to wanting one's own—one's own way, one's own space, one's own style, one's own income and security, one's own control of family and relationships. There is a strong tradition […] that espouses an individualism of context and relation.

John passes his anticommunity views on to Sam and Dean, who live and hunt on the margins of society, both the greater society and the hunter community as well. Though they have hunter friends and acquaintances, their father cautions them to keep their distance from most hunter gatherings. The freedom that Sam and Dean experience on the open road is a double-edged sword for both of them as Sam strives to find a normal life away from hunting and Dean longs for a real home. Yet, both brothers embody the myth of the rugged individual as they seek to live life on their own terms as well as die on their own terms.

Much folklore exists in American history with regard to how heroes should face their deaths. Heroic and sacrificial deaths often become the call to action for others: for example, "Remember the Alamo," which Sam Houston used to encourage his troops in Texas' fight for independence. Others used the same rallying cry ten years after the fact when the U.S. went to war with Mexico. Though a victory for the Mexican army under General Santa Anna, the siege and battle at the Alamo mission in February and March of 1836 established Jim Bowie, William Travis, Davy Crockett, and others as heroes of the Texas independence movement. Following Texas' annexation to the U.S., they became American martyrs and heroes, which allowed "Remember the Alamo" to be revived when going to war against Mexico in 1846.

Seeking revenge for those who die, whether in an established war or not, is certainly not a solely American phenomenon; feelings of revenge are a part of the human condition after all, but there are myriad examples throughout American history when revenge is the motive for all manner of quests and crusades. For example, cavalry men followed Teddy Roosevelt's charge up San Juan Hill to the shouts of "Remember the Maine!" and war was declared on Japan following the surprise attack on Pearl Harbor on that "day of infamy" December 7, 1941. The infamous date *Supernatural* fans know is November 2, 1983, the day that Azazel steps foot in Sam's nursery.

Mary Winchester's death leads directly to John Winchester's war with demonkind. John's anger, grief, and single-minded need for payback bring his sons into the "family business," and revenge then becomes the motivating factor in their lives. As Sam says in the pilot, "Dean, we were raised like warriors" (1.01). Their father's determination to hunt down and kill the demon who killed Mary, and John's desperation to keep his sons safe, lead to the boys living on their own much of the time, with Dean acting as mother, father, and brother for Sam. This pseudo-military training John gives the boys shows up in many conversations about pay grades, weaponry, and death.

In the first episode of Season Two, "In My Time of Dying" (2.01), Dean is mortally wounded and on life support when his reaper Tessa comes for him. He tells her that he cannot go with her as his family is counting on him in this current war. She tells him that he is not the "first soldier I've plucked from the field. They all feel the same. They can't leave. Victory hangs in the balance. But they're wrong. The battle goes on without them.... It's an honorable death, a warrior's death." Dean replies, "There's no such thing as an honorable death." Dean may not see honor in his death at that moment, but he is certainly willing to sacrifice his own life for Sam.

Later, in "All Hell Breaks Loose: Part 2" (2.22), when Dean has sold his soul to bring Sam back from the dead, Bobby notes the sacrificial family trait when he says, "What is it with you Winchesters, huh? You? Your dad. You're both just itching to throw yourselves down the pit." Dean reminds Bobby that he was brought back and should have been dead months earlier, saying that he wants his life to "mean something" through Sam's survival. For Dean, his whole life has been about protecting his younger brother, and when he "fails" in his mission to keep Sammy safe, he does the only thing that seems right at the time; he sacrifices his life and soul for Sam's because this is what gives his own life meaning.

All three of the Winchester men die sacrificial deaths. There is much American mythos about "dying with one's boots on," i.e., meeting death while standing, not lying in a hospital, or any other, bed. From Old West gunslingers to soldiers, the male idea of a heroic death is one that permeates American literature, both textual and visual. The "good death," dying in one's bed surrounded by family after a long life is not what John or Dean expect, but it is what Sam hopes for. John tells his boys in "Dead Man's Blood" (1.20) that he does not expect to live beyond the showdown with Azazel, and Dean assures Sam that he anticipates dying "on the job." Sam's longed for normal life is elusive for him as well.

All three Winchesters meet death on their feet more than once. The earliest example is in the Season One episode "Faith" (1.12) when Dean is electrocuted and suffers irreparable heart damage. Using humor, Dean remains stoic, insisting that Sam take care of the car "or I will haunt your ass." Knowing his fate, Dean checks himself out of the hospital ("where the nurses aren't even hot"), prepared to die on his own terms. Throughout the episode, Sam is determined to find some kind of cure for his brother, yet Dean resists Sam's efforts, pushing the younger man away any time he tries to help. Weakened by his damaged heart, Dean moves slowly and Sam offers his arm to help, yet Dean slaps him away saying, "get off me." The idea of being helpless or needing support is abhorrent to Dean, for it is the antithesis of his concept of what it is to be a man, to be a hunter, to be a Winchester. When he is "healed" by the Reverend Roy via a "reaper on a leash," and finds out that a young man has died in his place, he is angry at Sam for bringing him to this place and this result. Dying "on the job" or as a sacrifice for another, especially Sam, is one thing, but this for Dean feels wrong and gets in the way of his dying a "good death" as defined by his hunter's code.

Three sacrificial deaths in particular lead to further development of the story arc in the first several seasons of the series. The Winchester patriarch trades his life/soul for Dean's in Season Two's opener "In My Time of Dying," (2.01) while in the season's finale, Dean trades his soul to bring back Sam in "All Hell Breaks Loose Part 2" (2.22). Sam's sacrificial leap into Lucifer's pit in the Season Five finale, "Swan Song," (5.23) is the culmination of Eric Kripke's time at the show's helm. These three deaths are each important to *Supernatural's* narrative, but John's, in particular, sets up what is to come for the next three seasons.[2]

At the end of "In My Time of Dying," John insists on seeing with his own eyes that Dean has been pulled from the brink of death and will be all right. John then faces Azazel and hands over the Colt, willingly ready to accept his fate and keep his part of the deal. Dean did not see the way his father faced death, so he is left to wonder at the circumstances, whether his father met death the "right way," the way Dean expected him to. Dean's conversation with Sam in Season Two's "Crossroad Blues" (2.08) demonstrates this idea of meeting death on one's feet, or as Sam says later, "Blaze of Glory style." Dean's anguish at the thought of his father suffering so that he, Dean, could live is obvious as he struggles to understand John's sacrifice as Sam notes that John saved Dean's life, Dean says,

> Exactly. How am I supposed to live with that? You know the thought of him—wherever he is right now—I mean he spent his whole life chasing that yellow-eyed son of a bitch. He should've gone out fighting. That was supposed to be his legacy, you know? Not bargaining with the damn thing. Not this.

Sam notes that the many lives John has saved throughout his life and his passing on of what he has learned to his boys is John's legacy, and they should honor that by continuing what he began.

Sam's insistence that they continue to fight the good fight is taken to the extreme at the end of Season Two when Sam dies, and Dean, regardless of what he said earlier about not bargaining with demons, sells his soul to bring Sam back. Sam reminds Dean of his hypocrisy throughout Season Three as the younger brother hunts for a way to keep Dean from going to Hell at the end of his one-year deal. Dean once more resists Sam's help, and his trip to Hell and subsequent resurrection pave the way for the final showdown leading to the Apocalypse and Sam's great sacrifice.

At the end of Season Five with the final battle looming, Sam sees only one option. He must agree to be Lucifer's vessel, hoping to overwhelm the Devil long enough to hurl himself into the cage where he will be locked away forever with Satan himself. The climax of Season Five's "Swan Song" (5.22) and Sam's sacrificial death for all of humanity is aided by the presence of his older brother. It is only because of his love for Dean, the memories of their lives together, that allows Sam to overpower Lucifer and regain control of his body long enough to hurl himself, along with Lucifer's brother Michael, into the gaping maw that the Horsemen's rings have opened. This battle and sacrifice take place in Stull Cemetery, reminiscent, not of the lovely rural cemetery where Mary's headstone resides, but of Boot Hill where many an outlaw and cowboy made his final resting place.

When Sam, minus his soul, is resurrected by Castiel, it does not take Dean long to know that his brother is "not right." Once the problem is determined to be a missing soul, Dean does not hesitate to make intercession with Death the Horseman to see that Sam's soul is restored in "Appointment in Samarra"[3] (6.11). Once he has his little brother back with him, whole and intact, Dean again takes on the role that gives his life meaning: "watch(ing) out for Sammy." Dean's plan for himself is to meet his fate on his own terms.

In "Trial and Error," (8.14) while telling Sam that he needs his younger brother to be safe and live a long happy life, Dean says "I'll tell you what I do know; I'm going to die with a gun in my hand. That's what I have waitin' for me. That's *all* I have waitin' for me." Dean reiterates this many times throughout the series. In Season Twelve's "Celebrating the Life of Asa Fox" (12.06), Dean says that there is no better way to go out than on the job, and later in "Who We Are," (12.22) as the boys are locked in the Bunker losing breathable air, Sam asks Dean if this is the way he pictured them going out. Dean reminds him that, "You know it's not." Their frequent references to going out "guns blazing" is well suited to the show's American attitudes regarding masculinity, moral determination, and mortality. This is nowhere more evident than in the next few minutes of this episode when Dean is at last able to put a grenade launcher to good use blowing through the bunker's concrete wall and to a way out.

As they dig up a grave to salt and burn bones in "Into the Mystic," (11.11), Dean says, "So no retirement, huh?" Sam replies, "You're the one who's always wanted to go out 'Blaze of Glory' style, preferably while the Bon Jovi song is playing." Dean retorts with an Elton John lyric: "I'm a candle in the wind," and later in the season in "Alpha and Omega (11.23), Dean details his last wishes as he readies to go on a suicide mission to kill Amara, the Darkness.

As our heroes stand before Mary's grave marker in a Kansas rural cemetery, Sam seems to be going through the usual "final script" when he tells Dean that he does not have to go on this mission, and of course, Dean says he must. After telling Castiel that he, Dean, must "do this alone," he becomes upbeat, telling the group, "I want a big funeral. I'm talkin' epic: open bar, choir, Sabbath cover band, and Gary Busey reading the eulogy … and for my ashes, I like it here … yeah, you know as far as eternal resting places go." This peaceful setting is exactly what the original members of the Rural Cemetery Movement had in mind when they began their effort in Massachusetts. Dean's cavalier attitude is pure American bravado; another facet of dying with one's boots on is to be unconcerned with one's personal safety as long as others' lives are saved or the mission is completed successfully. This is particularly true as it relates to Dean's sense of responsibility to see that Sam remains safe.

At the very heart of *Supernatural* is the bond of the fraternal relationship. Dean's care for Sam and Sam's love for his older brother, the "two of them against the world," as Marie notes in "Fan Fiction," (10.05), all combine to tell a story of brotherly love that resonates for many reasons. Sam and Dean are representative of sibling relationships throughout literary history. Their bond and their battles teach us about family feuds, anger, and forgiveness. The American Civil War is often painted in this light of a family dispute, of brother against brother, and *Supernatural* often uses this metaphor as well as allusions to the war, especially as Sam and Dean trod the land where brother did battle brother.

Death's Release at the Site of the "Battle of Carthage"

In Season Five's "Abandon All Hope" (5.10), Sam and Dean go to Jasper, Missouri to try to head off Lucifer's release of the Horseman, or as Bobby Singer calls him, "The Pale Rider in the Flesh," "Big Daddy Reaper" and "The Angel of Death." According to the lore, Bobby says that, "The angel of death must be brought into this world at midnight through a place of awful carnage. Now, back during the Civil War, there was a battle in Carthage—a battle so intense the soldiers called it 'the battle of hellhole,'" but in reality, the Battle of Carthage was not exactly the bloodbath Bobby makes it out to be.

According to Kevin McClintock's article ("Hollywood Strikes Out Again"), the *Supernatural* writers got it all wrong. McClintock says, "It's a mere skirmish compared to colossal battles such as Gettysburg or Bull Run." The actual Battle of Carthage took place on July 5, 1861, a mere three months after the start of the war.

Civil War Trust notes that Union Col. Franz Sigel and his men were sent to the area to disperse a band of rebels. Governor Claiborne Jackson, along with his militiamen, battled with Sigel and his Union troops before Sigel received information that Confederate troops were on their way, though these were actually "unarmed recruits." After an artillery battle,

> Sigel ordered a withdrawal into the town. The Confederate pursuit climaxed with a firefight in the town square, where Jackson's men were ultimately unable to dislodge or destroy Sigel's force before he continued the retreat to Sarcoxie. The battle sustained Confederate hopes for the loyalties of the state and paved the way for the Battle of Wilson's Creek a month later.

A more likely battle to be called the "Battle of Hellhole," would be the Battle of Antietam, also known as the Battle of Sharpsburg depending upon what region of the country one is from (Antietam in the North and Sharpsburg in the South). With 22,717 casualties, Antietam is the site of the single bloodiest day in the four years of the war. Both McClellan's and Lee's troops were so badly bloodied, there was no clear winner following Lee's retreat back into Virginia, but Lincoln called it a victory, allowing him to issue his Emancipation Proclamation within days.

The *Supernatural* writers/researchers have logistics to overcome such as time and distance. Leaving Bobby's Sioux Falls, South Dakota home to head to Jasper County, Missouri in order to stop Lucifer requires that the site they travel to will be a reasonable distance. At a distance of 500 miles, it would certainly take several hours for Sam, Dean, Ellen, Jo, and Castiel to get to their destination, so finding a nearby historical battlefield may require some fudging of specific facts. Something not in dispute, however, is *Supernatural*'s tribute to Detroit's number one product.

American-Made Metal

The cars used in *Supernatural* are almost exclusively American-made and of the vintage variety. The Four Horsemen drive vehicles that were once the pride of Detroit aka Motown (War's cherry red Mustang, Famine's fleet of sleek, black SUVs, Pestilence's rattletrap AMC Pacer, and Death's pale Caddie).[4] These American-made cars, along with most of the vehicles used in *Supernatural*, provide the viewer a glimpse of an America that ruled the road. No other vehicle in *Supernatural* is as important, however, as Dean's 1967 Chevrolet Impala.

Known affectionately as "Baby," the sleek black automobile plays a significant role in most aspects of Sam and Dean's lives. At the end of Season One's finale, "Devil's Trap" (1.22), Baby is T-boned by a semi-truck whose driver has been possessed by a demon. In Season Two's opener, "In My Time of Dying" (2.01), the car and its occupants, Sam, Dean, and John, are shown severely battered and injured. While the men are airlifted to a hospital, Baby is taken to a police impound lot where Sam meets Bobby, who has driven his tow truck. When the two see Baby's condition, both men are filled with despair. Bobby suggests getting all of the weaponry and hunters' tools from the trunk and selling off the rest of the car to a scrap yard. Sam, however, insists that Dean will want to fix up the Impala. Standing as a metaphor for the elder Winchester brother, who is lying comatose in the hospital, Sam tells Bobby that, "If there's just one working part, that's enough. We're not going to just give up...." Bobby, recognizing Sam's personification of the car for Dean, agrees with a supportive, "Okay. You got it."

Baby's "near-death experience" early in the series would not be the last time that Dean would be forced to restore/repair his trusty steed. Sigmund Freud, writing in "Mourning and Melancholia," defines how grief and mourning may turn to melancholia, but that both begin with the "loss of a love object" (qtd. in Nylander 16). It may be safe to say that Dean's attachment to the Impala constitutes a relationship. In fact, Dean's identification with the car is so strong, that when he is forced to put her "on lockdown" for much of Season Seven, we see his distress many times. His disgust for the variety of cars he drives that season demonstrates that he is a one vehicle kind of guy. His loyalty to the car establishes her as a "love object," and he will seemingly spare no expense to repair her.

In the eponymously titled Season Eleven episode "Baby" (11.04), the Impala is shown to act as shelter, getaway vehicle, and an important member of the team. Dean's loss of Baby at any time throughout the series would affect him on a deep, psychological level, so if the Impala had been lost at any point in the series or sent to the scrap yard as Bobby suggests in "In My Time of Dying" (2.01), there is every possibility that Dean could have slipped into melancholia and not merely mourned the loss of a car, but of a piece of himself. Another iconic vehicle is one that belongs to none other than Death the Horseman, and his entrance is unforgettable.

Death's Epic Arrival

When we first meet Death the Horseman, it is in the aptly titled "Two Minutes to Midnight," (5.21). The other three Horsemen have been dispatched, their rings secured, and it is only Death whose ring will complete the set to unlock and relock Lucifer's cage. The deadline for the final showdown has arrived, and the doomsday clock is ticking.

Death arrives in a windswept Chicago as the "storm of the millennium" is getting underway. He "rides" his "pale horse": an off-white 1959 Cadillac. Death's ride, long and sleek complete with tailfins, seems as if it should be leading a cortege of hearses, but its driver arrives alone. The slow motion camera work adds to Death's leisurely exit from the car, and when we see him, well dressed in suit and top coat, his only accessories a walking stick and his ring, we immediately identify him as the modern western representation of Death: an undertaker. Death's mien carries with it an air of dignified melancholy; his skeletal features and deep set eyes offer both world weary sorrow and the wisdom of the ages. Death's arrival, to the strains of the Appalachian spiritual "O, Death," sung by Jen Titus, its dirge-like quality the perfect accompaniment, is the penultimate moment of the Horsemen's participation in the Apocalypse. When Death makes his appearance, we see him through a westernized, indeed American, lens because this is the only frame of reference the Winchesters, and we as viewers, have.

British born Julian Richings, who so graciously writes the foreword of this essay collection, portrays Death the Horseman, but not as the cloak wearing, scythe-wielding figure we often recognize. Though we do see more than one scythe associated with the character, Richings, as noted above, wears western clothing that could fit multiple centuries, speaks in a mid–Atlantic accent, giving him, as Richings himself has said, "an everyman" presence. This ability to blend in, to be ever-present, a mundane figure even, reminds us that death is all around us. Our mortality, try as we might to deny and delay, awaits us all and could be just around the corner. Death commands our respect and fear, lest we think too highly of ourselves, and yet, he is also pragmatic when he invites Dean to join him for some of Chicago's exceptional pizza.[5]

As modern Americans' intimacy with death has lessened, it is easier for us to "whistle past the graveyard," so to speak, something Dean actually does as he and Sam make their way through a cemetery in "Dead Men Don't Wear Plaid" (5.15). We live each day as if there will be many to follow, though in reality any one of them could be our last. Death, then, in his personification on *Supernatural,* reminds Dean, and we the viewers, that we are finite, that we have an expiration date, and that date is not known until it (and he?) comes for us.

American poet Emily Dickinson writes, "Because I could not stop for Death / He kindly stopped for me. / The Carriage held but just Ourselves / And Immortality / We slowly drove—He knew no haste / And I had put away / My labor and my leisure too, / For His Civility…" This poem seems so fitting for *Supernatural's* personification of Death in that he is civil, insists on courtesy, and will come for us whether we are ready or not.

Conclusion

Supernatural's celebration of all things American is a paean of love wrapped in a horror story. It is a tribute to the ideology and mythology that created the landscape that Sam and Dean traverse. The characters represent the ideals of freedom and the open road, the stalwart hero who faces the mysteries that lie just beyond the next bend. *Supernatural* is an anthem to legends that permeate our modern American culture. The stories and these characters resonate because America is a land built by peoples from the world over; these tales and legends spring from the very nature of what makes us human. It is our deepest fears told to us with an American wrapping. American culture, art, music, industry, masculinity, domesticity, and yes, especially death, present themselves through Sam and Dean's representations.

As Americans who traverse the heartland of the American landscape, how Sam and Dean et al. view and experience life and death tells us something about the American psyche. It is a commentary on the ways in which American ideals are celebrated and if never quite accomplished, at least strived for in the wider sense. Sam and Dean represent a long line of American heroes and antiheroes, rebels with and without a cause, road warriors who live on the margins of society, keeping that society safe while never really belonging to it. They face life and death on their feet, which is classic American mythos. Jared Padalecki and Jensen Ackles have hinted at how they see the Winchester boys' end in the finale of the series (which we now know will be in 2020), and that seems to mirror how Dean wants to go out: On their feet, boots on the ground, "Blaze of Glory style."

Notes

1. In Season Four's "Jump the Shark" (4.19), the funeral director has to tell Dean that the bodies he is investigating are not leaking blood but embalming fluid. This seems to be one of the few times the boys are confronted with embalmed corpses.
2. For more about the ways that significant deaths signal shifts in *Supernatural*'s narrative, see Erin M. Giannini's essay, "'When I come back, I'm gonna be pissed': Signaling Narrative and Character Shifts Through Death in *Supernatural*."
3. See Amanda Taylor's essay "'In My Time of Dying': Lessons on Grief in *Supernatural*" for a fuller exposition of this episode.
4. War drives a 1965 Ford Mustang Fastback. Famine's SUV is a Cadillac Escalade. Pestilence's AMC Hornet Wagon is the Pacer's 4-door model. Death's ride is a 1959 Cadillac Series 6200 Coupe. (Source: Supernatural Wiki)
5. See Amanda Taylor's essay "In My Time of Dying: Lessons on Grief in *Supernatural*" for more explication of this scene from "Two Minutes to Midnight."

Works Cited

"Abandon All Hope." *Supernatural: The Complete Fifth Season*, written by Ben Edlund, directed by Phil Sgriccia, Warner Home Video, 2009.
"All Hell Breaks Loose, Part 2." *Supernatural: The Complete Second Season*, written by Eric Kripke, directed by Kim Manners, Warner Home Video, 2007.
"Alpha and Omega." *Supernatural: The Complete Eleventh Season*, written by Andrew Dabb, directed by Phil Sgriccia, Warner Home Video, 2016.
"Appointment in Samarra." *Supernatural: The Complete Sixth Season*, written by Sera Gamble, directed by Mike Rohl, Warner Home Video, 2010.
"Baby." *Supernatural: The Complete Eleventh Season*, written by Robbie Thompson, directed by Thomas J. Wright, Warner Home Video, 2015.
"Bloodlust." *Supernatural: The Complete Second Season*, written by Eric Kripke and Sera Gamble, directed by Robert Singer, Warner Home Video, 2006.
"Brother's Keeper." *Supernatural: The Complete Tenth Season*, written by Jeremy Carver, directed by Phil Sgriccia, Warner Home Video, 2015.
"Carthage." *Civil War Trust*. 2017. https://www.civilwar.org/learn/civil-war/battles/carthage. Accessed 30 Jun. 2017.
"Children Shouldn't Play with Dead Things." *Supernatural: The Complete Second Season*, written by Eric Kripke and Raelle Tucker, directed by Kim Manners. Warner Home Video, 2006.
"Celebrating the Life of Asa Fox." *Supernatural: The Complete Twelfth Season*, written by Steve Yockey, directed by John Badham, Warner Home Video, 2016.

"Crossroad Blues." *Supernatural: The Complete Second Season*, written by Sera Gamble, directed by Steve Boyum, Warner Home Video, 2006.

"Dark Dynasty." *Supernatural: The Complete Tenth Season*, written by Eugenie Ross-Leming & Brad Buckner, directed by Robert Singer, Warner Home Video, 2015.

"Dead Man's Blood." *Supernatural: The Complete First Season*, written by Cathryn Humphris and John Shiban, directed by Tony Wharmby, Warner Home Video, 2006.

"Dead Men Don't Wear Plaid." *Supernatural: The Complete Fifth Season*, written by Jeremy Carver, directed by John F. Showalter, Warner Home Video, 2010.

"Devil's Trap." *Supernatural: The Complete First Season*, written by Eric Kripke, directed by Kim Manners, Warner Home Video, 2006.

Dickinson, Emily. "Because I Could Not Stop for Death." (479). *Poets.Org*. Academy of American Poets. 2017, https://www.poets.org/poetsorg/poem/because-i-could-not-stop-death-479. Accessed 21 Aug. 2017.

"Do You Believe in Miracles?" *Supernatural: The Complete Ninth Season,* written by Jeremy Carver, directed by Thomas J. Wright, Warner Home Video, 2014.

"Everybody Hates Hitler." *Supernatural: The Complete Eighth Season*, written by Ben Edlund, directed by Phil Sgriccia, Warner Home Video, 2013.

"Everybody Loves a Clown." *Supernatural: The Complete Second Season*, written by John Shiban, directed by Phil Sgriccia, Warner Home Video 2006.

"Exile on Main Street." *Supernatural: The Complete Sixth Season*, written by Sera Gamble, directed by Phil Sgriccia, Warner Home Video 2010.

"Faith." *Supernatural: The Complete First Season*, written by Sera Gamble and Raelle Tucker, directed by Allan Kroeker, Warner Home Video, 2006.

"Fan Fiction." *Supernatural: The Complete Tenth Season*, written by Robbie Thompson, directed by Phil Sgriccia, Warner Home Video, 2014.

Faust, Drew Gilpin. *This Republic of Suffering: Death and the American Civil War*, Vintage, 2008.

"In My Time of Dying." *Supernatural: The Complete Second Season,* written by Eric Kripke, directed by Kim Manners, Warner Home Video, 2006.

"Into the Mystic." *Supernatural: The Complete Eleventh Season*, written by Robbie Thompson, directed by John Badham, Warner Home Video, 2016.

Jackson, Charles O. "Attitudes to Death." *Journal of American Studies*. vol. 11 no. 3. Dec. 1977. pp. 297–312. www.jstor.org/stab;e/27553308. Accessed 30 May 2017.

"Jump the Shark." *Supernatural: The Complete Fourth Season*, written by Andrew Dabb and Andrew Loflin, directed by Phil Sgriccia, Warner Home Video, 2009.

Kripke, Eric, creator. *Supernatural*. Warner Home Video, 2005–2017.

McClintock, Kevin. "The Kevery: Hollywood Strikes Out Again." *The Carthage Press*. 24 Jul. 2012. http://www.carthagepress.com/article/20091125/news/311259972. Accessed 30 Jun. 2017.

McDermott, Robert A. "The Spiritual Mission of America." *ReVision*. Summer93. vol. 16. no 1 *Academic Search Premier*. web.b.ebscohost.com/ehost/detail/detail?vid=4&sid=3fb9c 2d7f9a-4561-a2b4f87d5ea0280%40sessionmgr104&bdata=JnNpdGU9ZWhvc3QtbGl2 ZQ%3d%3d#AN=9607260219&db=aph. Accessed 30 Jun. 2017.

"My Bloody Valentine." *Supernatural: The Complete Fifth Season*, written by Eric Kripke and Ben Edlund, directed by Mike Rohl, Warner Home Video, 2010.

Nylander, Susan R. *Whitman, Elegy, and the Nineteenth Century Culture of Death and Mourning,* 2009. California State U, San Bernardino, Master's Thesis.

"Pilot." *Supernatural: The Complete First Season,* written by Eric Kripke, directed by David Nutter, Warner Home Video, 2005.

"Sam, Interrupted." *Supernatural: The Complete Fifth Season,* written by Eric Kripke, Andrew Dabb, and Daniel Loflin, directed by James L. Conway, Warner Home Video, 2010.

"Swan Song." *Supernatural: The Complete Fifth Season*, written by Eric Kripke, directed by Steve Boyum, Warner Home Video, 2010.

"Swap Meat." *Supernatural: The Complete Fifth Season*, written by Eric Kripke, Julie Siege, Rebecca Dessertine, and Harvey Fedor, directed by Robert Singer, Warner Home Video, 2010.

"The Prisoner." *Supernatural: The Complete Tenth Season*, written by Andrew Dabb, directed by Thomas J. Wright, Warner Home Video, 2015.

"Trial and Error." *Supernatural: The Complete Eighth Season*, written by Andrew Dabb, directed by Kevin Parks, Warner Home Video, 2013.

"Two Minutes to Midnight." *Supernatural: The Complete Fifth Season,* written by Eric Kripke and Sera Gamble, directed by Phil Sgriccia, Warner Home Video, 2010.

"What Is and What Should Never Be." *Supernatural: The Complete Second Season,* written by Eric Kripke and Raelle Tucker, directed by Eric Kripke, Warner Home Video 2006.

"Who We Are." *Supernatural: The Complete Twelfth Season,* written by Robert Berens, directed by John F. Showalter, Warner Home Video, 2017.

Got Salt?

Human Remains and Haunting in Supernatural

REBECCA STONE GORDON

In addition to demonstrating that artisanal funeral pyres can be both practical and cathartic, the television series *Supernatural* advances provocative ideas about death. The long-running genre-bending horror series embraces what Lorna Jowett and Stacey Abbott call "...the inherently hybrid nature of television," blending traditional and modern monsters, myths, and urban legends (xiii). *Supernatural's* pilot episode, which premiered in 2005, plunges viewers into the story of brothers Sam and Dean Winchester as they embark on a quest to find their missing father, John, and avenge their mother, Mary. The Winchesters' straightforward-sounding mantra about "saving people, hunting things, the family business" turns out to be a bit murkier than it first seems, as the boundaries between human and monster prove quite porous. This essay focuses on an underlying premise of *Supernatural's* ghost stories, in which spirits are bound to their mortal remains or an intimate possession. This can have some decidedly dangerous consequences for both the living and the dead. It also raises ethical questions about the handling of human remains, even as it challenges us to think about alternatives to the American funeral industry's commodification of the body. Ghost stories, after all, are not for the ghosts.

In *Ghostland*, Colin Dickey writes that it does not matter whether we believe in ghosts or not, because "...ghost stories reveal the contours of our anxieties, the nature of our collective fears and desires, the things we can't talk about in any other way" (2). A long-running serial television show such as *Supernatural* has the opportunity to develop characters with rich interior lives. There are few recurring characters on the series, enabling a particularly tight focus on Sam and Dean. The Winchesters are always at the center of the narrative, Lorna Jowett and Stacey Abbott explain in *TV Horror*, even when an episode is ostensibly about someone else's crisis (50). In each episode, the circumstances of the case the Winchesters solve is a vehicle for revealing intimate details about their own personal struggles and interior lives. *Supernatural* is structured using what Jowett and Abbott call a "flexi-narrative that includes monster-of-the-week episodes, season arcs and ongoing relationship stories." (50) This ongoing brotherly relationship drama is enmeshed in the increasingly epic Winchester mythology.

Over time, the series itself becomes haunted by the Winchesters' struggles with their own humanity. Sam and Dean each struggle with what it means to be good or evil in different seasonal story arcs. This is a continuing source of narrative tension across the thirteen seasons, which Melissa Edmundson argues is a foundational aspect of the show's allure (9).[1] Julia Briggs could be describing *Supernatural* when she describes the work of the Gothic ghost story: "While much Victorian fiction veers between asserting family values and exposing their deceptions, the ghost story could do both at the same time" (181). The basic Gothic motifs, which form the backbone of the monster-of-the-week ghost stories, include buried secrets, isolated and decayed settings, intertextuality, family conflict, an excess of texts and textual materials, haunted objects, the instability of identity, and the precarity of bodily integrity. Derelict asylums, shuttered factories, lonely stretches of road, and modern condos built atop old, bypassed sewer systems are all locations which harbor secrets, spirits, and bodies. An element which distinguishes *Supernatural*'s ghosts from other types of ghost stories is the connection to the actual backbones of the ghosts.

Making human remains a source of animating power ties ghosts to their humanity and complicates their status as monsters. This is not passive or potential power that must be unlocked through magic.[2] Locks of real hair on a Victorian doll tether a soul to this mortal coil, enabling a young serial killer to continue her spree from beyond the grave ("Provenance"). A haunted kidney animates and controls mannequins, sending them on a murderous rampage to avenge a murdered woman ("Mannequin 3: The Reckoning"). Some are inherently evil in death as they were in life. Others demand attention, seek revenge, or reveal injustice. The repressed return, and they have business to attend to. Ghosts who demand justice for themselves are not the objectified corpses of crime dramas or police procedurals. The restless dead leverage the connection to their own remains to exert their will. In "The Usual Suspects" (2.07), a murder victim returns as a Death Omen. She leads Sam and a detective to the abandoned building where her skeletal remains are concealed behind a brick wall. The Winchesters solve the paranormal puzzle, but the victim essentially delivers her own remains to the police to expose the detective who murdered her before he can use his position of authority to harm other vulnerable women. As Sam points out, the Death Omen is the rare ghost who wants their remains to be found. Ghosts seek closure, but there are risks to revealing one's remains to hunters.

Don't Fear the Reaper

When Dean finds himself at death's door at the beginning of the second season, a reaper named Tessa attempts to escort him out of the veil. While Dean's body lies in a coma, Tessa lays out the case for why he should follow her, codifying the foundational ghost logic developed in the first season. Reapers do not know where souls go once they leave the veil between this world and the next. They cannot force a soul to leave. Tessa explains that most ghosts are the twisted souls of those who die too suddenly and violently for a reaper to find them. Other ghosts refuse to leave, bound by desire for vengeance or closure. Ghosts are trapped in or near the place they died, although some achieve a certain amount of mobility if their remains or the cherished object they are tethered to is moved. They all go mad over time and can do great harm to the living. "In My Time of Dying" (2.01) concludes with Dean waking from his coma, but it will not be the last time Dean visits the veil.

The meaning and social function of ghosts varies across cultures and time. (Davies 4). *Supernatural's* ghosts are usually unknown to those they haunt because it takes so long to develop their power. They are potentially dangerous, a problem to be solved rather than a social situation to be endured. Although Tessa does not explain this to Dean, it becomes apparent that helping a ghost come to terms with death or helping them get some form of justice will make it possible for a reaper to find them and escort them into the afterlife. In cases where they are too dangerous because their identity has become too fragmented, they must be, as Dean describes it, "ghost-killed." This is an act of total spiritual obliteration, the result of the salting and burning of their remains. Destroying human remains to liberate suffering souls advances an idea that grasping too tightly to vengeance or anger can create a psychological tar pit threatening harm to all who come near.

"Hook Man" (1.07) is the first episode in which the process of exhuming a grave, salting, and burning is shown onscreen. It does not stop the haunting in this case, as the ghost is still attached to the silver from his hook hand, but it establishes that Sam and Dean are accomplished grave diggers.[3] Ghosts strong enough to do harm have been dead for a long time, so their remains are depicted onscreen as desiccated or fully skeletonized. When they are burned, the camera rarely lingers on the remains themselves, instead cutting away to the dynamic image of the ghost. The spectral form is shown catching fire, turning to embers, exploding, or evaporating. The ghost's facial contortions suggest terror, fury, or agony. The act of exhuming and destroying human remains is an act of transgressive violence, and it is a leap of faith to ask viewers to sympathize with the desecrator rather than the desecrated, particularly in light of the long history of American grave desecration of marginalized populations for anatomical research.[4] The series largely sidesteps these ethical considerations within the narrative, instead focusing on the impact that this work has on Sam and Dean. Daniel Compora describes the Winchesters' struggle over the necessity to destroy monsters who suffer, particularly ghosts, arguing that they jeopardize the integrity of their own humanity each time they commit this act of violence (78).

In *Salt: A World History,* Mark Kurlansky traces the long history of salt as a symbol of purification. It is a frequently used item on *Supernatural,* used in both burning remains and creating protective barriers. Sam explains in "Roadkill," (2.16) "In most cultures salt's a symbol of purity, so it repels impure and unnatural things." Adding salt to cremation is a fictional embellishment, but the impulse to use fire as a purifying element can be traced to Ancient Greek mortuary practices.[5] In *Purified by Fire,* Stephen Prothero explains that Hindu texts, for example, specify that fire purifies both the body and the soul. In "Party On, Garth" (7.08), a hunter named Garth expresses skepticism over whether salting and burning will really free a spirit who doesn't wish to leave: "They've got ghosts in India, and they cremate everybody over there!" At this point in the series, it has become obvious that salting and burning remains is effective for older spirits, but does little to prevent the freshly dead from becoming ghosts, perhaps because they are still bound tightly enough to their identity to spurn their reaper and find something other than their remains to anchor themselves to.

Not all corpse-burning on the show is technically desecration. Corpses may also be burned in acts imbued with reverence, ritual, and respect during a hunter's funeral.

After John Winchester's death, viewers get their first glimpse of how hunters manage their dead when Sam and Dean build a pyre, wrap John in a shroud, and burn him in their own private ceremony. A hunter's funeral is a way to ensure that the dead maintain bodily integrity, paradoxically, through the obliteration of the body. The need for such measures is on brutal display in "The Magnificent Seven" (3.01). Sam, Dean, and Bobby work with hunting power couple Tamara and Isaac. Isaac is killed by demons who possess and reanimate him to terrorize Tamara. The goal of the hunter's funeral includes honoring the deceased, but the primary goal is to prevent the inhuman from usurping the humanity of the dead to inflict damage on the living.

Hunters are exceptionally skilled at wrapping bodies in beautiful rustic shrouds. The process of building the substantial structures that will burn long and hot enough to consume the bodies are, presumably a form of ritual. Death involves both social and physical removal of the dead from society, and the hunter's funeral is a solemn and respectful element in an otherwise violent and iconoclastic series. In keeping with philosopher Julia Kristeva's theory on the abjection of the corpse, this is a ritual that both renews contact with and then excludes the abject object from everyday life.

Prothero describes the goals of nineteenth-century cremation crusaders, who promoted cremation as the modern, efficient way to dispose of a body. Romanticizing funeral pyres was counter-productive to their message of scientific advancement. In *The Work of the Dead*, Thomas Laqueur describes their framing of cremation as "…the rapid release of a spirit from its fleshly prison" (537). By the end of the twentieth century, the funeral industry had colonized the cremation industry, managing to inject the singularly American zeal for embalming into cremation preparation and turning it into another step before burial rather than an alternative. As Americans seek more environmentally friendly, affordable, personalized ways to dispose of pets, human loved ones and themselves, the hunter's funeral presents a space to consider how disposal and memorialization can look outside the influence of the traditional funeral industry. In this, *Supernatural's* writers are in tune with the burgeoning "death positivity" movement.[6]

The Road So Far

Throughout Season One, haunting cases serve as an important vehicle for exposing Dean's emotional damage after the death of their mother, Mary. In these early episodes, Sam outwardly resents Dean for being what he perceives to be their father John's obedient soldier. Dean resents Sam's decision to leave the family to attend Stanford. In the pilot episode, Dean convinces Sam to leave Stanford for the weekend to look for John, who went missing while on a hunt. When Sam and Dean locate John's motel room, the walls are covered with newspaper clippings, drawings, and maps. Rachel Franks describes the modern murder mystery trope of the "murder board" as a modern twist on Gothic textual manipulation (34). It is a visual element that includes images of victims and a profusion of textual items such as receipts, newspaper clippings, and sketches. John's room is one giant murder board detailing the long history of disappearances on a desolate stretch of highway. In addition to these complex case files, hunters use antiquarian books, computer databases, and other sources of lore to sift through an overabundance of information in the hope of understanding the creature or ghost they hunt. Stopping a haunting is about more than putting a match to bones; it is also about putting a name and a story to the ghost. Ghosts don't get second obituaries in the local paper, so hunters' journals are the primary place where their stories are recorded and preserved.

Throughout the series, Sam and Dean are guided by their father's hunter's journal. John Winchester's journal is a combination diary, reference book, family heirloom, and *deus ex machina*. The journal guides Sam and Dean into and out of danger as the plot demands. Hunters' journals, libraries, case files, and murder boards form a body of lore that is unceasingly invoked, reinterpreted, and amended throughout the series. When a new case emerges and Sam begins sifting through the lore, the result is often what David Punter describes as "the attempt to validate that which cannot be validated" (3). The oral tradition of hunter's tales, the archives in the Men of Letters Bunker, and texts such as heavenly prophecies on tablets and Chuck Shurley's *Supernatural* book series constantly disrupt the authority of the lore and create new layers of intertextuality across the series.

Sam and Dean work the case John left behind to see if it will lead them to their father. They discover that the mysterious woman in white who lures men to their doom is the ghost of Constance Welch. As they put together the pieces of Constance's life, they learn that she murdered her children in a fit of rage because her husband was unfaithful. When her ghost appears on the side of the road, she both begs to be taken home and wails that she can never go home. Before Dean can break her earthly bond by burning her remains. She abducts Sam and attempts to kill him. He forces her to enter the abandoned Welch home, where her spectral children appear and drag her into the afterlife with them.[7] Like Constance, Sam is haunted by the past, but he believes that he has found a way to go home, making a new home with Jessica. When he returns to Stanford at the end of the weekend, however, he finds that he cannot go home either.

"Pilot" (1.01) opens with a flashback: the scene of Mary Winchester's death in the infant Sam's nursery. She is pinned to the ceiling, blood from a stomach wound blooming across her white nightgown. The episode ends with Jessica's death. She is similarly clad in a white nightgown, bloody, and pinned to the ceiling by the demonic force.[8] Jessica's death propels Sam back onto the road and into the hunter's life as he joins Dean to find both John and the murderous demon. Mary's character proves difficult to generalize about. She originally has no real identity of her own, existing only to motivate the Winchester men. In Season Four, it is revealed that she was a hunter before she met John, a part of her life kept secret from John. It was, in fact, a deal with a demon she made to save John's life that results in her death and Sam's infection with demon blood. In Season Eleven, God's sister, Amara, resurrects Mary to reward Dean for helping her reconcile with God. These developments introduce possible new layers of meaning onto the early episodes, but they do not change the nature of hauntings or the resolution of the monster-of-the-week episodes. One exception is the episode "Home" (1.09), in which it appears that Mary's spirit has continued to haunt the house in Lawrence where she died, despite her body burning to ash. This episode is an outlier in the overarching ghost logic of the series, and seems primarily designed to introduce Sam's demon-blood induced psychic powers rather than to give Mary's story any closure.

Although they are primarily on the road to find John during the first season, Dean makes many detours to hunt. At the start of "Dead in the Water" (1.03), Dean identifies another potential case—one in which people keep disappearing after drowning in a Wisconsin lake. Sam is concerned that John's trail is growing cold. He turns Dean's argument for pursuing the case against him as he points out, "People don't just disappear, Dean, other people just stop looking for them." Dean promises they'll find their Dad, but points out that they can also kill everything bad along the way. Dean exudes a confidence that all supernatural entities are evil, a conviction Sam struggles with. In Wisconsin, they meet the sheriff's grandson, Lucas, who witnessed his father's drowning in the lake. Lucas is too traumatized to speak, but he bonds with Dean. Dean confides to Lucas that he also witnessed a terrible death when he was a child, giving the viewer insight into the depths of trauma that exist below Dean's devil-may-care persona. This also affords Sam insight into his brother's grief and encourages him to be more compassionate.

The ghost in the lake is a murdered child named Peter. Peter's disappearance decades earlier remains unsolved. His mother cannot move on with her life because she does not know what became of her only child on the day he rode to the lake on his bicycle and never returned. Lucas is having nightmares and visions, which eventually reveal the location of Peter's buried bicycle. Peter is taking revenge on those who bullied and accidentally drowned him, killing the innocent family members of the now-grown men who kept his death a secret. To save Lucas, the sheriff confesses his role in Peter's death and offers himself to the ghost to atone for his sins. Peter drags the sheriff to the bottom of the lake and then seems to be at peace.

As they continue to hunt, Sam's guilt over Jessica's death threatens to consume him. Following a lead about mysterious deaths that began after a slumber party game of Bloody Mary, Sam and Dean uncover the story of a woman named Mary Worthington. Mary was murdered. She died trying to write the name of her murderer on her mirror, forming her connection to the antique mirror. The mirror was recently acquired by a local auction house, and Sam uncovers lore that some ghosts can move through mirrors. When Mary is summoned by someone with a guilty secret, she appears in their mirror as an uncanny reflection, inflicting a final moment of terror on her victim before she liquefies their eyes and kills them. As if Mary's tragic story isn't laden with enough Gothic motifs, the retired detective who worked her case kept her case files, adding a profusion of documentary material to the episode. Mary's focus on punishing those with guilty secrets makes Sam the perfect candidate to summon her. Dean believes Sam merely feels guilt that he wasn't there to prevent Jessica's death, but "Bloody Mary" (1.05) reveals Sam's secret to the viewer: he had visions of Jessica's death before it happened and did nothing to prevent it. Dean will not learn of Sam's visions for several more episodes.

Haunted or cursed objects are a common Gothic motif. Spiritual attachment to a material object that had deep meaning to the victim or contains some trace of their remains creates many narrative complications throughout the series, and these objects also require salting and burning to break their bond.[9] These attachments are also be exploited to gain control over a ghost in a number of episodes. In "Scoobynatural" (13.16), the animated homage/crossover *Scooby Doo* episode, the ghost of a child is bound to his pocket knife because it keeps him connected to his parents. Enslaved by an unscrupulous real estate developer who acquired the pocketknife, the ghost child implores Sam and Dean to recover the pocket knife and set him free, explaining that he has no control over his power or rage and does not mean to harm or kill people. This situation mirrors the season's story arc, in which Sam is attempting to help Lucifer's son Jack, a Nephilim, learn to control his own powers. Since objects are portable and can be inherited, sold, or transported into new contexts, this is a convenient storytelling device. It is also a convenient metaphor for the complicated relationship many people have with inherited property. To own an object connected to a ghost may feel like a curse, but these objects are surrogates for human remains and not technically cursed objects. On *Supernatural*, cursed objects have the conditions for causing harm imposed on them; they are tools or weapons.

On *Supernatural*, objects, especially antiques, carry with them the risk of a spectral home invasion. In "Provenance" (1.19), the object is a family portrait, a popular Gothic element. Sudden, unexpected intrusions by ghosts instantly change a home from a familiar place of refuge to a place of inexplicable horror and terror, the personification of what Freud describes as "unheimlich"—that which is simultaneously homely, yet not home (Dickey 17). In this episode a ghost intrudes on the peaceful home of a couple unfortunate enough to buy a haunted portrait at a charity auction and slashes their throats. Sam and Dean discover that the dour family in the portrait were murdered in their beds nearly a century ago by the father, Isaiah Merchant. Sam and Dean exhume, salt, and burn Isaiah's remains but the murders continue, revealing that Isaiah's adopted daughter, Melanie, is the malevolent entity. Isaiah adopted her after her own family was similarly slaughtered. Melanie was cremated. The painting regenerates itself after being salted and burned.

Fortunately for Sam and Dean, Sarah, the art dealer in possession of the painting, knows the history of Victorian dolls and explains that they were usually made with the child's own hair. Burning the doll stops Melanie's rampage. The episode is an opportunity for Sam's flirtation with Sarah to show he is healing from Jessica's death. It has important resonance with the previous episode, in which Sam learns how much pressure John placed on Dean to protect him when they were children. The cost of compromises and the consequences of trying to protect your family while saving others from evil are underlying themes of the entire series. When "Provenance" is read against later episodes, it takes on a more sinister subtext. John Winchester struggles with the possibility Sam's demon blood will make him evil and that John will have to choose between protecting Sam or losing everything, which resonates with Isaiah's story about trying to shelter a child whose evil nature ultimately costs him everything.

Institutional settings such as hospitals, asylums, and prisons are an opportunity to put multiple ghosts into the same location. In "Asylum" (1.10), Dr. Ellicott haunts the abandoned asylum he once ran. His ghost is powerful enough to infect trespassers, inciting them to act on their repressed rage. The asylum closed in the 1960s after patients rioted and killed Ellicott, whose remains were never recovered. At first, Sam and Dean perceive the threat to be the ghosts of the patients, but the patients are trying to warn the living, not harm them. Dean locates Ellicott's journal containing his notes about his secret experiments. He was abusing his power over these vulnerable patients and driving them to violent deaths in controversial "rage therapy" experiments. This is all recorded in his carefully illustrated journal, which bears a remarkable resemblance to a hunter's journal. Sam is an ideal target for Ellicott, as he seethes with rage over what he perceives to be John's unassailable power over Dean. Dean scrambles to find Ellicott's hidden laboratory and uncover Ellicott's remains. He struggles to salt and burn them as Sam tries to act on his murderous rage. Ellicott burns to cinder, Sam is released from possession, and the other ghosts seem to move on peacefully.

Another abandoned asylum holds more imprisoned ghosts of murdered patients as well as the ghosts of some local children. In "Advanced Thanatology" (13.05), the ghost of a mad doctor is attached to his plague mask collection. Burning the masks kills the doctor's ghost, but it does not free the captive ghosts who wander the halls. Dean cavalierly stops his own heart and instructs Sam not to revive him for three minutes. Although Dean's actions seem characteristically heroic yet impulsively stupid, his true motivation is barely concealed beneath the surface. His grief over the loss of his mother, again, and the death of his best friend, the angel Castiel, has broken his will to live. He is ready for Death to send him to The Empty, as the reaper Billie once told him would happen the next time he died.[10] Dean is surprised to find that Billie has been promoted to the job of Death. After a lengthy discussion about the important work the Winchesters still have to do, she sends Dean back to his body and sends a reaper to assist all of the trapped souls as a favor to him.

Like Death for Ghosts

The reaper mythology grows convoluted as the series progresses, but the basic premise that a ghost stuck in the veil can still move on if they find closure is consistent. Although the basic ghost lore was laid out piecemeal during the first season and codified in Dean's conversation with the reaper Tessa at the start of the second season, it was not until an episode at the midpoint of the second season that the emotional suffering of a ghost was fully explored. "Roadkill" (2.16) also exposes Dean's grief and unresolved guilt over his father's recent death, the price John paid to bring Dean out of his coma. The episode opens with a car accident, as Molly and David McNamara hit Farmer Greely and crash their car on an isolated stretch of highway. When Molly comes to, David is gone and Greely has a single-minded desire to harm Molly. Sam and Dean stop to help her. Sam explains to her that Greely is a ghost, trapped by strong emotions and unfinished business.

Molly is surprised at his sympathetic tone as he explains ghosts to her: "They weren't evil people. A lot of them were good ... just ... something happened to them. Something they couldn't control." Sam tells her salting and burning is "...like death for ghosts, but the truth is we still don't know, not for sure. I guess that's why we hold on to life so hard. Even the dead. We're all scared of the unknown." Sam is trying to come to terms with the possibility he may not be able to stop himself from "going Darkside," the consequence of being involuntarily infected with demon blood as an infant. Dean is grappling with his anger over his father's death and his own survivor's guilt. John sacrificed himself so that Dean could live, a violation of the natural order. Dean is aggressive and abrasive to Molly, unsympathetic to anything which violates the natural order.

Late in the episode, it is revealed that Molly is also a ghost. She was cremated after she died in the car accident, which actually happened fifteen years earlier, but she is unable to accept that she is dead. Each year on the anniversary of the accident, she and Ghost Greely appear on the side of the road. He enacts his revenge on her, capturing her and gruesomely torturing her in his cabin. Sam and Dean sought her out because they are trying to help her find peace. Although Sam shows her great kindness throughout the episode, she is subjected to the horror of Greely's ghost burning up in agony when his remains are salted and burned. Fortunately for Molly, after Sam and Dean show her that David is safe and loved and has moved on with his life, she gets to move on in a peaceful warm light.

Although Molly does not have any decaying remains to display and she does not burn away, Farmer Greely does graphically torture her in the episode. *Supernatural* is firmly in the horror genre, although body horror is more common in storylines involving embodied monsters or, later in the series, hellish torture. The remains depicted in haunting episodes are usually desiccated or skeletonized, but the bodies of a vengeful ghost's victims may be quite fresh. Sometimes, the series uses this fresh gore to provide comic relief. Stacey Abbott explores the relationship between body horror and slapstick comedy in *Supernatural*, showing how the horror genre frequently employs depictions of the dead body to evoke both terror and horror because both are "preoccupied with the body under attack" (6). While observing an autopsy at the beginning of "Yellow Fever," (4.06) Sam and Dean are accidentally splattered with "spleen juice" and other fluids while observing an autopsy of a man killed by what Bobby Singer identifies as a Buruburu, a type of Japanese ghost. Dean is afflicted with ghost sickness, a disease that is Gothic by its very nature. Over the course of 48 hours, the victim develops anxiety, hallucinations, paranoia, and, ultimately, death. Locating Luther, the source of the haunting, in a shuttered, decrepit sawmill, they piece together his story. Luther's brother implies that he was developmentally disabled, a gentle giant who was the janitor at the sawmill. He was falsely accused of murdering the secretary at the sawmill and subsequently road-hauled by her jealous husband. Luther died a tragic, brutal death while being dragged in chains down the road outside the mill. When his ghost manifests, he is shown as a large man cowering childlike in a corner in the sawmill.

As Dean's mental state deteriorates he gives voice to the absurdities of hunting and then mocks many of the shows tropes. He also begins to physically manifest symptoms such as a painful road rash and wood chips which mysteriously become stuck in his throat. Although these are played for comedy as Dean and the other infected victims scratch and act increasingly ridiculous in reaction to their growing paranoia, these symptoms reflect the violence inflicted upon Luther's body as he died. Dean hallucinates, the knowledge that he is lying to Sam about his time in Hell consuming him with guilt. He is terrified to confess to Sam what he did in Hell after he became a torturer, and he doesn't want Sam to feel guilt over the fact that Dean went to Hell because he made a deal to bring Sam back from the dead. In the meantime, Sam and Bobby must destroy Luther to liberate him from his torment, cure Dean's ghost sickness, and prevent anyone else from becoming infected. They must drag Luther's ghost down the road where he died in order to scare his ghost to death, revisiting this horrific violence on an innocent man. Dean is cured in the nick of time, but his relief is short-lived. At the end of the episode,

Dean is unsettled to see Sam's eyes flash a demonic yellow, a reminder that the paranoia and hallucinations he suffered during his ghost sickness were rooted in the realities of their lives.

Instant Swayze

Throughout the series, Bobby, who acts as a surrogate father to Sam and Dean, defends the natural order no matter how relieved he is each time Sam or Dean is resurrected after another cosmic misadventure. Bobby became a hunter after he was forced to kill his wife to save her from demon possession. When his wife is temporarily resurrected and he is given five days with her before she becomes a homicidal zombie, he shares that the pain of losing her again was not worth the joy of having her return. Bobby seems more committed than anyone else on the show to respecting the natural order of the universe. Until he dies. His decision to reject his reaper is monumental. Through Bobby, the violence and turmoil that fuel ghostly behavior is shown in a sympathetic light as Bobby struggles to control his power and his impulsive behavior.

Bobby's rationalizations for staying are borne of grief at the idea of losing Sam and Dean, fear of the unknown, and the desperate belief that his work is not yet done. Although Sam and Dean burn Bobby's remains, Bobby's long and extremely intimate relationship with his flask allows him to use it as an anchor for his soul. Conveniently, this is an object Dean fixates on, carrying the flask, and unknowingly, Bobby, around with him for the rest of the season. When a hunter named Garth suggests that Bobby's flask is haunted, Dean concedes this is theoretically possible. "Who knows more about being a ghost than Bobby? Instant Swayze!" ("Party On, Garth"). Nevertheless, Dean has trouble believing that Bobby ducked his reaper and does not believe that this is possible.[11]

In "Of Grave Importance" (7.19), a hunter named Annie is murdered by a ghost, who keeps her body in a hidden room in an abandoned mansion that was once a speakeasy. This powerful ghost is killing people and holding their spirits prisoner in the house to draw on their energy, preventing reapers from collecting their souls. When Dean arrives with Bobby's flask in tow, Annie and Bobby are reunited. She is upset about his decision to defy his reaper and confused about why he would choose to stay in this place "between existing and not." Bobby rationalizes his decision and bargains with her for understanding, denying the reality of his own death. Annie is resolute in her desire to move on, working the case to bring peace to the all of the ghosts trapped in the house.

Kristeva's work on abjection marks the corpse as abject both because of the physically repellent nature of decay and dissolution, but also because it is so visibly no longer "us." (4). While Kristeva is not saying that we can understand abjection by looking upon our own corpse, the scene where Annie's ghost finds her corpse hints at how unsettling that would be. Annie is understandably disturbed to find herself staring at her own bloody corpse. Bobby, who got some ghosting lessons from another ghost in the house, is now able to manifest at will, and reveals himself to Sam and Dean. They put all of the other ghosts in the house, including Annie, to rest, giving her the hunter's funeral she requested.[12] Over the rest of the season, Bobby's power grows, but a sense of uncontrollable rage grows along with it. Eventually, he realizes that he is an impediment to Sam and Dean's well-being as long as he refuses to move on, and he asks them to salt and burn his flask.

In an interesting twist, ghosts are not the only ones bound to their bones. Although demons and angels possess living people to use as earthly vessels, demons were once actually human. After a damned person dies and goes to Hell, they become a demon, but Bobby discovers that demons are really just "ghosts with egos," bound to their bones and susceptible to fiery obliteration. At the end of Season Seven, Dean is hurtled into Purgatory, the afterlife for monsters. His earthly body apparently makes the trip with him. Dean forms an uneasy alliance with Benny the vampire, pinning his own survival on a monster he usually hunts and kills. Benny helps Dean escape. Dean absorbs Benny's soul into his own body and carries him back to the earthly plane, literally and figuratively bearing the burden of his debt to Benny in "We Need to Talk About Kevin" (8.01). Dean travels to Louisiana and exhumes Benny's bones, honoring his promise and releasing Benny's soul to restore the vampire to corporeal form. Of course, Dean keeps this friendship secret from Sam, creating an entirely new cycle of brotherly angst and debates about monstrosity, humanity, and the natural order.

Conclusion

Death is an immutable part of the natural order, a truism often repeated on *Supernatural*. Yet, for all of their bravado and stoicism, the Winchesters subvert the natural order in order to protect their family on a regular basis. The consequences for upending the natural order lay the foundation for the Winchesters' more intimate encounters with death and their later encounters with Death. The series is heavily freighted with these demon deals and other ill-considered sacrifices. At the beginning of Season Two, John Winchester makes a deal with a demon that restores Dean to health but dooms John to Hell. When Dean learns what his father has done for him, it fuels a deep rage which manifests in a single-minded determination to uphold the natural order. This motivation only lasts until the end of the season, when Dean chooses to make his own demon deal in order to save Sam. The entanglements with demons, angels, and gods grow increasingly complex over the next thirteen seasons, underlaying all of the traumas and secrets that the writers peel like onions in the monster of the week episodes. The boundaries of the natural order enable the viewer to understand the gravity and consequences of later events, such as Bobby's decision to defy his reaper and remain in the veil. Seeing this as an act of resistance, Bobby gives voice to the bargaining and denial that are a natural part of grieving, but his status as a beloved character gives his struggle resonance far outside the boundaries of the show.[13]

Bobby's struggle gets to the heart of the question about what a television show about a family of monster hunters contribute to the conversation about death in contemporary American culture. Every *Supernatural* viewer has at least one thing in common: they, and everyone they know, are going to die. Sam and Dean's thinly disguised "chick-flick moments" play out under cover of the job, whether that involves trying to put the archangel Lucifer back into his cage or ganking the local ghost. They often speak of how "the life" only ends one way: dying bloody. These melodramatic monologues of martyrdom borrow some of the lazier conventions of Westerns and war movies, but at heart they acknowledge that a life well-lived is a life in which one is fully present. *Supernatural* advances the idea that grief and mourning make us human. That letting go and moving on is not the same as forgetting. That secrets and unfinished business poison relationships and doom families to repeat their mistakes, an act akin to haunting. While it's probably best not to take tips for do-it-yourself cremations from *Supernatural*, the implication that elaborate corpse preservation measures may be impediments to moving forward are worth contemplating. Impediments that are financial or psychological, that is. If you find yourself with a bloodthirsty ghost on your hands, remember: salt, then burn. A little lighter fluid seems to help.

NOTES

1. The Gothic nature of the show and the Winchester family saga is explored in depth in the essays in the volume Edmundson edited, *The Gothic Tradition in Supernatural.*

2. Body parts are also passive power sources in the show's mythology. Anyone with a little magical know-how can fashion them into weapons, tools, religious relics, or talismans. This is a different type of power than that exercised by the mortal remains of the deceased, who remain bound to their original identity.

3. In "The Real Ghostbusters" (5.19), Damien and Barnes, a pair of *Supernatural* fans doing some live action role playing (LARPing), are drawn into the horrifying job of exhuming graves with Sam and Dean, gasping for air and tending their blisters as they engage in this distasteful task.

4. There is a growing body of work on the history of these practices, including Katharine Park's *Secrets of Women: Gender, Generation and the Origins of Dissection* (Zone Books, 2010) and Michael Sappol's *A Traffic in Dead Bodies: Anatomy and Embodied Social History in Nineteenth-Century America.* (Princeton University Press, 2002).

5. In "Hollywood Babylon" (2.18), Sam and Dean infiltrate a haunted Hollywood movie

set. An argument breaks out on the set about the absurdity of ghosts fearing salt. A debate about the relative scariness of other condiments ensues, an example of the use of humor to sidestep practical interrogation of the show's phantasmic laws of physics.

6. Proponents such as mortician Caitlin Doughty, author of *Smoke Gets in Your Eyes: And Other Lessons from the Crematory* (W.W. Norton, 2015) and a co-founder of the Order of the Good Death, strive to demystify mortuary practices and educate the public about the range of alternative cultural and physical options for tending to the dead.

7. The episode merges a number of legends together, merging the phantom hitchhiker with the Mexican figure of La Llorona. Scholars such as Leow Hui Min Annabeth explores in depth the problematic way the episode appropriates this tale and places it within a series privileging White male masculinity in "Coloniality and the Chicana Gothic: Travelling Myths in the Pilot." *The Gothic Tradition in Supernatural*, edited by Melissa Edmundson, McFarland, 2016, pp. 91–102.

8. See Freddie Harris Ramsby's essay "'I prefer ladies with more experience': Virgins, Whores, and Post-Feminine Death in *Supernatural*" in this collection for a deeper exploration of the significance of Mary and Jessica's deaths.

9. Sam isn't surprised to find evidence of a haunting in a museum in Des Moines, Iowa, in "Family Feud," remarking that museums: "...are always filled with ADHD spirits and their tethers." (12.13).

10. Both Winchesters have died. A lot.

11. See Amanda Taylor's essay "'In My Time of Dying': Lessons on Grief in *Supernatural*" in this collection for further discussion of Bobby's refusal to go with his reaper.

12. The death and spectrality of Kevin Tran plays out differently after he is murdered in the Bunker after Metatron has sealed the doors to Heaven. Sam and Dean are not merely haunted psychologically for their complicity in Kevin's death and their inability to protect him; they are actually haunted.

13. For more on grieving, see Amanda Taylor's essay "In My Time of Dying: Lessons on Grief in *Supernatural*."

WORKS CITED

Abbott, Stacey. "Rabbits' Feet and Spleen Juice: The Comic Strategies of TV Horror." *TV Goes to Hell: An Unofficial Roadmap of Supernatural*, edited by Stacey Abbott and David Lavery, ECW, 2011, pp. 3–17.

"All Hell Breaks Loose: Part 2." *Supernatural: The Complete Second Season*, written by Eric Kripke, directed by Kim Manners, Warner Home Video, 2007.

"Asylum." *Supernatural: The Complete First Season*, written by Richard Hatem, directed by Guy Bee, Warner Home Video, 2006.

"Bloody Mary." *Supernatural: The Complete First Season*, written by Ron Milbauer and Terri Hughes Burton, directed by Peter Ellis, Warner Home Video, 2006.

Briggs, Julia. "The Ghost Story." *A New Companion to the Gothic*, edited by David Punter, Blackwell, 2012, pp. 176–185.

Compora, Daniel. "Gothic Imaginings: Folkloric Roots." *The Gothic Tradition in Supernatural: Essays on the Television Series*, edited by Melissa Edmundson, McFarland, 2016, pp. 75–88.

Davies, Owen. *The Haunted: A Social History of Ghosts*. Palgrave Macmillan, 2007.

Dickey, Colin. *Ghostland: An American History in Haunted Places*. Viking, 2016.

Edmundson, Melissa. "Introduction." *The Gothic Tradition in Supernatural: Essays on the Television Series*, edited by Melissa Edmundson, McFarland, 2016, pp. 1–12.

"Dead in the Water." *Supernatural: The Complete First Season*, written by Eric Kripke and Sera Gamble, directed by Kim Manners, Warner Home Video, 2006.

Franks, Rachel. "Murder Across the Board: Murder Boards as a Liminal Space for the Dead on Popular Television." *Aeternum: The Journal of Contemporary Gothic Studies*, vol. 3, issue 1, 2016, pp. 33–48.

"Home." *Supernatural: The Complete First Season*, written by Eric Kripke, directed by Ken Girotti, Warner Home Video, 2006.

"Hook Man." *Supernatural: The Complete First Season,* written by Eric Kripke and John Shiban, directed by David Jackson, Warner Home Video, 2006.

"In My Time of Dying." *Supernatural: The Complete Second Season,* written by Eric Kripke, directed by Kim Manners. Warner Home Video 2007.

Jowett, Lorna, and Stacey Abbott. *TV Horror.* I.B. Tauris, 2013.

Kristeva, Julia. *Powers of Horror: An Essay in Abjection,* translated by Leon Rouding, Columbia UP, 1982.

Kurlansky, Mark. *Salt: A World History.* Penguin, 2003.

Laqueur, Thomas. *The Work of the Dead: A Cultural History of Mortal Remains.* Princeton UP, 2015.

"The Magnificent Seven." *Supernatural: The Complete Third Season,* written by Eric Kripke, directed by Kim Manners, Warner Home Video, 2008.

"Of Grave Importance." *Supernatural: The Complete Seventh Season,* written by Brad Buckner and Eugenie Ross-Leming, directed by Tim Andrew, Warner Home Video, 2012.

"Party On, Garth." *Supernatural: The Complete Seventh Season,* written by Adam Glass, directed by Phil Sgriccia, Warner Home Video, 2012.

"Pilot." *Supernatural: The Complete First Season,* written by Erik Kripke, directed by David Nutter, Warner Home Video, 2006.

Prothero, Stephen. *Purified by Fire: A History of Cremation in America.* U of California P, 2001.

"Provenance." *Supernatural: The Complete First Season,* written by David Ehrman, directed by Phil Sgriccia, Warner Home Video, 2006.

Punter, David. "Introduction: The Ghost of a History." *a New Companion to the Gothic,* edited by David Punter, Blackwell, 2012, pp. 1–9.

"Roadkill." *Supernatural: The Complete Second Season,* written by Raelle Tucker, directed by Charles Beeson, Warner Home Video, 2007.

"Scoobynatural." *Supernatural: The Complete Thirteenth Season,* Warner Home Video, 2018. written by Jeremy Adams and Jim Krieg, directed by Robert Singer, CW, 29 Mar. 2018.

"The Usual Suspects." *Supernatural: The Complete Second Season,* written by Cathryn Humphris, directed by Mike Rohl, Warner Home Video, 2007.

"Weekend at Bobby's." *Supernatural: The Complete Sixth Season,* written by Andrew Dabb and Daniel Loflin, directed by Jensen Ackles, Warner Home Video, 2011.

"We Need to Talk About Kevin." *Supernatural: The Complete Eighth Season,* written by Jeremy Carver, directed by Robert Singer, Warner Home Video, 2013.

A Familiar Soundscape

Existentialism, Winchester Exceptionalism and the Evolution of Death in Supernatural

SARAH ELAINE NEILL

Death plays many roles in *Supernatural*. It is a narrative catalyst, an omnipresent threat, an ally, an end and a beginning, a force for good and a tool for evil. Like the Winchester brothers, death has evolved throughout the seasons, becoming more complex and dynamic with every plot twist. Trespassing the boundaries of goodness and morality in order to question their very existence, death and the Winchesters lead us to reflect upon our expectations and assess our own cultural norms. Indeed, although the series often plays with dualities (e.g., natural/supernatural, heaven/hell, life/death, good/evil), it is the way that false dichotomies are examined and rejected that speaks to the show's deeply philosophical nature and hints at its enduring tenure and cult-classic status among fans. The value of *Supernatural* is not in the answers that it gives, but the questions it asks.

After more than a dozen years in broadcast, *Supernatural* has shown death to be, in many ways, the third central character alongside Sam and Dean Winchester. The entire premise of *Supernatural* is built upon death. From Mary to John, Ellen, Jo, Bobby, and Charlie, each loss further changes the Winchesters and redefines their relationship, deepening their resolve to save each other at any cost. Sam and Dean's identities—as individuals, as brothers, and as hunters—are therefore forged out of death. But death, unlike the brothers, is not visibly personified until the end of Season Five—the last of the Kripke years—and so has no dialogue, but "speaks" only through sound. Death (with the exception of the Horseman, who is but one physical manifestation of the larger concept) is therefore an acousmetre, ever-present in diegetic noise (what the characters can hear) and non-diegetic music and sound (what the viewer can hear, but the characters cannot), but lacking a discernable source.[1] The brothers' dynamic relationship with death, which is both the impetus for their identity and an enemy force, is therefore primarily apparent in the soundtrack, where otherwise hidden meanings are brought into relief.

The contrast and interplay between what is seen and what is heard reveals how the Winchesters embody American ideas toward death and dying. The Winchesters, in their attempts to escape, overcome, cheat, transfigure, and repeatedly deny their own deaths, are a metaphor for threads of existentialism and exceptionalism running through the core of modern America. Existentialist anxieties about afterlife, the meaning of life and humanity, and the immortality of a soul are a staple of Western philosophy that has shaped contemporary American culture, so it comes as no surprise that they are evident in *Supernatural*, a product of that same culture. Within the safety of *Supernatural*, we encounter death as Sam and Dean die (repeatedly).

As they are revived and resurrected, we become lulled into comfort that death is not real, and that perhaps we too could cheat it again and again like they have. In this way, the exceptionalism that ensures Sam and Dean's survival, and therefore the continuation of *Supernatural*,[2] also appeals to our need to believe that we are extraordinary and our culture is somehow beyond reproach. Simultaneously, existentialist doubts that any meaning exists outside of what we make for ourselves nag at our convictions of our own exceptionalism. The tension between these two concepts is particularly apparent in the way that the brothers negotiate a relationship with death. As I argue in this essay, music is one lens through which to analyze this tension, given the acousmetric nature of death throughout the series. What I refer to as the Winchester musical theme (discussed in detail later) is a critical case study for exploring how Sam and Dean relate to death.

Because existentialism is at the core of *Supernatural*, it is deeply ingrained into each aspect of the show, including sound and music. In some cases, as in the Winchester theme, which links the brothers with death, or Azazel's theme, which represents the evil side of the supernatural and foreshadows Sam's struggle balancing his powers with his morality, music is in clear-cut melodies that accompany recurring existentialist themes on screen. At other times—and because confrontation with existentialist questions is so prevalent and frequent—these moments are accompanied by silence or non-melodic sound. Practically speaking, it would be heavy-handed to have a musical theme enter every single time Sam and Dean grapple with death or existentialism. Nevertheless, there are numerous significant instances of critical moments where the brothers' exceptionalist convictions, existentialist fears, and musical material collide with death in the narrative. In this way, the normalcy of these existentialist pursuits are reinforced in the soundtrack, further establishing their centrality to *Supernatural* as Sam and Dean wrestle with existentialism, even if they themselves do not always ultimately reach purely existentialist answers.

The unofficial tagline of the show—"saving people, hunting things, the family business"—first spoken by Dean in "Wendigo" (1.02) and foreshadowed in the boys' first confrontation in the pilot, sets the tone for the presumed normative relationship between the Winchesters and death. People (humans) must be saved and kept alive, while things (the supernatural) should be hunted and killed. The division seems clear. Death is punishment; life is precious. Maintaining the partition between good and evil through death is the boys' *raison d'être*, even after they fulfill their mission to find and destroy Mary and Jessica's killer, the demon Azazel ("Devil's Trap"). But the distinction becomes increasingly muddled as seasons go on and death is shown to be reversible, impermanent, and vague. Dean's resurrection in "Lazarus Rising" (4.01), his revival as a demon in "Do You Believe in Miracles?" (9.23), Bobby's escape from his Heaven in "Inside Man" (10.17), the death of Death in "Brother's Keeper" (10.23), and the return of Mary Winchester in Season Twelve are such turning points.

Driver Picks the Music: Sound and Narrative Truth in Film

Although the primary focus of this essay is the centrality of death in the Winchesters' identity as expressed through their musical representation, it is important to note that when music accompanies moving image, it may have a number of functions, which can and often do overlap. Both diegetic and non-diegetic music can set time and place, create atmosphere, reference other works or genres, represent a character or idea, align the listener with a particular character or an omniscient narrator, and add to, comment upon, or critique some element of the narrative.[3] A vestige of film's lineage from opera, melodrama, and other stage works, musical themes are commonly used to represent individual characters or concepts and the developments that they undergo.[4]

Supernatural pulls from the rich tradition of horror film music, using sound to further heighten or incite fear and terror in the listener, such as when sudden, loud noises amplify startling images, or when open-ended or atonal musical motifs represent uncertainty or unboundedness. Ever intertextually clever, *Supernatural* is also a clear descendent of the marriage between heavy metal and horror film that grew out of the 1980s (e.g., Dario Argento's 1985 film *Phenomena*). Using both the Gruska/Lennertz original score and pre-composed works—usually classic rock—sound is used in the series to provide context, give information, and empathetically resonate what would otherwise remain unspoken or silenced (i.e., to give insight into the psychology or thoughts of a particular character).[5]

Sound inhabits a particular space within film, which grants certain powers and privileges; it is both within and separated from the narrative. As a result, sound can call attention to the narrative, either through critique or amplification. That is, the music may either highlight a stark contrast to make a point, or it might emphasize a consistent message in tandem with the image. No matter the origin, as Isabella van Elferen has argued in her study of Gothic music, "sound suggests presence even when this presence is invisible or intangible" (4). Sound that is disembodied is eerie, but it is also powerful. Unbounded by physical limitations, acousmatic sound can move throughout time and space. This is true in "Inside Man" (10.17) when Sam and Castiel contact Bobby via the radio in his Heaven. Sound can permeate the life/death boundary, which is why Sam and Bobby can talk to each other, but their physical or spiritual selves cannot. Castiel must act as intermediary as Sam cannot enter Heaven and Bobby cannot leave it. In this way, sound and music can represent or make known what is otherwise unknowable. Through this capability to reveal the invisible, sound is more truthful than image. When what we hear does not conform to what we see in film, we trust our ears above all else.

Sound can move through boundaries, as in the case of Bobby's radio in Heaven, but it can also create them. In horror film, the division between safe and unsafe often takes a physical boundary, with the walls of a house dividing the natural from the unnatural, either as a haven, as in the farmhouse in *Night of the Living Dead* (1968), or a cage, as in *The Amityville Horror* (1979) and countless other haunted house narratives. Sound also subtly indicates the partition between normalcy and threat. The concept of home has seen considerable discussion in *Supernatural* literature, with the Impala (Baby) as a four-door home amid the boys' rootlessness. Indeed, this should come as no surprise, given that it was God (Chuck) himself who noted this in "Swan Song" (5.22), narrating: "It had never occurred to them [Dean and Sam] that, sure, maybe they never really had a roof and four walls. But they were never, in fact, homeless." As Susan A. George has argued in her analysis of Dean's relationship to Baby, the Impala stands both as a representation of postindustrial American masculinity and as a refuge in the otherwise harsh life of the itinerant hunter (148).

While *Supernatural* certainly employs visual safe spaces, it also relies significantly on sound to create shelter and signify well-being, or lack thereof, both to the audience and the Winchesters. Although the original score and pre-existing canon overlap in function throughout the series, in general, classic rock is used diegetically (i.e., it is heard by the characters and has a physical source within the scene) to represent reality and normalcy. The Gruska/

Lennertz score, in contrast, is used to represent inner, psychological states, supernatural beings, and the audience's own fear. The use of music to create safe havens in *Supernatural* is as much a reaction to fan engagement as it is a characteristic of the horror genre.

Defining home through tropes of sound or image reinforces the dynamic relationship that *Supernatural* has with its audience. When the brothers are settled in the Impala and Dean has the music blasting, we know that everything is back to "normal," or it should be. When something clearly is amiss— such as the unrelenting repetition of Asia's "Heat of the Moment" in "Mystery Spot" (3.11)[6]—the audience feels it even more acutely precisely because of the contrast. In "Mystery Spot" and throughout the series, music is a locator for time and space. "Heat of the Moment" represents the inescapable "moment" of the cursed Tuesday, while "Back in Time" by Huey Lewis and the News signifies the narrative's return to a consecutive timeline after Sam's confrontation with the Trickster/Loki/Gabriel. Not only are the songs chronological (1982 and 1985, respectively), but the lyric content indicates first nostalgic longing for a moment in the past and then return to an established and normative time. Furthermore, attentive fans will read the intertextual homage to Marty McFly waking up in his own time in 1985's *Back to the Future* as Sam's eyes open on Wednesday with Dean alive and everything as expected.

One especially poignant use of music as an aural indicator of the boundary between normalcy and the uncanny is in the final moments of "Devil's Trap" (1.22). Having narrowly escaped an encounter with Azazel that left Dean, Sam, and John badly injured and emotionally raw, the Winchesters are in the Impala on the way to the hospital, radio playing quietly. Sam sees a dying Dean in the rearview mirror and reassures him that they are less than ten minutes from the hospital when an 18-wheeler, driven by a demon-possessed trucker, violently plows into the side of the car. We see the moment of impact four times in quick succession and watch the Impala pushed helplessly down an embankment. The only sound is screeching metal and the roar of the semi as the screen fades to black. The black eyes of the driver and the limp, bloody bodies of father and sons are foregrounded by what should be comforting classic rock ("Bad Moon Rising" by Creedence Clearwater Revival in the broadcast version and "Backwater Rising" by Tom Coerver in the Netflix version), but instead is an uncanny reminder that even what we believed to be safe is not.[7] The car that was a place of refuge mere moments ago is now a family casket.

Recognizing how classic rock is used in the series to create and develop sonic familiarity is relatively clear-cut because those songs are pre-existing and self-contained. The audience will likely know the song already, so they are more aware of the sound in the first place and are attuned to how the music and image interact. Original compositions, especially when arranged in a more traditional film score style for symphony orchestra, are better at going unnoticed by a casual viewer who is used to film music working as "sonic wallpaper." By this same logic, it is the motifs of the Gruska/Lennertz score—consistent over thirteen seasons—which are most relevant for a nuanced analysis of the relationship between the Winchester brothers and death. Like classic rock, which indicates the status quo for the brothers, or, as Castiel notes, "no paradise, no hell, just more of the same" ("Swan Song"), the original score also employs sonic familiarity to create aural homes, familiarize the foreign, and draw connections between seemingly opposing concepts.

The Winchester Musical Theme

By far the most frequently employed and long-lasting musical theme, which I refer to as the Winchester theme for convenience, debuts thirty minutes into "Devil's Trap" (1.22) as Dean reflects on the lengths he is capable of going in order to preserve his family. Credited to Gruska, the theme is the Winchesters' sonic fingerprint.[8] Although family is at the center of the Winchester identity, their definition of family both stretches beyond and excludes blood relations. As Dean says to Crowley in "Inside Man" (10.17) when Crowley argues that he and Rowena are "family" and "blood": "Well that's not the same thing. A wise man once told me 'Family don't end in blood,' but it doesn't there either." This was a lesson that both Sam and Dean learned the hard way in Season Six, when their maternal grandfather, Samuel Campbell, and his relatives chose to align with Crowley against the brothers ("Family Matters").

The Winchester family comprises Sam and Dean at the center, along with their parents, but it also extends to Ellen and Jo, Castiel, Bobby, Charlie, and others, and the musical theme works as a shorthand to reinforce these relationships in collaboration with dialogue and visuals, or in their absence. From its first iteration, the Winchester theme represents not only the brothers' dedication to each other over all else, especially in the face of death, but also their threatened humanity as they transgress moral and ethical boundaries in trying to stay alive together. In this way, the theme encapsulates the brothers' identity and relationship to death, and foreshadows the limitations of their "humans should live, monsters should die" code.

The Winchester theme is not simply an aural marker to let the audience know when and how Sam and Dean love each other (any *Supernatural* fan knows that is the baseline of their relationship), but to provide narrative information, especially when the image and dialogue are incomplete or inconsistent with the true situation. One such example is "The Prisoner" (10.22) when

Mark-of-Cain Dean mercilessly beats Castiel. As the Winchester theme swells in solo cello, it not only acts as striking counterpoint to the bloody and brutal images, but as a commentary both on Castiel's status as part of the Winchester family and Dean's impending loss of humanity. Although Dean shows no sign of caring for Castiel, except when he decides not to stab him with the angel blade, the accompanying music tells us that the real, un-cursed Dean is suffering in this moment as well. Seasoned fans will recognize the theme and its history of being paired with images indicating deep emotional bonding and a desire to do the right thing by the Winchester code. Here we trust our ears over our eyes to reveal the truth. Similarly, earlier in the season in "Soul Survivor" (10.03), as Sam struggles with rehabilitating demon Dean, the Winchester theme plays as he walks through Dean's room and looks through photos of them and their parents, indicating Sam's mourning Dean's death and lost humanity.

The theme itself is musically representative of the Winchesters in a number of ways. Set in minor mode, the theme taps into common assumptions in the collective Western psyche about minor keys representing longing or melancholy. Without the raised leading tone and ending on an unfulfilling half cadence it sounds even more rootless and ungrounded. Like the boys' physical home, the tonal home of the melody is just out of reach. In the second phrase, which is sometimes omitted in later iterations or references, the opening C minor arpeggio stretches toward the upper octave, unable to surpass the B-flat that also defined its lower range. With the simplicity of a folk melody, the Winchester theme succinctly represents what typifies the brothers: searching for stability amid a world that is both familiar and foreign. And, in keeping with existentialist philosophy, it reflects a necessity to create meaning and boundaries where there otherwise would be none. Although the first time the theme appears it is in solo piano in C minor, it undergoes a series of alterations in instrumentation, rhythm, tonality, and interval content. Each variation adds a layer of meaning to the visual and narrative context. But for the purposes of analyzing the Winchesters' relationship with death, it is the fact that the theme appears at certain times that is of the most importance, rather than the changes that it undergoes.

The Winchester theme is born out of confrontation with loss, either of life or humanity. When John dies ("In My Time of Dying"), when Dean believes Sam is fatally infected with the Croatoan virus ("Croatoan"), and then when Sam dies in Dean's arms ("All Hell Breaks Loose: Part 2"), the Winchester theme is sounded. Likewise, Sam's sacrifice in "Swan Song" (5.22), Dean's death at the hands of Metatron ("Do You Believe in Miracles?"), and Mary's resurrection ("Keep Calm and Carry On") and struggle adapting to life with her adult sons ("The Foundry") are all accompanied by the theme. In each instance, additional meanings adhere to the melody and are later referenced simultaneously in the mind of the listener. Almost without realizing it, the audience is conditioned to equate the Winchesters' identities with loss and death. Although Sam and Dean posture themselves as battling death, in reality it is an essential part of them—perhaps the most essential part. The Winchesters without the constant threat of death would not really be the Winchesters at all.

Form and Void, the Darkness, the Empty: American Existentialism

The brothers' resistance toward death, even as it is an intrinsic part of an inevitable end for them, speaks not only to inherited cultural assumptions about life and death, but also to *Supernatural's* existentialist framework. Before assessing the ways in which Sam and Dean navigate their own mortality, it is crucial to contextualize *Supernatural* within American culture in general and American attitudes towards death and dying in particular. One reason that the brothers' quest to preserve life (especially their own) at all costs seems so natural and unquestionable is that the majority of the audience shares the same assumptions. It is perhaps too obvious to even state that in American culture, so much as we can speak of it as unified, life is understood to be inherently valuable and should be protected and prolonged as much as possible. While Americans by no means monopolize preoccupation with immortality, it is nevertheless clear that the default stance in America is to fear and avoid death, which we understand as a tragedy or loss. We treat death as if it were a disease that could be cured. For this reason, the Winchester theme is inescapably bittersweet. It represents the bonds of family and the constant threat that death poses to those relationships.

Based on Nielsen ratings, *Supernatural's* key demographic is adults (especially women) ages 18–49. These viewers would have been born, at the earliest, in the mid–1960s—a critically important point in the timeline of death and dying in America. As scholar and author of *The Good Death*, Ann Neumann, notes:

> For the first time in human history, the definition of death changed in the 1970s. Up until then, death had meant the almost simultaneous end of heartbeat, breathing, and brain function. But a revolution in medicine took place in that decade, developing innovations that could keep the lungs and heart functioning indefinitely. Respirators and defibrillators had winnowed the definition of death down to brain function alone. And nobody—not doctors, lawyers, patients, or families—knew what that meant [12].

In a relatively short amount of time, death was postponed and institutionalized. Within several generations, Americans no longer died at home surrounded by family, but in care facilities tended to by doctors and nurses. Living longer, dying in institutions after considerable medical intervention, without having to face our own mortality the same way our great-grandparents did, we have become alienated from our own deaths. According to U.S. Census data from 1999, an American born in 1980 has a life expectancy of about 74 years, whereas their grandparents (assuming 30 years for a generation) would have only had an average of 54 years. This rapid increase in life expectancy is a mirage of the fountain of youth. As Neumann argues, "We live in an era where death is not real to us; it's something that happens to other people, and so we kid ourselves that it can be avoided" (47). And, yet everyone knows rationally that they will die, making the concept of death tantalizingly uncanny. This fascination with and abhorrence of death make it the perfect subject for exploration in television, where we can live and relive through our most beloved characters, practicing death but never truly confronting it.

The idea of death in America changed drastically in the past fifty years, with cases like Karen Ann Quinlan and Terri Schaivo forcing the question of what it means to be alive, and when death should come after we have artificially abated it. In our quest for immortality, we have unintentionally opened Pandora's box and now face essential disputes about humanity. If life support can sustain a person's body, perhaps indefinitely, what does it mean to be alive, to be human? These same fundamental inquiries into the nature of humanity are at the core of *Supernatural*. Instead of mechanical invention, though, there are curses and supernatural forces that offer immortality at the cost of humanity. Demons, vampires, and Mark-of-Cain inflicted Dean may all live forever, but are their lives worth living? Not to mention the case of Mary Winchester, resurrected after thirty-three years. When, backed by the Winchester theme, Mary mournfully recalls the bliss of being with her young sons in Heaven ("The Foundry"), we find ourselves asking whether it is truly a kinder fate to be alive at all.

With American views on death and dying as a backdrop, *Supernatural* navigates questions of what it means to be human and how to live life authentically. The brothers continuously struggle to take control in a world that they are repeatedly told is predetermined. From the Apocalypse narrative to the Mark of Cain, the Winchesters make it their business to subvert destiny. Although at times both Sam and Dean have taken up existentialist tropes, it is not the characters in *Supernatural* that prove the show to be existentialist, but the values that are implicitly questioned. *Supernatural*'s existentialism is not the casual cultural existentialism of the black turtleneck bedecked beatnik, but the deep questioning of what life means and how it should be lived: belief in free will and authenticity above all else. Although it was a philosophical movement originating in continental Europe in the late nineteenth century, the foundational themes of existentialism have profoundly impacted

American culture and the modern experience. Within *Supernatural*, these ideas are frequently brought to our attention through iterations of the familiar Winchester theme.

Some Specifics of Existentialism

To speak of existentialism (or of any -ism) we must begin from an understanding that there was no such thing according to those philosophers considered to be the founders of the movement (e.g., Kierkegaard, Heidegger, Sartre, de Beauvoir, Camus, Jaspers). Indeed, existentialism was no centrally organized movement or school at all, and many key existentialist philosophers rejected the label. Therefore, although there are similarities that tie existentialist philosophers together, there are also considerable disagreements between them. For the purposes of this study, I work with generalities that do not necessarily reflect the complexity of existentialism, but which allow for discussion within the framework of a broadcast show that has adopted elements of the philosophy and successfully used them to engage millions of viewers. Likewise, it is not important for this discussion whether a certain trope in *Supernatural* is really more in line with one philosopher or another, but that the show interacts with and negotiates the legacy of existentialism writ large.

Existentialism centers around several main topics: freedom, authenticity, death, anxiety, and morality. While it would seem at first glance that existentialism is a primarily negative philosophy, it is something altogether different than nihilism. Nihilism says that life is meaningless, even pointless; existentialism acknowledges the absurdity (pointlessness) of life, but argues that it is the human subject who gives life meaning. Our ability to create meaning in life is both a gift and a curse. Without an external meaning or set of morals, we have infinite possibilities ahead of us. So, too, do we have infinite choices, which we alone pursue after confrontation with the absurd (i.e., the realization that life has no prescribed meaning other than what we give it).

The unpleasant consequence of absolute control is the existential anguish that accompanies it. If we are truly free to choose, as existentialism posits, then the results of our actions are fully our own responsibility. Choice is predicated by the idea that reason alone will never lead to a resolution, only to uncertainty, at which point we must make a decision of our own volition. It is here that existentialist thought departs from the rationalism and belief in pure reason of the Enlightenment era. There are no absolutes and no objectivity in existentialism. Or, rather, knowing absolutes and objectivity will not give the full picture of the human experience. Existence is more than the facts of natural (or supernatural) science, the moral truths of religion, or the amalgamation of the two.

Existence begins and ends with the human subject. To try to find resolution either in scientific fact or dogmatic belief would be, to an existentialist, to submit to inauthenticity. An individual must come to their own authentic truth as a result of their choices, which can neither be arrived at by pure reason nor blind faith. For Sam and Dean, this means defining their own moral code, which they must constantly revise in the face of new obstacles. While their world shows some indication of divinity, they can never really trust that Heaven has their best interest at heart, and they certainly do not subscribe to any notions of destiny. They also cannot simply rationalize their way through the complex landscape of their moral conundrums. Ultimately, they make a choice and stand by it. As a fatally injured Dean tells the reaper, Tessa, in "In My Time of Dying" (2.01) when she resigns herself to fate: "Well, that's crap. You always have a choice. You can either roll over and die, or you can keep fighting, no matter what."

Over the course of thirteen seasons, *Supernatural* has become increasingly existentialist. The initial "humans should live, monsters should die" of Season One is challenged early in Season Two. Struggling to keep the division between monster and human clear, the brothers disagree on whether to kill a nest of vampires that does not feed on humans ("Bloodlust"). Sam's mysterious visions, which begin in the first season as the result of ingesting demon blood as an infant, show him to be at least partially supernatural, if still human. In Season Four, this story arc comes to a head when Dean confronts Sam about the psychic abilities that he has gained from drinking demon blood ("Metamorphosis"). "Do you even know how far off the reservation you've gone? How far from normal? From human?" Dean challenges Sam, rejecting Sam's argument that he is in fact doing the right thing and saving lives. For Dean, the difference between monster and human, good and evil, has always been more black and white than for Sam. When he sees his brother move from one side to the other, Dean doesn't understand nuance, he only sees a human becoming a monster: "If I didn't know you, I would want to hunt you." The embodiment of free will and self-determination, Dean lives his life dictated by rules that he believes to be morally correct and justifiable, but which Sam and the narrative continuously challenge.

If morality is a set of rules defining good and evil, the absence of these rules generates both freedom and disorientation. Yet, even if there are no external rules, societal forces create norms in order to structure behavior and belief. When an individual relies only on these norms, without confronting absurdity, they are living what an existentialist would call an inauthentic life. Consider, as an oversimplified example, a hypothetical community in which everyone only wears blue because they just know it is the right color for clothing. If you were to visit this place as an outsider, you would find the belief strange, maybe even pointless or absurd. You might say to a townsperson that they were being uncritically conformist. They might counter that they choose what blue clothes to wear each day. When you show up wearing red, they tell you that you are wearing a bad color, and they know this because that's just the way it is. Blue is good; not blue is bad. Maybe wearing red is grounds for imprisonment, torture, or execution. To you, it would seem ridiculous: obviously the rule is constructed and not universal. It is something that was made up at some point, and so it could just as easily be unmade.

Now imagine that instead of dictating the color of clothing, the rule dictated what body parts men or women must cover with their clothing. Perhaps we could rationalize this rule as a cultural difference or the result of an institutional dress code. It is not as clearly nonsensical as the first example. Most reasonable people would understand it as constructed, but still legitimate. But what about a more ambiguous moral dilemma: does a human being have the legal and ethical right to choose the means and circumstances of their own death without implicating their physician or loved ones in a crime? Contemporary debate shows Americans are far from agreement on the issue. Some see a man-made rule that can be changed, while others see an ethical obligation to save a life as long as possible. What, then, of an even more immutable moral: the seemingly unanimous condemnation of murder, with the implied importance of preserving life, so deeply ingrained as inherently wrong that we generally do not even think to contemplate it. The average well-adjusted person does not ask why it is considered wrong to kill because we believe we already know that it must be.

Like Sam challenging Dean's blind loyalty to their father in the early seasons, or the brothers' rejection of the strict rules and hierarchical structure of Heaven, existentialism argues that all of these rules are the same in type, if not degree. From the blue clothes to dress codes and physician-assisted death, each ethical standard—no matter how inscrutable it may seem—only has meaning because we give it meaning, according to an existentialist viewpoint. These norms, whether we call them morals, laws, rules, or commandments, are man-made. Humans need to create meaning and order in their lives, to organize the chaos, but this meaning is neither intrinsically correct nor universally true.

In the blue-wearing town, it is easy to face the absurd, because we are outsiders and it is an imaginary location that can be entered and left. Morality, on the other hand, is part of a world that we cannot escape or be objective toward, and so it seems to be beyond scrutiny. Confronting the blue rule does not shake your entire worldview. Asking why we value life, what does it mean to be good or evil, or how we know what is right or wrong—these questions can rattle our beliefs and throw us into disorienting existential angst. And, humans do not tolerate existential dread well. We do our best to move away from it, often settling back into the rules that we know, finding them both restricting and comforting.

This is inauthenticity. It is what Sam and Dean continuously bump up against in negotiating their mission as hunters. At some points, like when Dean—Winchester theme in the background—reassures a drunken Sam that he will kill him before letting him turn into a monster ("Playthings"), convictions and logic run out, and the Winchesters must embrace their existential dread and make a decision. Dean, for example, lives by a code, at least at first: the supernatural must be eliminated. Yet, when he encounters the supernatural in Sam, the dissonance between family and duty becomes incompatible, and he is forced to confront, in a moment of existential dread, the conflict between Winchester exceptionalism and his core beliefs. In this confrontation, Dean chooses Sam, adjusting his philosophy about what must live or die.

To believe that other forces dictate our actions and avoid confronting our own freedom of choice is to deny our authenticity. Sam and Dean straddle the line of authenticity by stubbornly defending their own right to define themselves. A combination of the quintessential belief in the American dream that defined so much of industrial and post-industrial American life and existentialist free will, the boys repeatedly insist on controlling their own image. Whether wresting their identity from militant angels or rabid fans (e.g., at a *Supernatural* convention in "The Real Ghostbusters"), Sam and Dean reject the labels that are thrust upon them by others. As Sam pleads with metamorphosing Rugaru in "Metamorphosis" (4.04): "It doesn't matter what you are; it only matters what you do. It's your choice." Yet, for the average person, it is far easier to disappear into the everyday and accept these manmade boundaries than to continuously encounter the terrifying depths of our own freedom. Failing to face mortality and the fact all life inevitably ends in death is one such moment of inauthenticity. *Supernatural* has played with the boundary between life and death, facing the inevitability while also averting it. This circling around the question of death's role in life gives the show its existentialist underpinning, even when Sam and Dean themselves act in ways inconsistent with existentialism.

What's Dead Should Stay Dead: Resurrection, Immortality, Winchester Exceptionalism

Unequivocally, the most problematic aspect of the brothers' relationship with death is their repeated resurrections, bordering on immortality. Despite believing that the strict division between life and death should not be trespassed and that "what's dead should stay dead" (Dean, "Children Shouldn't Play with Dead Things"; Bobby, "All Hell Breaks Loose: Part 2"), the Winchesters and their loved ones are frequently revived in *deus ex machina* fashion. Early revivals come at a steep cost, usually trading one life for another through demon deals, but in the later seasons, life is restored through divine intervention. Castiel pulls Dean from Hell ("Lazarus Rising"), the brothers are mysteriously transported to a plane right above where Lucifer explodes into earth ("Lucifer Rising"), Castiel revives Bobby in "Swan Song" (5.22) with a touch on the forehead, and Charlie is revived by Ezekiel/Gadreel ("Slumber Party").

With each revival, the underlying morality of Winchester exceptionalism is called into question. As the brothers perform existentialism through the rejection of the so-called natural order, we cannot help but notice how they seem to skirt the rules of life and death that so tragically affect others around them. As Death the Horseman tells Dean in "Appointment in Samarra" (6.11): "You and your brother keep coming back. You're an affront to the balance of the universe, and you cause disruption on a global scale." Likewise, we, the audience, are pressured to examine our own morality and the meaning that we create from *Supernatural*, as we hope that Sam and Dean survive while remaining relatively indifferent to the consequences of this survival within the narrative.

Easily the most extreme example of a Winchester cheating death is "Mystery Spot" (3.11) Gabriel, as the Trickster, kills Dean over a hundred times to prove to Sam that death is inevitable. Ultimately, however, Dean survives Tuesday and the narrative moves on. Gabriel's intervention is one of several times that Angels manipulate time to convince the Winchesters of their predestined fate. Zachariah and Michael also employed this method ("The End"; "The Song Remains the Same") to pressure the brothers into reenacting Michael and Lucifer's fraternal battle. These manipulations raised the question of whether any of the times that Sam and Dean have died were real, or if they were further exploitations of the human mind. Unlike other character deaths portrayed on the show, Sam and Dean have never been reaped or deposited into their own personal Heaven, although they have allegedly visited Heaven before. As Ash relays in "Dark Side of the Moon" (5.16) "This ain't the first time here. I mean, you boys die more than anyone I've ever met." Each time Sam and Dean visited Heaven before, their memory was wiped clean by angels. Yet, if angels have the ability to manipulate time and space and to create alternate realities and influence consciousness, perhaps the Winchesters have never actually died at all, but have only experienced angel-induced hallucinations. Indeed, if the series ends with Sam and Dean still alive, perhaps they never will actually die.

It is the cost of survival that has the most ethical implications for the series. As Dean confesses during the first instance of the Winchester theme, the lengths the brothers are willing to go to in order to save each other often cannot be justified. In addition to all those who died while possessed, or as casualties of soulless Sam or Mark-of-Cain Dean, there are also deaths by negligence or indifference. One such example is when Sam lures a man into a demon-deal that gets him killed in order to locate Crowley and demon–Dean ("Soul Survivor"). These casualties simultaneously undermine the moral code that the Winchesters purport to live by, and seem to further alienate them from the possibility of death, even as their aural identity becomes more intertwined with it. In this way, the narrative provides an existentialist critique toward the artificiality of morals while also reflecting the contradiction of American cultural attitudes about death.

Endings Are Impossible

In Seasons Eleven and Twelve, the stakes had never been higher for the Winchesters to stay alive. When Dean kills Death the Horseman in the ultimate act of free will ("Brother's Keeper"), he saves Sam at the cost of the world by unleashing the Darkness. In a world without Death the Horseman, but where people still die, a reaper, Billie, appears in "Form and Void" (11.02) to give an ultimatum on Winchester exceptionalism. First as an acousmetre, she sings an a cappella version of the folk song "O, Death" that accompanied the first appearance of the Horseman in "Two Minutes to Midnight" (5.21). Invoking the permanence and power of death through familiar but (temporarily) disembodied sound, Billie threatens Sam that he and Dean will experience no afterlife, no Heaven or Hell, only nothingness. Tapping into the deep existentialist understanding of death as emptiness, the repetition of "O Death" calls into question the sustainability of Winchester exceptionalism. The reliance on free will that allowed Sam and Dean to survive and colored their previous relationship with death—ultimately allowing Dean to kill Death the Horseman—now echoes back with existential dread.

Billie's threat strips the brothers of their sense of security when facing death. If they will neither be revived nor experience an afterlife, their next deaths will be truly final. Religious frameworks of a soul outliving a body provide comfort and even an eagerness to experience death. *Supernatural* is a secular show, but plays on religious themes from the Judeo-Christian tradition regarding death and afterlife, most notably Heaven, Hell, and Purgatory. Importantly, there is no everlasting comfort in any of these locations. Even Heaven, which should be paradise, is a sterile and bureaucratic complex. Each soul is locked in a personal Heaven, closely monitored by robotic angels obsessed with hierarchy and dogma. As Ash describes it, "Like a butt-load of places all crammed together. Like Disneyland except without all the anti–Semitism" ("Dark Side of the Moon"). If peace and freedom are mutually exclusive, as Castiel suggests in "Swan Song" (5.22)—"I mean it, Dean. What would you rather have: peace or freedom?"—then Heaven is the epitome of ignorant captivity. It is no wonder Sam and Dean are resistant. Heaven seems hardly better than the Djinn-induced hallucination Dean suffered in "What Is and What Should Never Be" (2.20).

Combined with Billie's warning that she will throw the brothers out into the Empty, the bleak picture of eternal salvation is yet another indication of existentialism at work within the series. Even when her threat is rendered impotent as Castiel kills her to save the Winchesters, whom he says are too important to the world ("First Blood"), the possibility of a final and existential death still lingers in the narrative. Indeed, with no real indication that any afterlife would be preferable to nothingness, the brothers are left longing for the familiar: no Heaven, no Hell, just more of the same, to reference Castiel in "Swan Song" (5.22). As an audience, no matter the ethical costs and moral trespasses, we also find ourselves wanting the same—a series that never dies— once again bringing into focus our wish for immortality. Even as the Winchester theme definitively links the brothers with death sonically, viewers hope for endless moments on the road, Baby purring, and classic rock on the radio.

NOTES

1. Michel Chion, *Audio-vision, Sound on Screen*, ed. Claudia Gorbman (British Film Institute: 1994). Chion attributes certain power and mystery to the acousmetre, because it is only heard and not seen. This is consistent with death in *Supernatural*, which is eerie and threatening, versus Death the Horseman, who is oddly comforting through his calm demeanor and penchant for junk food.

2. See Erin M. Giannini's essay "'When I come back, I'm gonna be pissed': Signaling Narrative and Character Shifts through Death in *Supernatural*" in this collection for an exploration of how character death and resurrection ensures the continuation of the series.

3. For further discussion, see Claudia Gorbman's seminal 1987 book, *Unheard Melodies: Narrative Film Music*.

4. Many scholars link Wagnerian *Leitmotiv* techniques directly to seminal Hollywood composers, such as Bernard Herrmann, as part of the quintessential film music tradition.

5. I use the term "classic rock" following the precedent set by other *Supernatural* scholars, such as Gregory J. Robinson and Stan Beeler.

6. See Michail-Chrysovalantis Markodimitrakis' essay "Dean's Groundhog Day: Negotiating the Inevitability of Death via *Supernatural*" for a fuller explication of this episode.

7. There are a number of instances where pre-existing music was changed from the original airdate to Netflix syndication (e.g., in "Faith" [1.12], Deathrider's "Death in the Valley" replaced Blue Öyster Cult's "Don't Fear the Reaper"). This is almost certainly a result of copyright limitations.

8. In triple meter, the Winchester theme occurs initially as a rising C minor arpeggio, falling back to middle C, wavering down to B-flat and back before outlining another C minor arpeggio—this time rising to the B-flat to suggest a minor seventh chord—before drifting down to pause on the implied, but unconfirmed, dominant (G, in C minor). The range of the theme is a single octave.

WORKS CITED

Abbott, Stacey, and David Lavery, editors. *TV Goes to Hell: An Unofficial Road Map of Supernatural*. ECW, 2011.

Aho, Kevin. *Existentialism: An Introduction*. Polity, 2014.

"All Hell Breaks Loose: Part 2." *Supernatural: The Complete Second Season*, story by Eric

Kripke and Michael T. Moore, teleplay by Eric Kripke, directed by Kim Manners, Warner Home Video, 2007.
The Amityville Horror. Written by Sandor Stern, directed by Stuart Rosenberg, American International Pictures, 1979.
"Appointment in Samarra." *Supernatural: The Complete Sixth Season*, written by Sera Gamble and Robert Singer, directed by Mike Rohl, Warner Home Video, 2011.
Asia. "Heat of the Moment." *Asia*, Geffen, 1982.
Beeler, Stan. "Two Greasers and a Muscle Car: Music and Character Development in *Supernatural.*" *TV Goes to Hell: An Unofficial Road Map of Supernatural*, edited by Stacey Abbott and David Lavery, ECW, 2011, pp. 18–32.
"Bloodlust." *Supernatural: The Complete Second Season*, written by Sera Gamble, directed by Robert Singer, Warner Home Video, 2007.
"Brother's Keeper." *Supernatural: The Complete Tenth Season*, written by Jeremy Carver, directed by Phil Sgriccia, Warner Home Video, 2015.
Buben, Adam. *Meaning and Mortality in Kierkegaard and Heidegger: Origins of the Existential Philosophy of Death.* Northwestern UP, 2016.
"Children Shouldn't Play with Dead Things." *Supernatural: The Complete Second Season*, written by Raelle Tucker, directed by Kim Manners, Warner Home Video, 2007.
Chion, Michel. *Audio-Vision, Sound on Screen.* Edited by Claudia Gorbman, British Film Institute, 1994.
Cox, Gary. *The Existentialist's Guide to Death, the Universe, and Nothingness.* A&C Black Academic and Professional, 2011.
"Croatoan." *Supernatural: The Complete Second Season*, written by John Shiban, directed by Robert Singer, Warner Home Video, 2007.
Crowell, Steven, editor. *The Cambridge Companion to Existentialism.* Cambridge, 2012.
"Dark Side of the Moon." *Supernatural: The Complete Fifth Season*, written by Andrew Dabb and Daniel Loflin, directed by Jeff Woolnough, Warner Home Video, 2010.
Dastur, Françoise. *How Are We to Confront Death?: An Introduction to Philosophy.* Translated by Robert Vallier, Fordham UP, 2012.
"Devil's Trap." *Supernatural: The Complete First Season*, written by Eric Kripke, directed by Kim Manners, Warner Home Video, 2006.
"Do You Believe in Miracles?" *Supernatural: The Complete Ninth Season*, written by Jeremy Carver, directed by Thomas J. Wright, Warner Home Video, 2014.
"The End." *Supernatural: The Complete Fifth Season*, written by Ben Edlund, directed by Steve Boyum, Warner Home Video, 2010.
"Family Matters." *Supernatural: The Complete Sixth Season*, written by Andrew Dabb and Daniel Loflin, directed by Guy Bee, Warner Home Video, 2011.
"First Blood." *Supernatural: The Complete Twelfth Season*, written by Andrew Dabb, directed by Robert Singer, Warner Home Video, 2017.
Foresman, Galen A., editor. *Supernatural and Philosophy: Metaphysics and Monsters ... for Idjits.* John Wiley & Sons, 2013.
"Form and Void." *Supernatural: The Complete Eleventh Season*, written by Andrew Dabb, directed by Phil Sgriccia, Warner Home Video, 2016.
"The Foundry." *Supernatural: The Complete Twelfth Season*, written by Robert Berens, directed by Robert Singer, Warner Home Video, 2017.
George, Susan A. "A Man and His 1967 Impala: *Supernatural*, U.S. Car Culture, and the Masculinity of Dean Winchester." *Supernatural, Humanity and the Soul: On the Highway to Hell and Back*, edited by Susan A. George and Regina M. Hansen, Palgrave Macmillan, 2014, pp. 141–154.
Gorbman, Claudia. *Unheard Melodies: Narrative Film Music.* Indiana UP, 1987.
Gruska, Jay, and Christopher Lennertz. *Supernatural: Original Television Soundtrack, Seasons 1–5.* Watchtower Entertainment, 2010.
Halfyard, Janet K. *Sounds of Fear and Wonder: Music in Cult TV.* I.B. Tauris, 2016.
Hayward, Philip, editor. *Terror Tracks: Music, Sound and Horror Cinema.* Equinox, 2009.
Huey Lewis and the News. "Back in Time." *Back to the Future: Music from the Motion Picture Soundtrack*, Chrysalis, 1985.

"In My Time of Dying." *Supernatural: The Complete Second Season,* written by Eric Kripke, directed by Kim Manners, Warner Home Video, 2007.

"Inside Man." *Supernatural: The Complete Tenth* Season, written by Andrew Dabb, directed by Rashaad Ernesto Green, Warner Home Video, 2015.

Joralemon, Donald. *Mortal Dilemmas: The Troubled Landscape of Death in America.* Taylor and Francis, 2016.

"Keep Calm and Carry On." *Supernatural: The Complete Twelfth* Season, written by Andrew Dabb, directed by Phil Sgriccia, Warner Home Video, 2017.

Knight, Nicholas. *Supernatural: The Official Companion, Season 1.* Titan, 2007.

"Lazarus Rising." *Supernatural: The Complete Fourth Season,* written by Eric Kripke, directed by Kim Manners, Warner Home Video, 2009.

"Lucifer Rising." *Supernatural: The Complete Fourth Season,* written by Eric Kripke, directed by Eric Kripke, Warner Home Video, 2009.

Malpas, Jeff, and Robert C. Solomon. *Death and Philosophy.* Routledge, 1998.

"Metamorphosis." *Supernatural: The Complete Fourth Season,* written by Cathryn Humphris, directed by Kim Manners, Warner Home Video, 2009.

"Mystery Spot." *Supernatural: The Complete Third Season,* story by Jeremy Carver and Emily McLaughlin, teleplay by Jeremy Carver, directed by Kim Manners, Warner Home Video, 2008.

Nagari, Benjamin. *Music as Image: Analytical Psychology and Music in Film.* Routledge, 2016.

Neumann, Ann. *The Good Death: An Exploration of Dying in America.* Beacon, 2016.

Night of the Living Dead. Written by George A. Romero and Jack Russo, directed by George A. Romero, The Walter Reade Organization, 1968.

Phenomena. Story by Franco Ferrini and Dario Argento. Directed by Dario Argento, Titanus, 1985.

"Playthings." *Supernatural: The Complete Second Season,* written by Matt Witten, directed by Charles Beeson, Warner Home Video, 2007.

"The Prisoner." *Supernatural: The Complete Tenth Season,* written by Andrew Dabb, directed by Thomas J. Wright, Warner Home Video 2015.

"The Real Ghostbusters." *Supernatural: The Complete Fifth Season,* story by Nancy Weiner, teleplay by Eric Kripke, directed by James L. Conway, Warner Home Video, 2010.

Reed, David. *Supernatural: Bobby Singer's Guide to Hunting.* It Books, 2011.

Reynolds, Jack. *Understanding Existentialism.* Acumen, 2006.

Robinson, Gregory J. "Metal and Rust: Postindustrial White Masculinity and *Supernatural's* Classic Rock Canon." *Supernatural, Humanity and the Soul: On the Highway to Hell and Back,* edited by Susan A. George and Regina M. Hansen, Palgrave Macmillan, 2014, pp. 197–210.

"Slumber Party." *Supernatural: The Complete Ninth Season,* written by Robbie Thompson, directed by Robert Singer, Warner Home Video, 2014.

"The Song Remains the Same." *Supernatural: The Complete Fifth Season,* written by Sera Gamble and Nancy Weiner, directed by Steve Boyum, Warner Home Video, 2010.

"Soul Survivor." *Supernatural: The Complete Tenth Season,* written by Brad Buckner and Eugenie Ross-Leming, directed by Jensen Ackles, Warner Home Video, 2015.

"Swan Song." *Supernatural: The Complete Fifth Season,* story by Eric Gewitz, teleplay by Eric Kripke, directed by Steve Boyum, Warner Home Video, 2010..

"Two Minutes to Midnight." *Supernatural: The Complete Fifth Season,* written by Sera Gamble, directed by Phil Sgriccia, Warner Home Video, 2010.

Van Elferen, Isabella. *Gothic Music: The Sounds of the Uncanny.* U of Wales P: 2012.

"Wendigo." *Supernatural: The Complete First* Season, story by Ron Milbauer and Terri Hughes Burton, teleplay by Eric Kripke, directed by David Nutter, Warner Home Video, 2006.

"What Is and What Should Never Be." *Supernatural: The Complete Second Season,* written by Raelle Tucker, directed by Eric Kripke, Warner Home Video, 2007.

Folklore and Mythology

Blood, Death and "Demonic Germ Warfare"

Family and the Legend of Roanoke in Supernatural

REBECCA M. LUSH

In the episode "Croatoan" (2.09) from Season Two of *Supernatural*, the Winchester brothers confront death and the fear of dying in both a physical and metaphorical context. While physical death is the most prominent threat in the episode, there is also the subtext of death as disappearing from cultural memory and national mythologies. The episode takes its title from the historical accounts and subsequent myths regarding the "Lost Colony" of Roanoke, which in turn helps foreground the Winchesters' journey within myths of American genesis. The historical and mythical Roanoke and the disappearance of the English colonists represent lost colonial desires and aspirations that focus on the familial losses sustained by the colonists' seeming death and disappearance.

I argue that in "Croatoan," the Winchesters re-enact and attempt to change the outcomes of past events from colonial American history. However, these attempts ultimately fail, and the brothers are doomed to repeat and even reinforce the mistakes of the past despite their best efforts to right perceived wrongs. The themes of death and family in the "Croatoan" storyline foster an allegorical reading of the Winchesters as a critical symbol for the nation.

To situate my reading, I begin with an overview of the existing scholarship on *Supernatural* with an eye towards genre explorations related to Gothic and horror. I then provide historical context about the early English North American colony of Roanoke and its transmission history in later literary retellings that direct attention to colonial nostalgia and idealized notions of family. Next, I consider in particular how the 1588 account by Thomas Harriot uses the metaphor of "invisible bullets" to describe death from disease. This description resonates with the show's use of "demonic germ warfare" to describe the Croatoan virus. I conclude with an extended analysis of the episode "Croatoan," focusing on scenes of violence, bloodshed, and death.

Supernatural *as American Gothic Television*

Supernatural first aired in 2005 and has since been classified by scholars and viewers as a "cult television" show, a status that acknowledges its popularity but, more significantly, its devoted fan following. While *Supernatural* studies is a relatively new academic subfield, the increasing number of studies about the show has distinct scholarly trends. Some of the earliest academic considerations focus on fan media analyses as well as issues of gender and sexuality. Another significant academic approach has been unpacking the show's relationship to folklore studies. Additionally, *Supernatural* has clear roots in the Gothic and horror traditions and also uses humor to deliver episodes that have a postmodern sensibility due to their open discussions of narrative conventions and audience expectations. Given my particular analysis of death and American mythologies, I expand on previous *Supernatural* scholarship to consider how the show uniquely combines the major approaches used in analyzing American Gothic television: family trauma and national guilt.

More specifically, my own focus on death and colonial American history in the "Croatoan" material in *Supernatural* builds on some of the work started by Loew and Klein & Shackelford. This work examines how the show handles issues of cultural othering and how the show addresses the legacy of colonization as an event and social structure. Loew focuses specifically on the questions related to Chicana feminism. Klein & Shackelford consider in part how the supernatural creatures take the place of Native peoples and outlaws. I consider how the show raises questions about othering and violence on the American frontier by redefining who is Other. When colonial scenarios get re-enacted, the show recasts colonial actions as literally demonic, which shifts the historical responsibility for the agents of death in early America by extension. Since one of the central concerns of "Croatoan" is the ethics of killing and whether the switch from human to Other can justify death, these earlier postcolonial analyses carry special significance to unpacking how the episode comments on death, violence, and disappearance.

The relationship between folklore and death, broadly defined, has special significance when considering how *Supernatural* retells American myths and legends. Folkloric considerations of the show typically consider how it addresses variants and expands on the folklore canon by enacting yet another performance or iteration of key folk stories. The process of folkloric transmission attempts to defer the "death" of a story by passing it down across time. *Supernatural*'s intertextual nature fosters narrative arcs that explore both the transmission of oral traditions and convoluted death-centric archival materials. This intertextuality, or the process of drawing relationships between texts, creates a meta-awareness and results in a richer narrative.[1]

The reimagining of Roanoke in "Croatoan" continues the show's intertextuality and folkloric focus and provides a repetition that should resonate with many U.S. American viewers. When Sam initially recounts the story of Roanoke, Dean registers hearing it before, even though at first he doesn't recognize the word "Croatoan." The brothers' conversation likely parallels the experience for many viewers as they are also reminded of a previously repressed lesson about American history. As Daniel Compora has noted, "By populating their universe with characters with actual folkloric origins, the creators of *Supernatural* tap into existing cultural fears and beliefs, lending an air of authenticity and familiarity to the tales being shared" (80). Compora additionally situates the show's use of folkloric materials as consistent with the United States as a "death-denying society" where tales of ghostly returns and hauntings tie into real fears about death and averting death (78).

Death and violence have a particularly unique position in American literature and myths of American nationhood, which makes *Supernatural* an apt example of contemporary American Gothic. Richard Slotkin has argued that the American literary tradition, particularly as it relates to the quintessentially American genre of the Western, articulates a mythic national identity and presence via what he terms "regeneration through violence." In Slotkin's view, violence does not signal loss but, rather, provides a moment of cultural rebirth. His definition of what he refers to as the "myth of the hunter" considers the specifically American context of the frontier and defines the hunter as "a figure who embodies the Christian moral and social law that the hunter both defends and tries to avoid and who therefore, like the Indian opponent, is at once the hero's anima and his soul's most feared enemy" (179). The applicability of Slotkin's "regeneration through violence" to *Supernatural* is overwhelming. The Winchesters are hunters, and the paradoxical relationship between hero and opponent very easily maps onto the show's complicated binaries of "human vs. monster/inhuman" and "good vs. evil." In Slotkin's hunter myth, death initiates a new identity but one that rests on fears and anxieties about violence.

The Uncanny Restaging of Death and Disappearance

The anxiety over death and violence such as those Slotkin identifies in relation to national identity writ large exist on a micro-scale in the familial trauma of the uncanny home of American Gothic. "Croatoan" represents an uncanny space to explore the trauma of the home but also the nation as a symbolic home. Renee Bergland's notion of the national uncanny, which considers how "the interior logic of the modern nation requires that citizens be haunted," describes the paradoxical relationship necessary in American Gothic texts (4). The uncanny as used in Gothic studies typically refers to the concept of the *unheimlich*, which translates to "unhomely," as defined by Freud. For Freud, the uncanny corresponds to the disconcerting sensation when something that should be familiar and safe becomes unfamiliar and unsettling or even threatening. Bergland notes recurring patterns in early examples of American Gothic that simultaneously "acknowledge the American horror and celebrate the American triumph" (16).

Helen Wheatley likewise links national anxieties with the American Gothic, especially in American Gothic television. While horror and Gothic television programs foster a special uncanny relationship in the way viewers consume tales of terror in the comfort of their home, for Wheatley, American Gothic television fetishizes the idea of family more so than British Gothic (24). Wheatley also sees American Gothic television as having two main structural approaches to the genre: firstly, using the form to express national guilt, or secondly, focusing on the everyday "image of the family and familial trauma" (123).

Supernatural links these two approaches, particularly in an episode such as "Croatoan" where family undergirds Dean's resistance to killing Sam. As Wheatley further argues, the "extreme veneration of the American family created an inevitable fictional response, in the exposure of the American family's underside" (124). In "Croatoan," this underside includes confronting violent family histories and exposing historical violence. It also highlights the death of comforting national mythologies that have functioned to hide suppressed colonial violence and deaths. Finally, and more specifically, "Croatoan" explores the anxiety that the idealized, middle-class nuclear family could disappear.

The "Real" Legend of Roanoke and Folkloric Imaginings

The story of the historical "Lost Colony" provides an example of colonial amnesia, and amnesia itself indicates the death or disappearance of memory. The negative effects of the English colonial project in North America have been ignored or mythologized in subsequent retellings of the Roanoke experience due to the focus on the disappearance of the colonists rather than the methods of colonization or their impact on local indigenous communities.[2]

Colonists sought to make the Roanoke colony the first permanent English settlement in North America; the English renamed the territory "Virginia" in honor of Queen Elizabeth, who reigned at the time. Subsequent authors celebrated the birth of Virginia Dare, the first English child to be born on American soil, in romanticized epic poems and stories that lament an origins story for the U.S. that never was. The redirected focus on the loss of English families in later retellings shifts the focus of the English colonial project from that of a political and economic venture to one focused on family. The "death" or loss of English families in the New World also signals a loss of identity— the colonized land ceases to have a clearly English and proto–U.S. American identity and, instead, becomes a space of instability.

The story of the "Lost Colony" is an American historical mystery that has haunted the nation's popular imagination for centuries, particularly in the literary legacy that it has inspired. In 1584, under a charter granted to Sir Walter Raleigh, the English first attempted to establish a permanent colonial outpost in North America in what we recognize today as the Outer Banks region of North Carolina. A subsequent group of English colonists (90 men, 17 women, and 9 children) that arrived in 1587 has become mythologized in American history, literature, and culture since it seemingly disappeared from the historical record. Due to English politics and need for naval power at home in 1588 (the famed "Spanish Armada" year), no ships returned to the Roanoke colony until 1590. The envoy in 1590 arrived at a colony without colonists. Just where these colonists went, whether they died, or whether they joined with local Native peoples (most likely the Roanoke Indians) has been the subject of much historical scrutiny and even conspiracy theories spurred in part by the tantalizing clue that the word "Croatoan" was left inscribed by the colonists.

The historical Roanoke is a site of multiple colonial disappearances, but the third and final one has been the most mysterious. Sixteenth-century accounts of the Roanoke colony highlight its tenuous position and give hints that not all is well between colonists and indigenous peoples. Colonial accounts set up these conflicts in ways that foreshadow the various disappearances of the colonists. In the description of the third voyage to Roanoke by Ralph Lane, Sir Richard Grenville finds the colony "desolate" since all of the men left to return to England with Sir Francis Drake. The English colonists left with Drake because they feared a lack of supplies, but, perhaps more tellingly, the men feel desperate to leave because "the hand of God came upon them for the cruelty and outrages committed by some of them against the native inhabitants of that country" (Hakluyt 304). Grenville then left behind fifteen English men at the deserted Roanoke colony to maintain the English colonial claim to the land. A further voyage of colonists, the one that included women and children, landed in Roanoke to find Grenville's fifteen men also gone.

Thomas Harriot's most well-known historical account of Roanoke similarly hints at disquiet in the English colony. Harriot suggests that his contemporaries' reports are inaccurate because they found Roanoke to be "miserable," which led to "envious, malicious, and slanderous reports ... by our own countrymen besides" (6).[3] The historical archive then paints Roanoke as an unstable space as the turnover in colonists inhabiting it is quite high and the stories about it convey conflicting points of view.

Yet, incomplete historical proof leads to rich and imaginative literary recreations and suppositions. Earlier periods of American literature also reimagined this colonial mystery long before *Supernatural* added its version to the mix. Novelists and poets in the late nineteenth century through the early twentieth century were transfixed by Virginia Dare, a child born in the English colony to one of the families from the 1587 expedition. Stories about Dare typically include romanticized and melodramatic events from her supposed survival into adulthood among the Indians.[4] In some poems and novels, she is even imagined as a direct ancestor of Pocahontas, an attempt to naturalize white citizens as having nativity to North America.[5] The many retellings of the Roanoke story, many of which focused around Virginia Dare, reveal a desire to establish family as the root of folk definitions of national identity; the inferred death and disappearance of Dare and other English colonists reflect how the rhetoric of family can obscure colonial actions.

Who's Afraid of Virginia Dare? Frontier Violence and the Myth of Family

Historical fiction novels and narrative poems, particularly from the nineteenth century and early twentieth century, shift the focus more decidedly to lamenting the loss of proto–American families and their assumed deaths. For example, in the foreword to *The Legend of Virginia Dare*, Sallie Southall Cotten asserts that the lost colony is a "tragedy" in the history of American colonization. Her narrative poem reimagines colonial Roanoke as an English domestic space where after "Many long months pass in busy home-making/ Sweet English customs prevail on the isle" (27). The English family is subsequently under threat in her dramatic description: "Mother and child, as in Bethlehem story,/Flee from the hate of their blood-thirsty foes" and "Suddenly with whoop of murder/Wily Indians swarmed around them" (34). Cotten's text yokes together family trauma with national trauma and makes the English family sympathetic to Christian readers through Cotten's biblical comparison. The loss of the English family as presented by Cotten is analogous to the loss of the nascent American nation. Cotten creates a binary between English and Native in order to unfold a tale of frontier violence, death, and erasure.

While earlier fictional imaginings of Roanoke often highlight the hardships faced by colonists and lament their mysterious fate, more contemporary engagements with this mystery consider the complexity of the English North American colonial project. *Supernatural*'s "Croatoan" episode portrays bloodthirsty and dangerous characters who usher murder and death into small town America. However, whether we are to read these characters as proxies for English settlers or Native peoples is left ambiguous. The historical Roanoke can be considered a frontier story, one that explores the relationship between colonist and Native; similarly, the episode "Croatoan" evokes a frontier context, albeit metaphorically. Frontier narratives traditionally highlight danger and the potential for violence. Whether it is about people facing the rigors of the wilderness or about conflict between colonist/settlers and indigenous peoples, the frontier story often centers on surviving and trying to defy death.

The episode largely avoids reproducing an "us vs. them" binary common in frontier literature, which positions the Native as Other, and instead attributes violence to the entire community. The episode initially gestures towards stereotypical shorthand for Native characters, particularly when describing how one man's neighbor, Mr. Rogers (yes, that is indeed a humorous nod to children's television program *Mister Rogers' Neighborhood*) comes at him "with a hatchet." Overall, the episode references the frontier and colonial contexts without expanding on the complex racial politics of the historic Roanoke colony. In some ways, then, "Croatoan" anticipates more recent moves in retelling the story of Roanoke, such as Season Six of *American Horror Story* where the English colonists are portrayed as bloodthirsty and violent and, therefore, the source of their own death, destruction, and subsequent disappearance.

Invisible Bullets: Disease as a Weapon and Violence as Contagion

One of the earliest accounts of the Roanoke colony describes disease as a weapon of death and destruction. Thomas Harriot's 1588 text *A Briefe and True Report of the Newfoundland of Virginia* describes a rash of mysterious deaths among the southeastern Algonquian that the Native people report as being the result of "invisible bullets" (29). Harriot's text reminds us that germs played a significant role in the clash between English and Native at Roanoke and that death and disappearance in the colonial record was closely tied to disease and infection. While contemporary scholars now acknowledge that what Harriot describes could be explained with a basic understanding of disease vectors, the language used by Harriot is important in positing a link between disease and violence, a link that "Croatoan" also picks up on and expands in its reimagining.[6] After the English arrive, Roanoke Algonquian informants tell Harriot that their people become sick and many die, which he records as "Those that were immediately to come after us [the English] they [the Natives] imagined to be in the air, yet invisible and without bodies, and that they by our entreaty and for the love of us did make the people to die in that sort as they did by shooting invisible bullets into them" (29).[7]

The Harriot quote has several areas of relevance for the episode "Croatoan" because the show also considers sickness as a weapon and ponders the nature of the visibility of bodies. Harriot's recording of "invisible bullets" can be seen as an act of absurd transcription—an English recorder captures a non–English cultural viewpoint despite his lack of cultural understanding. The Native informants speaking to Harriot describe how they become sick from the English, even though they cannot see any visible means of this sort of "attack." While Harriot's text and other historical accounts of Roanoke from the 1580s often hint at discord in colonist and indigenous relationships, the invisible bullets passage cements disease as a tool of colonization and as a force of destruction. Again, it's important to note that the Roanoke colonists would not have understood disease vectors and immunity, thus their spreading of disease does not carry the same sense of intent as later periods in American history; nevertheless, the result is a complex story about death and colonial contact.

Sixteenth-century authors Harriot, Barlowe, and Lane all relay stories about colonial Roanoke that gesture toward various ways Native and English perish in the pursuit of England's colonial project but treat the discussion of English casualties separately. *Supernatural* retells this story, as well, but places the notion of disease as a weapon at the forefront. Whereas Harriot's text shows an unintentional use of disease during colonial conflict, "Croatoan" shows the use of disease to be intentional and makes the virus an explicit weapon, or as Sam describes it, "demonic germ warfare." *Supernatural*'s Croatoan virus as a form of demonic warfare when considered in conjunction with the Roanoke Colony, therefore, implicitly raises questions about the ethics of the English colonial project and provides contemporary critique about the nation's past.

Rivergrove as the New "Roanoke" Out West

"Croatoan," set in Rivergrove, Oregon, draws inspiration from American history and mythology and provides a rich consideration of the multiple meanings and contexts for "death." The episode provides veiled commentary on the death and destruction carried out as part of the English colonial project in North America as well as on the fears of death as a form of disappearance and cultural erasure. Sam and Dean may usually fight demons and other aspects of the supernatural, but in "Croatoan," they have to grapple with the lesser-known aspects of America's colonial identity and the fear of losing their own familial identity.

The themes in "Croatoan" parallel the colonial anxieties of the Roanoke tale. The episode begins with Sam noticing the word "Croatoan" carved into a wooden telephone pole and then providing Dean—who initially appears to know nothing about that word—with a quick refresher course on Roanoke's history. Troubles soon escalate as the townspeople contract a demonic blood-borne pathogen that turns them into killers; those infected disappear seemingly into thin air by the episode's end, leaving the Winchesters wondering about the townspeople's fate. Throughout the episode, the brothers often express fears of being "wiped out overnight" and talk about how the threat of "demonic germ warfare" may force everyone in town to resort to violence and inhuman behavior.

Interestingly, the threat and role of death in "Croatoan" is unique from other handlings of the same subject matter in *Supernatural*: death is not only omnipresent and threatening but also carries with it a finality and erasure that destabilizes the Winchesters' sense of mission and purpose. Throughout the series, death is oftentimes a temporary state for the protagonists Sam and Dean, but the association of death with disappearance in "Croatoan" also changes its narrative role. Additionally, in this episode, death can also mean becoming non-human, or a "thing." In that respect, "Croatoan" highlights Sam and Dean's awareness and fear of how their own increasing volatility undermines their family mantra of "saving people, hunting things." In other words, the episode shows death to be both literal and metaphoric; those infected lose their previous identity and experience a metaphoric death, even though their bodies continue to function. The demonic virus demonstrates that all people are susceptible to carrying the germs of monstrosity, violence, and erasure within them.

Colonial Ghosts: Death, Disappearance and Haunted Returns

By taking its title from the historical accounts and subsequent myths regarding the "Lost Colony" of Roanoke, the episode reflects Postcolonial Gothic concerns that consider how colonial encounters are a repressed cultural memory that return to haunt later generations. As defined by Hughes & Smith, the Postcolonial Gothic portrays colonial encounters as "a catalyst to corrupt, to confuse or to redefine the boundaries of power, knowledge and ownership" (1). In sum, Gothic representations of the legacy of colonial history tend to show how both the colonizer and colonized continue to suffer from either guilt or oppression as a result of the imbalance of power and violence implicit in colonization.

In colonial American literature and the national imagination more generally, the disappearance of the English colonists from Roanoke provides a particularly Gothic historical and literary moment, especially regarding the involvement of Native American peoples. In many fictionalized retellings, Native peoples are obliquely implicated in the disappearance of the English in Roanoke. However, the historical Roanoke story is a rare moment in early American literature where the roles of English and Native are reversed. Most literature describing colonial U.S. encounters emphasizes the death and cultural losses of Native peoples, which renders them ghostly figures of the past with no future in the emerging U.S. republic, such as in James Fenimore Cooper's *Last of the Mohicans*. By contrast, the Roanoke story places the English in the role of the disappeared and, therefore, ghostly figures.

Supernatural's "Croatoan" is just one in a long line of creative reimaginings and departures from the historical record. In the tale of the "Lost Colony," death is assumed but never proven, allowing for many creative suppositions but also anxiety regarding historical certainty and legacy. In short, the Roanoke colony has become a uniquely American folkloric tradition with subsequent generations retelling and modifying the historical tale, continuously adding new explanations for the colonists' disappearance. These retellings change as cultural values change and as scholarly inquiry becomes infused with the popular imagination. The legend of Roanoke becomes an excellent subject for *Supernatural*'s own play with American folklore motifs. The related themes of death and loss of family common in Roanoke retellings help develop the show's unique and contentious relationship to death defined broadly.

The Roanoke story evokes a context in which death can mean disappearing but also a haunting return, much in the way that the Winchesters themselves (and as of Season Twelve their mother, Mary, as well) may die but are able to return. It is important to point out from the outset that "Croatoan" does not explain the fate of the townspeople who disappear in present day Rivergrove, Oregon; we do not know if they have died, exist in a separate dimension, or some other possibility. Thus, *Supernatural* creates its own unresolved legend, mimicking the structural format of the Roanoke myth and heavily suggesting death without confirming it.

The episode's interests in the inhumanity and brutality of those infected also comments on the oftentimes-overlooked destruction and cultural threat the English Roanoke colonists posed to the indigenous population. Nineteenth- and early twentieth-century fictional retellings of the Roanoke story lament the disappearance of the colonists and idealize them without acknowledging the messier and grotesque realities of the colonial project. The episode

"Croatoan" does not simply lament a town that disappeared but also highlights the chaos and destruction that ensues prior to the disappearances. Unlike in early folkloric narratives, the people who disappear in "Croatoan" are not represented as idealized victims but as rather complicated people who commit heinous acts (albeit under demonic influence). The show therefore implicitly asks us to reconsider the veneration of family and symbols of nationhood. Viewers are encouraged to root for Sam and Dean to survive despite the brothers' role in the death and disappearance of the townspeople. Yet, the episode does not allow viewers to passively enjoy the narrative. Sam continually questions Dean on the ethics of the methods used to stop the demonic virus. What is the cost of "saving people, hunting things" when the line between people and thing is continuously blurred?

"Demonic Germ Warfare" and the "Death" of Family and Community in Supernatural

In "Croatoan" the blood-borne, demonic Croatoan virus strikes terror into the protagonists, but as a plot device, the virus enables multiple metaphorical readings that comment on American anxieties past and present. While scholars working from cultural studies approaches assert that monsters and monstrosity are "available for any number of meanings" and that "monstrosity is historically conditioned" (Halberstam 2 and 6), monstrosity can also provide a language to make visible repressed notions or systems that strike fear into people. In short, the Croatoan virus in *Supernatural* expresses the monstrosity of social forces (in this case, colonialism) by showing how they threaten the integrity of the individual human body (via blood infection).

Death is foregrounded as the main concern of the episode, especially since the "previously on" segment recaps Sam's "death visions" from prior episodes. The Winchesters arrive in Rivergrove precisely because Sam has a vision of Dean attempting to kill a young man. Sam's vision includes a young man shouting "I swear it's not in me," hinting that the threat will be something invisible to the unaided-eye, something that lurks beneath the skin and, thus, can potentially pass as human.

The first scene set in Rivergrove highlights the space as an example of idealized small-town Americana but also focuses on the medical clinic, which foreshadows the importance of disease in the episode's exploration of death. Once the Winchesters arrive, we get a camera pan of the town area and see a quaint town street filled with small shops and locals walking home with shopping bags, fixing vintage trucks and engaging in the maintenance of canoes and fishing equipment. The local medical clinic looms large in the center background and is clearly in focus when Sam and Dean first start questioning a local about the whereabouts of the young man who matches the description from Sam's vision. The scene cuts back and forth between the Winchesters and their informant, and the visual background of each speaker hints towards their survival, or not, later in the episode. Sam and Dean are associated with the medical clinic, a space that prevents and treats disease and, therefore, represents a safe haven from the virus. Their informant, a local Marine and fisherman, sits on a rustic front porch with peeling paint, a setting that connotes the kind of small-town family space that is most fragile and under threat in this episode, as the peeling paint suggests.

The episode's repetition of the incised word "Croatoan" from colonial history establishes early in the episode's narrative the significance of metaphoric deaths (as disappearance) and isolation. The relocation and repetition of the carved word "Croatoan" in this episode highlights how Roanoke is a space evocative of a particular context as opposed to a specific geographical location. While Oregon is a long way from North Carolina, the episode portrays an updated version of one of the most iconographic features of the Roanoke story. Instead of "Croatoan" being inscribed on a tree in the forest, we see it inscribed into the bark of a utility pole in a town space. The inscription onto an object that delivers power and services is significant. The modern-day utility pole represents the raw material needed to power Rivergrove, sustaining the homes and businesses of its inhabitants and linking them to the outside world.

Inscribing "Croatoan" on the pole not only provides an overt modernization of the lost colony story, but it also suggests that what is in danger of disappearing is life in the town as we know it as well as the ability to communicate and, metaphorically, remain visible to others. The word "Croatoan" is placed conspicuously on an object that ensures Rivergrove is part of a wider network of other locations in the state and the wider U.S. Unsurprisingly, after spotting "Croatoan" on the utility pole, the brothers realize the phone booth by the pole is out of order and that they also have no cell service. They have no connection to the outside world—they have become isolated in a manner analogous to how the early English colonists were isolated from their homeland of England. The implied malfunctioning utility pole also being metaphorically infected with the Croatoan virus throws into question a symbol of westward "progress."

Sam and Dean's subsequent conversation upon seeing the word "Croatoan" reminds the audience of how certain events or ideas function as a shorthand for larger national concerns and guilt. While Sam's humorous jab that Dean does not remember school but rather *Schoolhouse Rock* provides a moment of levity, *Schoolhouse Rock* functions as a shorthand for history curriculum just as the lost colony functions as a shorthand for larger national anxieties and concerns. As Stacey Abbott has argued, "verbal comedy is used in *Supernatural* primarily as a means for Sam and Dean to maintain control" and Sam's humorous critique functions in this way (9). The *Schoolhouse Rock* joke affords Sam a modicum of power before he goes into further detail about the vagaries of American history that he has no agency over. As Sam continues to explain, the Roanoke story includes colonists who were seemingly "wiped out overnight" and that some theories include "Indian raids, disease, but no one knows what really happened."

Domestic Violence and Deaths: Demonic Forces and Folklore vs. "Fakelore"

The first scene of violence and death occurs in an uncanny space—what should be the idealized American family home. Following the leads gained in their first interview with a local townsman, Sam and Dean go to the Tanner house to inquire about Duane, the subject of Sam's most recent "death vision." The single-family home, complete with a backyard and cheeky signs such as "born to fish, forced to work" and colorful good luck horseshoes, strikes Dean as "creepy" and a "little too Stepford." Again, one of the brothers deploys verbal comedy to maintain control over a puzzling and dangerous situation.

What then ensues is a scene of domestic violence. Mrs. Tanner, the household's mother, is held against her will by her husband and son. The two men violently attack her and try to infect her with the Croatoan virus by bleeding onto her open wounds. She is gagged with a kitchen towel, and the pristine background of the kitchen contrasts with the bright red blood. Sam and Dean, as usual, save the day and wrest Mrs. Tanner to safety while Dean ends up shooting Mr. Tanner, resulting in the man's death. As Mrs. Tanner later says, "one minute they were my husband and son and the next they had the devil in them."

Situating the first scene of blood loss and death within what should be an ideal home reveals what is symbolically at stake in the episode—the integrity and survival of the much-venerated nuclear American family. The mother is held against her will in the kitchen, a domestic space associated with care of the family. Instead of the kitchen being a place that provides sustenance, it has become a place of violence and death. The first casualty then is the idea of the home and family, and the second casualty is the literal death of the father, Mr. Tanner. The uncanny as a translation of Freud's idea of the unhomely figures importantly here. The home has become un-homelike and, since this is a Gothic television series, we as viewers are more likely to see this scene unfold on a television screen within our own home, which subtly extends the anxiety about home and family to our own living rooms. Additionally, the infected blood from the virus can represent violence but can also stand in for family line and lineage, which reinforces the episode's exploration of the death of family.

The Winchesters surmise that their father's theory that "Croatoan" was the name of a plague and pestilence demon may indeed have credence, which makes the entire episode an exercise in ostension, or folkloric enactment, and underscores the cyclical nature of American anxieties about death and disappearance. Catherine Tosenberger has argued that *Supernatural* treats folklore in a manner that allows the audience to hear assorted variants from Sam and Dean's research or recollection and then performs or re-enacts those same folkloric stories before our eyes, "both diegetically and metatextually in a process known as ostension."

Additionally, Mikel J. Koven has explored the show's use of folklore versus fakelore[8] and sees the series' attention to contextualization and its desire to place most folkloric storylines within their appropriate cultural context as the show's attempts to resist the production of fakelore (189). However, Koven concedes that television variants ultimately must make a choice about what variant is most "authentic" when depicting the folklore monster: "the television narrative demands some kind of concretized lore to literally represent the week's monster. The inchoate folklore must be, somehow, physically embodied" (191). Since in "Croatoan" the monster is not corporeal but is rather a virus, the episode maintains a sense of open-endedness regarding variant explanations for why the English colonists and the Rivergrove residents disappear.

The episode portrays the demonic virus as killing the identities of its victims, a loss that then spurs the victims onto violent acts that lead to the deaths of other townspeople. Since the virus attacks identity first, familial bonds and identities become unstable and unclear. Sam and Dean disagree on whether being infected means one stays human, or if, in Dean's words, being infected makes you an "it." Eventually, Sam starts to agree with Dean, stating towards the end of the episode, after he fears he himself has become infected, that "I'm not gonna become one of those things." This also engenders a role reversal for Dean. For most of the episode, Dean supports killing those stricken with the demonic virus because in his eyes, they are no longer human. However, when Sam appears to have been infected, Dean realizes that they aren't just fighting a generalized demonic threat; they are fighting a demonic virus that also threatens the notion of family and identity. Despite his prior belief, Dean refuses to accept that Sam's infection would mean he is no longer the same person, no longer his brother.

By the end of the episode, "Croatoan" reinforces the difficulty in discerning human from demon, and the disappearance of all involved means that their true identities will remain a mystery. The metaphoric death of the townspeople's human identities makes those typically presented as ideal Othered and dangerous. Noël Carroll defines monstrosity in many ways, including the notion that the monster defies categorization, what Carroll dubs the interstitial. Carroll also defines what he terms the fission figure, which is the monster that vacillates between two states, such as human and demon. The people of Rivergrove defy categorization along the lines of Carroll's theory and can therefore be deemed monstrous. The modern-day re-enactment of the Roanoke story casts everyone as either monsters or potential monsters, which undercuts romanticized notions of founding English families disappearing. At the end of the episode, Dean asks Sam, "Where the hell did everybody go?" and reminds the audience that the Winchesters remain the last standing family and humans in the area. In effect, Sam and Dean re-enact the role of folkloric Roanoke colonists who must integrate with other communities in order to survive. There is nothing left but for the brothers to hit the road and find a new monster to fight.

While what happened to the historical English colonists in Roanoke at the end of the sixteenth century will likely remain mysterious and open to interpretation, one thing is certain: America's enduring fascination with this story has no end in sight. Similarly, the episode "Croatoan" offers a very unsatisfactory resolution—we learn that the event largely unfolded as a way to test whether or not Sam was immune to the virus, and could be a proper carrier of demon blood for the antagonists' machinations. Sam and Dean never determine the fate of the disappeared townspeople and cannot tell whether or not they are dead. Even when the series returns to the Croatoan virus storyline in Season Five, the whereabouts of the Rivergrove residents are never addressed.

While the road so far for Sam and Dean has taken many twists and turns, as of Season Thirteen, the core theme of the show is still the fear of family members dying or disappearing. The Croatoan virus shows that no one is immune to the darker side of humanity (or inhumanity), and thus the idealized notion of the family is always under threat. While the infected inhabitants of Rivergrove disappear seemingly into thin air just like the English colonists before them, the anxiety of their disappearance and the threat it symbolizes to the venerated notion of the idealized family and national identity remains.

The disappearance of the historical colonists and the fictional residents of Rivergrove functions as a death since their stories only exist as part of the past, not the present or future. The structure of *Supernatural* casts Sam and Dean in the roles of those who must remember the deceased or disappeared so that they can continue their work in the show of safeguarding humanity from the monstrous, demonic, and even the heavenly. "Croatoan" casts them as the keepers of the "real" story of Roanoke and highlights that the disappearance of English colonists does not mean the death of the anxieties and problems inherited from the colonial past to the present. "Croatoan" is a relatively early example in this long running series of how the show positions Sam and Dean as the holders of American social and national mythological narratives, which the series later makes materially explicit and symbolic in their literal inheritance and reclamation of the Men of Letters bunker along with its extensive occult library. "Croatoan" establishes the significance of American history to the present work of the Winchesters and provides yet another example of how the show considers multiple aspects to the oft-quoted phrase "family don't end with blood" as a way to cope with death.

NOTES

1. In addition to "Croatoan," the episode "Bedtime Stories" (3.05) is an especially clear example of the series' interrogation of how folkloric culture, such as fairy tales, portrays death and violence.

2. I refer here to folkloric, creative, and theatrical/filmic retellings not academic studies. Colonial American studies have long addressed the complex power negotiations between the English and Native peoples and increasingly attempt to decolonize academic views of indigenous peoples as marginal and instead acknowledge their centrality. See in particular *A New World: England's First View of America* edited by Kim Sloan and Joyce Chaplin's *Subject Matter*. For an example of decolonizing academic approaches to the study of colonial Native America see Betty Booth Donahue *Bradford's Indian Book* and Jace Weaver *The Red Atlantic*.

3. Spelling modernized. The 1590 text renders the quote as: "enuious, malicious, and slaûderous reports … by our owne countrey men besides."

4. These literary texts use the generic term "Indian" and do not provide tribal specificity—a generalization by these authors that help contemporary scholars see these as the dominant culture's construct of how they see Native peoples as opposed to being reflective of what theorist Gerald Vizenor terms "the tribal real."

5. There are several reasons to see this as mere fantasy not the least of which includes each woman's date of birth. Dare was born in 1587 and Pocahontas was likely born ca. 1596.

6. While the parallel between *Supernatural*'s Croatoan virus and Harriot's "invisible bullets" is uncanny, it is unclear if Harriot was a direct source for the show's writers. For a thorough discussion of the exchange of medical knowledge and understanding between the English and the Roanoke Algonquians see the chapter "Epidemic, Encounter, and Colonial Promotion in Virginia" in Kelly Wisecup's *Medical Encounters: Knowledge and Identity in Early American Literatures*.

7. Spelling modernized. The 1590 text renders the quote as: "Those that were immediately to come after vs [the English] they [the Natives] imagined to be in the aire, yet inuisible & without bodies, & that they by our intreaty & for the loue of vs did make the people to die in that sort as they did by shooting inuisible bullets into them."

8. A term coined by Richard M. Dorson to describe narratives that attempt to insinuate oral traditions and generational passing down but are actually new literary creations.

WORKS CITED

Abbott, Stacey. "Rabbits' Feet and Spleen Juice: The Comic Strategies of TV Horror." *TV Goes to Hell: An Unofficial Road Map of Supernatural*, edited by Stacey Abbott and David Lavery. ECW, 2011, pp. 3–17.

American Horry Story: Roanoke. Created by Ryan Murphy and Brad Falchuk, FX, 2016.

"Bedtime Stories." *Supernatural: The Complete Third Season*, written by Cathryn Humphris, directed by Mike Rohl, Warner Home Video, 2008.

Bergland, Renee. *The National Uncanny: Indian Ghosts and American Subjects.* UP of New England, 2000.

Carroll, Noel. *The Philosophy of Horror: Or, Paradoxes of the Heart*. Routledge, 1990.

Chaplin, Joyce. *Subject Matter: Technology, the Body, and Science on the Anglo-American Frontier, 1500–1676*. Harvard UP, 2003.

Compora, Daniel P. "Gothic Imaginings: Folkloric Roots." *The Gothic Tradition in* Supernatural: *Essays on the Television Series*, edited by Melissa Edmundson. McFarland, 2016, pp. 75–90.

Cooper, James Fenimore. *The Last of the Mohicans*. Penguin, 1986.

Cotten, Sally Southall. *The Legend of Virginia Dare*. Roanoke Island Historical Assoc., 1937.

"Croatoan." *Supernatural: The Complete Second Season*, written by John Shiban, directed by Robert Singer, Warner Home Video, 2007.

"The Devil You Know." *Supernatural: The Complete Fifth Season*, written by Ben Edlund, directed by Robert Singer, Warner Home Video, 2010.

Donahue, Betty Booth. *Bradford's Indian Book*. UP of Florida, 2014.

Dorson, Richard M. "Folklore and Fake Lore," *The American Mercury*, March 1950, pp. 335–42.

"The End." *Supernatural: The Complete Fifth Season*, written by Ben Edlund, directed by Steve Boyum, Warner Home Video, 2010.

Freud, Sigmund. *The Uncanny*. Translated by David McLintock. Penguin, 2003.

Hakluyt, Richard. *Voyages and Discoveries*. Penguin, 1985.

Halberstam, J. *Skin Shows: Gothic Horror and the Technology of Monsters*. Duke UP, 1995.

Harriot, Thomas. *A Briefe and True Report of the New Found Land of Virginia*. Dover, 972.

Hughes, William, and Andrew Smith. "Postcolonial Gothic." *Gothic Studies* vol. 5, no. 2, 2003, pp. 1–96. *ProQuest*. Accessed 7 Jan. 2017.

Klein, Michael J., and Kristi L. Shackelford. "'Hey Sammy, we're not in Kansas anymore': The Frontier Motif in *Supernatural*." *Undead in the West: Vampires, Zombies, Mummies, And Ghosts on the Cinematic Frontier*, edited by Cynthia J. Miller and A. Bowdoin Van Riper. Scarecrow, 2012, pp. 19–32.

Koven, Mikel J., and Gunnella Thorgeirsdottir, "Televisual Folklore: Rescuing *Supernatural from the* Fakelore *Realm*." *TV Goes to Hell: An Unofficial Road Map of Supernatural*, edited by Stacey Abbott and David Lavery. ECW, 2011, pp. 187–200.

Leow, Hui Min Annabeth. "Coloniality and the Chicana Gothic: Travelling Myths in the Pilot" *The Gothic Tradition in* Supernatural: *Essays on the Television Series*, edited by Melissa Edmundson. McFarland, 2016, pp. 91–102.

Nielsen, E.J. "Wearing the Woman in White: The Doomed Lives and Afterlives of Women." *The Gothic Tradition in* Supernatural: *Essays on the Television Series*, edited by Melissa Edmundson. McFarland, 2016, pp. 103–113.

Sloan, Kim. *A New World: England's First View of America*. U of North Carolina P, 2007.

Slotkin, Richard. *Regeneration Through Violence: The Mythology of the American Frontier: 1600–1860*. Wesleyan UP, 1973.

Tosenberger, Catherine. "'Kinda like the folklore of its day': *Supernatural,* Fairy Tales, and Ostension." *Transformative Works and Cultures,* no. 4, 2010. http://dx.doi.org/10.3983/twc.2010.0174. Accessed 29 Dec. 2016.

"Two Minutes to Midnight." *Supernatural: The Complete Fifth Season*, written by Sera Gamble, directed by Phil Sgriccia, Warner Home Video, 2010.

Vizenor, Gerald. *Manifest Manners: Postindian Warriors of Survivance*. Wesleyan UP, 1993.

Weaver, Jace. *The Red Atlantic: American Indigenes and the Making of the Modern World, 1000–1927*. U of North Carolina P, 2017.

Wheatley, Helen. *Gothic Television*. Manchester UP, 2006.

Wisecup, Kelly. *Medical Encounters: Knowledge and Identity in Early American Literatures*. U of Massachusetts P, 2013.

Wheelin' and Dealin'

Crossroads Mythology, Deal-Making and Death in Supernatural

RACHEAL HARRIS

Be it a biological pattern or familial predisposition, making deals with demons is intrinsic to Winchester DNA. Grounded in folklore belief and urban legend, deal-making involves summoning a demonic entity to bargain for favor or assistance. The price of this exchange is frequently the soul. As such, in order to pay their debt, the individual must die. Although the moment of death is open for negotiation, the invariable consequence of such an inter-action is damnation. But what does this inclination toward deal-making and its relationship to death signify about the folklore of *Supernatural* and how the Winchester family enact this folklore?

Demonic dealing and crossroad pacts are initially introduced as an avenue via which John and Dean Winchester attempt to guarantee the terms and circumstances around their individual deaths. How the concept is intro-duced is specific to the grounding of the series in traditional Southern folklore beliefs and impacts how death later comes to be understood and experienced. Deal-making is not specific to John and Dean but to all members of the Win-chester clan—blood relatives and otherwise. As the series progresses, the relationship which Sam and Dean have to their deceased kin, along with their obligation to each other, plays a more vital role in how deal-making is under-taken. So too, as the brothers continue in their pattern of dealing, dying and being resurrected, it becomes clear that making a deal with a demon brings no guarantee of happiness in life or permanence in death.

Examining the deals struck by members of the Winchester clan and those closest to them, I conclude that within the series, the deal is a form of cur-rency. The value of this currency is most apparent when it is read in relation to death. In turn, how death is understood relates exclusively to the rural folklore beliefs in which the series makes its foundation. American folklore, particularly concepts of crossroad dealing, conjuration, and zombification, provides a framework through which much of the discussion on supernatural elements and entities are introduced within the series. American folklore will be used here to explore the landscape of deal-making and the relationship it shares with *Supernatural's* larger depiction of Americanism and American folklore beliefs, particularly the understanding of death and what happens to the soul after death. Ultimately, I argue that it is regional specific beliefs and folklore superstitions of the American South which have the greatest influence on how death is depicted within *Supernatural*.

Supernatural *and "Flexible" Folklore*

First, however, it is necessary to briefly explore *Supernatural's* relationship to folklore in general. Shanna Swendson compares the narrative of Sam and Dean to a modern retelling of Grimm's fairy tales (350). She contends that where the role of the Brothers Grimm was to record regional lore so that it might be remembered by future generations, in the case of the Brothers Winchester, archetypal or ancient lore is re-examined against present cultural ideas and beliefs. From this framework it is restructured for the modern audience, giving a new lease on life to a fusion of history, folklore, and urban mythology which might otherwise be forgotten. When Winchester lore is applied in the modern world, it becomes an artistic representation of fact.

In the long term, the risk to this approach is that it presents a filtered view of the historically accurate roots of the series. This may impact how specific folklore motifs are remembered historically and culturally. Within the series, this sentiment is present in the episode "Hell House" (1.17) when Sam and Dean encounter the spirit of Mordechai Murdoch, which represents a pastiche of urban legends. Murdoch, having no direct link to history or lore, exists as a growing and changing entity. Rather than having a basis in history, folklore, or urban legend, belief alone makes him real. For the brothers, the lack of established lore complicates Murdoch's exorcism. This episode is important because it is a metaphor for the mythology or lore of the larger series.

Additionally, Koven & Thorgeirsdottir assess *Supernatural* within the folklore/fakelore framework, concluding that *Supernatural* recasts folklore to make it relative to the larger plot of the series, rather than de-contextualizing it purely for narrative value. Their observations are instrumental in establishing how we might approach the ways folklore and urban legends, particularly in relation to their respective ideas on death, are used within the series.

For example, in "Crossroad Blues" (2.08), we see evidence of this recasting in the representation of the ritual which Sam and Dean undertake to summon the Crossroad Demon. While visual elements like the literal crossroads and the tribute box find a home in authentic legend, the appearance of the comely female demon, along with the idea of sealing a deal with a kiss, are particular to the series' interpretation of deal-making.

The recasting of folklore is repeated in this episode with the introduction of Goofer dust into the narrative. When George Darrow gifts the bag of Goofer dust to Sam, he references it as a protective element. In traditional folklore practice, brick dust is used for this purpose, whereas Goofer dust (composed of graveyard dirt and sometimes bone and hair) is associated with black magic as opposed to protection conjure (Anderson 112). The nefarious nature of Goofer dust precludes it from being used or even sought by most practitioners. In *Supernatural*, it is because of its elements that it is misappropriated into the Southern lore of the narrative. While this could be seen as *Supernatural* getting something "wrong," it is more useful to see this as an example of the flexible relationship the series has to folklore.

At no point do I wish to suggest that *Supernatural* is exclusive in its use of Southern lore when discussing the spirit world or afterlife. There are various examples of wider American folklore found throughout the series. For instance, "Red Sky at Morning" (3.06) exhibits an East-Coast feel in both setting and content, with the sea providing the folklore context for the haunting of Sea Pines, Massachusetts by a clipper and its crew. So too, many of the episodes which employ the use of poppets, hex bags, witchcraft paraphernalia, such as "Malleus Maleficarum" (3.09), and plotlines that focus around the history of witchcraft within the broader scope of American history, such as "It's the Great Pumpkin, Sam Winchester," (4.07), bear more in common with beliefs specific to the Pacific Northwest. The second episode of the series, "Wendigo" (1.02), draws heavily upon Native American lore in its discussion of the Wendigo mythology. Similar lore is seen again in "Bugs" (1.08), while the relationship between the Croatoan virus and the real-life mystery of the lost Roanoke colony in "Croatoan" (2.09) are indicative of how broader American history and legend are interwoven throughout the series.[1]

In these examples, death narratives which feature within the plot relate closely to the fundamental religious beliefs of the first settlers rather than the Roman Catholic inspired ideas in which hoodoo and Southern lore grounds itself. It is these concepts which I focus on in the remainder of my analysis. My reasoning for this approach lies in the fact that, apart from the Croatoan story arc, examples of wider folklore belief feature primarily in stand-alone or "monster of the week" episodes. In contrast, episodes which are heavily influenced by Southern specific lore and/or Roman Catholicism provide the foundation for narrative arcs which expand across multiple seasons of the series as well as expansive attitudes toward death and dying. I will focus my attention to Southern-specific folklore.

Southern Folklore

Anthropologist Zora Neale Hurston spent much of her career investigating the folklore beliefs of the American South and Haiti. What her studies revealed about these locales was that the purpose of their specific folklore was to provide context to the present, while the sharing of stories across generations explained the role of the individual in relation to immediate family and wider community (30–33). Secondary to this, folklore existed alongside region specific ideas about religion and the afterlife. These religious beliefs were a fusion of the African religions, brought to America by way of Haiti and Africa, and Roman Catholicism, into which all Southern slaves were baptized (Garry & Hansen, 336–340). Perhaps best recognized today as hoodoo, these beliefs draw heavily on the interaction between living and dead, with a pronounced focus on the importance of family, lineage, and obligation.

While Dean and Sam may hail from Kansas, thus owing more to the legacy of the quintessential Midwestern cowboy (Klein and Shackelford, 20; Valenzano & Engstrom, 558–559) than the southern hoodoo priest or priestess, many of their encounters with dying as well as supernatural beings are strongly linked to those Southern belief systems. We see throughout the series that their pattern of living, dying, and being resurrected links them to the Old South more so than to the region of their births. When introduced in "Pilot" (1.01), Dean remarks that he has "been down in New Orleans on a voodoo thing." This statement immediately introduces Southern mythology into the narrative, establishing a cultural framework and context from which wider mythologies will grow. This is further solidified in the episode "Faith" (1.12)when Sam suggests turning to a hoodoo doctor to prevent Dean from dying prematurely.

Seeking out this avenue of assistance, despite a general opposition to much of the supernatural world, suggests an inclination on the part of both Sam and Dean towards trusting healing techniques which are based in conjuration and spell work. Dean objects to Sam's attempt to use hoodoo to heal him and is prepared to die, until a reaper restores him to health. It is not a coincidence that the reaper, a personified form of death, is introduced against the hoodoo backdrop. Its inclusion here foreshadows the ongoing relationship which hoodoo belief and death will share, particularly in Dean and Sam's early experiences with dying.

Unlike other supernatural belief systems, hoodoo is something that both brothers believe in enough to trust with their lives. Their belief is further highlighted in the episode "Playthings" (2.11) in which hoodoo lore is explored as a preventative force, employed to repel a vengeful spirit. Unlike other forms of ritual, such as witchcraft, hoodoo is not associated with evil elements. Sam and Dean are not surprised by or opposed to its presence in the hotel. The use of the Five Spot symbol, itself specific to hoodoo culture, is first recognized by Sam, who concludes that hoodoo is involved in the supernatural occurrences. Dean later discovers that the elderly owner of the property had a Creole nanny in her childhood, concluding that her skills in hoodoo conjure must have come from this authentic source.

At the end of the episode, it is not Sam and Dean who drive away the ghost. Rather, it is the grandmother, Rose, who makes a deal with her dead sister Maggie's spirit: Rose will remain on the property so long as her own daughter and granddaughter are able to leave unharmed. Rose's sacrifice foreshadows the sacrifices that Sam and Dean will make for each other in later episodes. At the core of these sacrifices is a strong sense of familial obligation. This too, plays an essential role in Southern belief systems. Familial obligation is interwoven with many of the folklore beliefs that influence the *Supernatural* narrative and form the bond between Sam and Dean. To more fully appreciate Sam and Dean's penchant for making (demon) deals to save family, it is necessary to examine the concept of ancestor reverence.

Ancestor Lore: How Sam and Dean Understand Their Role in the Winchester Clan

Ancestor reverence plays a prominent role in many folklore beliefs. Ancestor reverence is at the core of the Winchester family narrative, which is used to create the mythical landscape in which Sam and Dean fulfill their destined roles as hunters. Connected to their parents and forebears through the Winchester legacy that is passed on to them through John, primarily via his written words, the boys use their history to justify their present occupation as hunters. Interacting with the journal allows the brothers to establish who they are within the lineage of their family line by reading themselves against those who came before. Similarly, John's notes on how to kill a range of evil entities can be viewed as a form of ancestral intercession. Although he is not present, it is his recorded experiences which allow Sam and Dean to save lives and hunt things with a degree of success.

During their encounter with the Shtriga in "Something Wicked" (1.18), the journal acts as a reminder of the unending relationship between past and present. In this instance, Dean is reminded of an incident in his childhood when he failed to protect Sam, a misstep which almost resulted in Sam's death. Encountering the Shtriga again in their adulthood, Dean is granted an opportunity to atone for his (perceived) prior shortcomings. Dean concludes that John did not kill the monster specifically because it is Dean's fate to do it. Only in doing so can he affirm himself as a member of the family. Outside of its comment on the importance of familial responsibility, the episode highlights Dean's belief that it is his job to save Sam, regardless of the cost to his own life. This belief is central to the Winchester family ideology and dictates Dean's first foray into deal-making. Subsequently it is his dealing which leads to his death. These elements: dealing, death and later, resurrection, form the holy trinity of Winchester lore.

As John's journal bridges father to sons, so does the Impala, better known as Baby.[2] This connection has similarly been a topic of academic studies on the series. Arguments have been made that the Impala functions as a sign of legacy (Fechter 299–300), hyper-masculinity (Beeler 53–55), and as an updated version of the Gothic castle (Knowles 39–40). Although Dean is the owner of the car, it becomes a stand-in for John, specifically as an avenue through which Dean vents his rage at John, both for dying and for selling his soul. Despite this rage, Dean cannot forsake the tie to John. It is his only remaining connection to his father. Instead, he rebuilds the Impala on several occasions, even after it has been damaged almost to the point of being useless.

For Sam too, the car is a place in which family bonds are felt strongly. Knowing that he will die, Dean spends his last months on earth bonding with Sam over how to make repairs on the car in "Fresh Blood" (3.07). Promising that he will look after Baby, Sam inherits the vehicle after Dean is sent to Hell in "No Rest for the Wicked" (3.16). Returning to Earth after being resurrected by Castiel in "Lazarus Rising" (4.01), Dean is horrified to find that Sam has made alterations to the interior of the vehicle by installing an iPod dock. The modern technology is starkly opposed to the car itself (a classic car from the 1960s) as well as being at odds with the ancestral bond which the Impala represents.

Sam's ancestral ties to the Impala are later represented in the memory of his childhood, which saves him from possession in "Swan Song" (5.22). Looking at the green army man which has been jammed into the rear door's ashtray, Sam reconnects to his humanity via the childhood memory of how the figure came to be there. This recollection, recounted for the audience in a voiceover by Chuck Shurley, leads to the reconnection of Sam's present self to his familial duty and his role as a hunter within the Winchester clan while also forming the final chapter in one book of the Winchester Gospel. Sam's remembrance also functions to strengthen his link to Dean, thus preventing Dean from being killed in the battle between Lucifer and Michael. Sam willingly sacrifices himself by jumping into the pit and into (certain) death. Like his brother before him, Sam sacrifices his own life to ensure that Dean can continue living. As *Supernatural* so often reminds us, however, death is rarely an ending. While for Dean, a return from death to life is relative to his future alignment with the archangel Michael, for Sam, resurrection relates to a past that is tied to the underworld.

Unlike Dean, Sam's ancestral bonds are impacted by the relationship he forms with Azazel. Although the demon is not his kin in the traditional sense, the fact that they are linked via demon blood is integral to the perception that Sam has of himself and his role within the Winchester family unit. To Sam, the value of his soul, compared to that of John, Mary, or Dean, differs because of the relationship he has shared with demonic entities through ingesting demon blood. Inasmuch, Sam sees himself as an outcast. Castiel heightens this belief by taking an intentionally antagonistic stance towards Sam throughout Season Four, implying that Sam cannot be trusted because he is inherently aligned with Lucifer. Although Sam and Dean reconcile, there is a perpetual sense that Sam does not precisely fit the mold of his ancestral line.

In the episode "Sharp Teeth" (9.12), Sam accuses Dean of treating family bonds as a "cure all" for their fractious relationship, illustrating his resentment that familial ties supersede all else and that his real sense of otherness is never addressed. At several points, Sam attempts to use death as an avenue to escape these feelings. Dean's commitment to Sam, which is linked to his own understanding of his role in the family, continues to prevent Sam from staying dead. Thus, a repetitive cycle begins in which Sam and Dean are sacrificing their lives for each other, only to be resurrected back into the hunting lifestyle. To some extent, this torture can be read as punishment for the sins of their forebears, particularly Mary and John, who both wagered their souls in deals with demonic entities.

Deal-making is introduced along with the legend of the Colt, toward the end of the first season. The combination of the richly Midwestern mythology of the Colt legend fuses the regional narratives of Sam and Dean firmly with those of the South. Still, it is not until the episode "Crossroad Blues" (2.08) that the deal-making concept is explored in detail and then with specific reference to American folklore belief.

Dealing and Death

No member of the Winchester family deals or dies with more frequency than Dean. Putting aside the many deaths he suffers while caught in the

Trickster's time loop in "Mystery Spot" (3.11), Dean's experiences of death and resurrection reveal the most about the changing attitudes which the Winchesters have toward dying.[3] Like most normal humans, the object of the hunter is to stay alive. Although he admits that members of the hunting community frequently have a short life span, Dean is no exception to this rule. His first encounter with impending death in the episode "Faith" (1.12) reveals that while Dean is willing to die as a consequence of his heroism, he does not wish to. After the events of "In My Time of Dying" (2.01), however, once he realizes that John has traded his life to save him, Dean's attitude takes a stark turn. Although he does not seek death as such, the guilt he feels over his father's sacrifice darkens his view toward living. It sets Dean on a path where he is destined to repeat the very behavior that not only led to John's death but also to Dean's own guilt. In doing so, Dean passes this guilt on to the only surviving member of his family—Sam. This does not bring Dean peace, however, not even in death.

Dean strikes his first deal in traditional folklore fashion—at a crossroads in "All Hell Breaks Loose: Part 2" (2.22). We will return to the historical authenticity of this act shortly. This initial act of bartering involves the exchange of his soul for Sam's resurrection after Sam is knifed in the back. Rather than the instant death suffered by John in "In My Time of Dying" (2.01), or the more common ten years of life granted to Mary in "In the Beginning" (4.03) and the deal-makers in "Crossroad Blues" (2.08), Dean receives a single year in return for his soul. The countdown to his death begins as soon as Sam is resurrected. Knowing that his death will occur at a specific date and time, rather than being freeing, has the opposite effect. It hangs over Dean like a shadow, impacting his motivations to hunt and his attitude towards life. The assurance of death causes him to be careless, which is often where the comedic relief of Season Three presents itself, but once Hellhounds start baying at his heels, he breaks down and admits fear.

At this point in his journey, death is a punishment for Dean, something which he fears because he knows it is intimately linked to Hell, torture, and the slow transition into a demon. When he does die, he suffers the very worst of this fate as he is tortured on the rack for decades. This ends only when he agrees to torture other souls in return, as we learn in "Family Remains" (4.11). Unexpectedly returned to life, the perfect memory of these events functions as a heavier weight than the guilt he felt before. This leads to his antagonistic relationship with the Horseman Death and the reaper Tessa. As his encounters with each of these characters becomes more frequent, it becomes clearer that Dean hates them because he envies them. As he watches those closest to him die and often go to Heaven, death becomes something which he attempts to barter for as a reward or release from the pain of his life as a hunter. He longs for comfort and peace but fears that this will never come because of the sins he has committed in Hell. Dean's attitude is complicated by the fact that after his initial deal, he no longer has the ability to use his soul as a bartering chip. After his actions in Hell, he is also known to many of the demons there, and they continue to taunt him after his return to earth. The events of "On the Head of a Pin" (4.16) force Dean to confront the part he played in torturing souls in Hell, but this does little to help him reconcile these actions. The realization that it was he and not John who is responsible for breaking the first seal on Lucifer's cage adds to his torment.

From a folklore perspective or even a religious viewpoint, what Dean fails to realize is that his "sins" are not merely his own, instead they echo the sins committed by his parents before him and the generations of hunters before them. As a member of the Winchester lineage, the life force of his ancestors flows through him. Much the same as in folklore belief, it is their actions that have brought him to the place and time in which he finds himself (Haskins 33). If he were to realize this, he might also see that looking to them for guidance might alleviate much of his suffering and accommodate his path to righteousness. As the last pure-blooded Winchester, it is Dean's purpose to carry the history of his family and to atone for it. Only after this mission has been accomplished can he finally experience a good death.[4] That is the real "family business," and that is his destiny.

In opposition to his brother, Sam's experiences with death have been a mirror of his *inability* to make a deal. From his perspective, this relates to his exposure to demon blood, something he is deeply conflicted about. Sam's encounters with dying, rather than an exchange, are always an attempt at atonement. Through his self-sacrifice, he aims to make himself worthy of being able to deal his soul and to be a true member of the Winchester lineage.

This is perhaps most painfully highlighted in "Lazarus Rising" (4.01) when Sam admits that he tried to negotiate to have Dean brought back to life but that "no demons would deal." Having to articulate this, and to admit to it in front of Bobby, is the starting point in the division between the brothers. When it is later revealed to the boys that Mary, like John, died as the result of having made a demonic pact, Sam's feeling of otherness is even more pronounced. It is this friction which provides the narrative tension for the rest of the fourth season. With neither brother wanting to carry on without the other, they become each other's greatest weakness. That demons, angels, and the hunting community know this, makes the Winchester boys a constant target for retribution. To kill one will punish the other. As a result, Sam and Dean become stuck in a loop, in which deal-making leads to death. which leads to resurrection.[5] This loop begins with Dean's first demon deal in "All Hell Breaks Loose: Part 2" (2.22) and takes on added significance once we better understand the evolution of crossroads lore in *Supernatural*.

Lore of the Crossroads

Crossroads have a long association with divination and fortune telling. Metaphorically, they are a representation of life difficulties and hard decisions. Reading this against the turmoil of Sam and Dean Winchester, we can say that their entire life is lived at a crossroads. For the superstitious, a crossroads is a place where realms intersect, where the living cross over, and where the dead might be summoned back to this realm (Alvarado 255). From out of this idea grows the hoodoo perspective, which is that crossroads have an intimate link to undead spirits and/or loa gods. These gods form a pantheon of deities and act as intermediaries between mortals and God. They can be bartered with; however, this generally has little to do with soul-selling (Filan, 151).

There are a variety of gods on whom one might call for assistance at a crossroad, though it is traditionally only Papa Legba (or Papa Lebas as he is sometimes known) who is associated with crossroads divination. Unlike a demon, Legba is called upon for assistance and guidance in times of stress. He is a liaison between humanity and the other loa. In his syncretized form, he is represented by Saint Peter or Saint Anthony (among others), which further enforces his image as intermediary. Although Legba is not known to have an interest in soul selling, he is a petro loa. It is the nature of petro loa to have a bawdy and raucous sense of humor. Such character traits are discussed frequently in literature related to spirit possession, in which a specific loa will ride their devotees, making them perform lewd acts in the process (Hurston, 349).

The liveliness of the loa is perhaps most clearly seen in the late addition of Crowley to the recurring character line-up. Introduced in Season Five's "Abandon All Hope" (5.10) as the King of the Crossroads, Crowley embodies the humorous aspect of the loa's qualities, bringing him in line with the standard crossroad mythology. Crowley's sense of humor is apparent from his initial appearance, manifesting itself in the deal he makes with Bobby Singer, which he insists be sealed with a kiss. Much to Bobby's chagrin, Sam and Dean learn of the deal through Crowley, who has captured the moment on his phone's camera ("Two Minutes to Midnight"). In later seasons, Crowley is frequently responsible for injecting humor into the plot, a feat which is accomplished through his joviality and mockery. To some degree, Castiel forms a similar function, although the comedic aspect of his character is related to his inability to understand human motivations. In contrast, Crowley understands them all too well, and it is manipulation of human desire and weakness that makes him such a formidable ally.

Bobby's deal with Crowley, while costing him his soul, is approached very differently than Dean's deal or Sam's inability to deal. Ethically, we can argue that Bobby's deal, unlike that of John or Dean, was undertaken selflessly. This is highlighted by the fact that Crowley restores to Bobby the use of his legs even though Bobby failed to request this for himself. We will return to this act of mercy in a moment. In contrast, John's deal was made to save Dean. This appears to be selfless on the surface, although when we consider his dying words to Dean, we see that it was John's own fear of having to kill his youngest son which played a role. It is also possible that John's regret over his own absenteeism in the lives of Dean and Sam motivated his sacrifice, thus deepening the selfish motivations behind it. Similarly, Dean's deal was not only to restore Sam but also to absolve his own guilt in failing to protect his younger brother. Sam highlights this in Season Three after Dean rebuffs attempts to free him from the deal. Dean does not want to go on without his brother, but he also feels the weight of having been the recipient of life at the cost of his father's soul. The attempt to assuage this guilt leads him to self-sacrifice but this, too, is a selfish act and one that leads to his damnation.

Bobby's deal is in service not only to Sam and Dean but also the preservation of mankind. Where Dean's actions allow Sam to bring on the Apocalypse, Bobby, as the surrogate father/mentor, offers himself in salvation of humanity. Thus, his motivations are selfless. Crowley takes mercy on Bobby by healing his broken spine and allowing him full bodied movement. There is little doubt that failure to do so would have rendered Bobby useless during the battle. In this sense, we see again an element of the loa gods, who are not inclined to punish deal makers but rather to take pity on them and their frailties.

The Living Dead: Dean, Sam and Zombification Lore

An alternative reading of hoodoo/folklore influences on *Supernatural* leads to parallels between Dean, Sam, and the concept of the zombie. Zombification has long been a part of Southern folklore, having distinct ties to the Haitian belief systems that were brought to America through the slave population of that area. Distancing ourselves from the image of the zombie within the landscape of current popular culture, within *Supernatural* and the regional framework of zombification, we see that because of their serial deal-making, both brothers adopt traits which resemble those of the zombie.

In Haiti, the zombie is a trapped soul that has been cursed and has lost control of both its body and free will, rendering it a powerless automaton (Hurston 279–280). Zombification traps the cursed individual in servitude to their master. Unlike the historic master/slave relationship in which the slave has control of their own body but not their own life, in zombification, the spirit of the zombie retains awareness whilst being locked into its own unresponsive body. Zombification might best be likened to medically diagnosed "locked-in" syndrome, in which the mind is aware while the body is unresponsive. Appearing in a death-like state then, the zombie is forced to carry out the will of their master. Locked within the prison of their body, the victim eventually loses all sense of self, becoming a mindless, tortured vessel, almost like the soul which has become a demon.

Depending on the variant of the belief, in some instances a zombie curse can be broken or counteracted with the use of conjure. In other examples, there is no cure, and the soul is damned to work until the body decays. While there are conflicting beliefs around the fate of the soul after death, common lore stipulates that the holder of the zombie retains ownership of the soul, ensuring that the afflicted is never at rest. This fate, worse than death or damnation, is the primary reason why zombification remains one of the most feared curses that can befall an individual.

Dean

Dean's resurrection from Hell in Season Four renders him a type of zombie. Michael, the archangel, holds his curse. Although Dean's deal is made with a demon and his contract held by Lilith, it is God's will that Castiel raise Dean to life. This usurps the original contract and the original contract holder. Since God is absent from the series at this point, Castiel takes on the role of the puppeteer insofar as it is he who attempts to steer Dean towards the fulfillment of Michael's wishes. Although he is not fully aware of it at the time, acting on the orders of God, Castiel resurrects Dean with the intent that Dean will become the chosen vessel for Michael. Surrendering his body in this way would remove Dean's ability for control, leaving him at the complete mercy of the angel possessing him.[6] The purpose of being a vessel, along with the intent of Michael, are inconsequential to Dean, who perceives angel possession as a form of surrender. Thus, he declines to become a willing participant in that destiny.

As Castiel becomes more sympathetic to Dean, the role of puppeteer is transferred to Zachariah. Unlike the bond Dean shares with Castiel, though, his relationship with Zachariah is antagonistic. This becomes influential in Dean's ability to avoid the "curse" of becoming a vessel. Unlike the deal that had him sent to Hell, Dean sees his resurrection not as a bartering agreement or pact but as something forced upon him. This fact allows him to break the "curse" of his own zombification.

Dean again becomes a type of zombie when he accepts of the Mark of Cain in Season Nine. Under the influence of the Mark, which is understood as a curse from God, he is powerless to fight the forces that control his body and his psyche. Unlike his struggle with the angels over becoming the vessel for Michael, the Mark of Cain exists within him as an uncontrollable entity. Although Dean accepts the Mark from his forefather, the biblical Cain of Genesis, he is quick to learn that, much like zombification, the Mark controls him. Whereas he was largely able to barter with demons for the resurrection of Sam, or the angels over his preordained fate as a vessel, Dean is in complete servitude to Cain's curse. The surrender of his free will leaves him stricken in the sense that soul-bartering did not and, even as a character with such a strong sense of free will, Dean almost succumbs to being cursed.

The peak of Dean's suffering is reached in "Brother's Keeper" (10.23), during which he begs and tries to barter for death. Much like a victim of zombification, he has the presence of mind to see what is happening to him and to even chart his own decline into madness; yet, he is unable to stop it. Just like the zombie, Dean wants release, wants death, yet there is no avenue, other than the complete deterioration of his body, through which he can achieve this. The process of this deterioration is slow and not without impact on his mental faculties. As such, even if he were able to achieve death, there is no guarantee that his soul would be in a state to transcend to Heaven or any other place of peace.

Sam

Sam, too, does not escape a certain amount of zombification throughout *Supernatural*. Notably, the soullessness he experiences throughout Season Six presents a similar condition to that of being a zombie. Moving through his life without the hindrance of his soul, Sam, while being highly capable as a hunter, is merely going through the motions of a predetermined role. Getting no joy or satisfaction from helping the people he encounters, and similarly, no joy from killing demons, Sam forfeits his sense of self. This makes him merely an empty shell, and, much like a victim of zombification, he is powerless to fully engage in the world around him.

In Season Eight, when Sam is possessed by an angel under the pretense of being healed, his body becomes the kind of "meat suit." The term "meat suit" has always been an object of derision for both brothers. Although Sam is conscious and in control of his actions for some of the time, there are moments in which he is rendered helpless within his own body. In these moments, Sam is at the mercy of the angel; he is merely a tool through which the angel can undertake his own nefarious work—Sam becomes like the living dead. Unlike the impact of his soullessness, however, the possession plays a more detrimental role on Sam in the long term because of his relationship to Dean. Although not in control of his brother's faculties, it is only through Dean's invitation that the angel was able to enter Sam's body, making him a zombie. It is only due to Crowley's intercession that Sam can free himself from the curse. The use of demonic connections to achieve his freedom is itself, a source of bartering, which brings the concept of soul value and pact making back into the fore. In this instance, it is again Dean who is responsible for paying the cost of Sam's freedom. Although it is Dean who was ultimately responsible for making the deal with the angel in the first place, his actions, as always, were inspired by the concept of self-sacrifice.

Conclusion

Due to the numerous encounters which Dean and Sam have with death and dying, their own and each other's, the audience is reminded that the Winchesters' fates are intimately linked to their role within the "family business." Theirs is a pattern of sacrifice which has been repeating throughout generations and one which, despite their attempts to change fate or to intercede with their ancestry, continues with negative consequences. These repetitive decisions and their predictable outcomes are central to the larger arc of *Supernatural*: deal-making, death, and resurrection.

NOTES

1. For a more in depth look at "Croatoan" (2.09), see Rebecca M. Lush's essay "Blood, Death, and Demonic Germ Warfare: Family and the Legend of Roanoke in *Supernatural*."

2. Interestingly, Baby also serves to connect Dean with a newly resurrected Mary in "Keep Calm and Carry On" (12.01). As Dean shows Mary around the bunker, he takes her to Baby. Mary's eyes light up at the sight of the familiar car. She walks to Baby, caressing the car as though it were John, and leans into the backseat window and verbally greets the car. Dean, opposite of Mary, looks fondly at the backseat, then makes the uncomfortable connection between his own sexual encounters in the car and the fact that his parents also had sex in the car.

3. See Michail-Chrysovalantis Markodimitrakis' essay "Dean's Groundhog Day: Negotiating the Inevitability of Death via *Supernatural*" in this collection for a deeper explication of this episode.

4. See Susan Nylander's essay "Death, American Style: Americana and a Cultural History of Death" in this collection for a fuller discussion of the concept of "good death."

5. See Jessica George's essay "Death, Resurrection, and the Monstrous Evolution of the Winchesters" and Erin M. Giannini's essay "When I come back, I'm gonna be pissed: Signaling Narrative and Character Shifts through Death in *Supernatural*" in this collection for more on resurrection in the series.

6. Intriguingly, Dean agrees to be Michael's vessel at the end of Season Thirteen in "Let the Good Times Roll" (13.23), with the caveat that Dean remain "in the driver's seat." The deal is made to save Sam, who is in the clutches of a full-powered and angry Lucifer, and, predictably, ends with Michael taking full control of Dean's body. The transition from Dean to Michael is made clear—signaled by Dean's clear pain and anguished cry of "We had a deal!"—and holds great possibility for Season Fourteen's storylines. The editors and author look forward to seeing what happens.

WORKS CITED

"Abandon All Hope." *Supernatural: The Complete Fifth Season*, written by Ben Edlund, directed by Phil Sgriccia, Warner Home Video, 2010.

Abbott, Stacey. "Then: The Road So Far." *TV Goes to Hell: An Unofficial Road Map of Supernatural*, edited by Stacey Abbott and David Lavery. ECW, 2011, pp. 6–17.

"All Hell Breaks Loose: Part 1." *Supernatural: The Complete Second Season*, Written by Sera Gamble, directed by Robert Singer, Warner Home Video, 2007.

"All Hell Breaks Loose: Part 2." *Supernatural: The Complete Second Season*, written by Eric Kripke, directed by Kim Manners, Warner Home Video, 2007.

Alvarado, Denise. *The Voodoo Hoodoo Spellbook*. Weiser, 2011.

Anderson, Jeffrey E. *The Voodoo Encyclopedia: Magic, Ritual and Religion*. ABC Clio, 2015.

Beeler, Stan. "Two Greasers and a Muscle Car: Music and Character Development in Supernatural." *TV Goes to Hell: An Unofficial Road Map of* Supernatural, edited by Stacey Abbott and David Lavery, ECW, 2011, pp. 40–57.

"Brother's Keeper." *Supernatural: The Complete Tenth Season*, written by Jeremy Carver, directed by Phil Sgriccia, Warner Home Video, 2015.

"Bugs." *Supernatural: The Complete First Season*, written by Rachel Nave and Bill Coakley, directed by Kim Manners, Warner Home Video, 2005.

"Croatoan." *Supernatural: The Complete Second Season*, written by John Shiban, directed by Robert Singer, Warner Home Video, 2007.

"Crossroad Blues." *Supernatural: The Complete Second Season*, written by Sera Gamble, directed by Steve Boyum, Warner Home Video, 2007.

"Death's Door." *Supernatural: The Complete Seventh Season*, written by Sera Gamble, directed by Robert Singer, Warner Home Video, 2012.

"Do You Believe in Miracles?" *Supernatural: The Complete Ninth Season*, written by Jeremy Carver, directed by Thomas J. Wright, Warner Home Video, 2014.

Engstrom, Erika, and Joseph M. Valenzano III. "Cowboys, Angels, and Demons: American Exceptionalism and the Frontier Myth in CW's *Supernatural*," *Communications Quarterly*, vol. 62, no. 5, 2014, pp. 147–165.

_____. *Television, Religion and Supernatural: Hunting Monsters Finding Gods*, Lexington, 2014.

"Faith." *Supernatural: The Complete First Season*, written by Raelle Tucker and Sera Gamble, directed by Allan Kroeker, Warner Home Video, 2006.

Fechter, Mary. "Riding Down the Highway: Why the Impala Is the Third Main Character." *In the Hunt: Unauthorized Essays on Supernatural*, edited by Leah Wilson. Benbella, 2013, pp. 297–308.

Filan, Kanaz *The New Orleans Voodoo Handbook*. Destiny, 2011.

Foresman, Galen A. "What the Hell Is Going On?" *Supernatural and Philosophy Metaphysics and Monsters ... for Idjits*. Edited by Galen A. Foresman. Wiley Blackwell, 2013, pp. 49–61.

"Fresh Blood." *Supernatural: The Complete Third Season*, written by Sera Gamble, directed by Kim Manners, Warner Home Video, 2008.

"Fresh Bones." *X Files: The Complete Second Season*, written by Howard Gordon, directed by Rob Bowan, Fox, 1995.

Garry, Jane, and El-Shamy Hasan. *Archetypes and Motifs in Folklore and Literature: A Handbook*. M.E. Sharp, 2005.

Giannini, Erin. "'There's nothing more dangerous than some a-hole who thinks he's on a holy mission': Using and (Dis)-Abusing Religious and Economic Authority on *Supernatural*." *TV Goes to Hell: An Unofficial Road Map of* Supernatural, edited by Stacey Abbott and David Lavery. ECW, 2011, pp. 236–253.

Haskins, Jim. *Voodoo & Hoodoo*. Original Publications, 1978.

"Hell House." *Supernatural: The Complete First Season*, written by Trey Callaway, directed by Chris Long, Warner Home Video, 2006.

"Home." *Supernatural: The Complete First Season*, written by Eric Kripke, directed by Ken Girotti, Warner Home Video, 2006.

Hurston, Zora Neale. *Of Mules and Men*. 1935. Harper Collin, 2008.

_____. *Tell My Horse*. 1938. HarperCollins, 2008.

"I Think I'm Gonna Like It Here." *Supernatural: The Complete Ninth Season*, written by Jeremy Carver, directed by John Showalter, Warner Home Video, 2014.

"In My Time of Dying." *Supernatural: The Complete Second Season*, written by Eric Kripke, directed by Kim Manners, Warner Home Video, 2007.

"In the Beginning." *Supernatural: The Complete Fourth Season*, written by Jeremy Carver, directed by Steve Boyum, Warner Home Video, 2009.

"It's the Great Pumpkin, Sam Winchester." *Supernatural: The Complete Fourth Season*, written by Julie Siege, directed by Charles Beeson, Warner Home Video, 2009.

"Keep Calm and Carry On." *Supernatural: The Complete Twelfth Season*, written by Andrew Dabb, directed by Robert Singer, Warner Home Video, 2017.

Klein, Michael J., and Kristi L. Shackelford. "'Hey Sammy, we're not in Kansas anymore,' The Frontier Motif in *Supernatural*." *Undead in the West: Vampires, Zombies, Mummies, and Ghosts on the Cinematic Frontier*, edited by Cynthia J. Miller and A. Bowdoin Van Riper. Scarecrow, 2012, pp. 19–32.

Knowles, Thomas. "The Automobile as Moving Castle." *The Gothic Tradition in Supernatural Essays on the Television Series*, edited by Melissa Edmundson. McFarland, 2016, pp. 35–49.

Koven, Mikel J., and Gunnella Thorgeirsdottir, "Televisual Folklore: Rescuing *Supernatural* from the Fakelore Realm." *TV Goes to Hell: An Unofficial Road Map of Supernatural*, edited by Stacey Abbott and David Lavery. ECW, 2011, pp. 187–200.

"Lazarus Rising." *Supernatural: The Complete Fourth Season*, written by Eric Kripke, directed by Kim Manners, Warner Home Video, 2009.

"Let the Good Times Roll." *Supernatural: The Complete Thirteenth Season*, written by Andrew Dabb, directed by Robert Singer, Warner Home Video, 2018.

"Malleus Maleficarum." *Supernatural: The Complete Third Season*, written by Ben Edlund, directed by Robert Singer, Warner Home Video, 2008.

"Mystery Spot." *Supernatural: The Complete Third Season*, written by Jeremy Carver, directed by Kim Manners, Warner Home Video, 2008.

"No Rest for the Wicked." *Supernatural: The Complete Third Season*, written Eric Kripke, directed by Kim Manners, Warner Home Video, 2008.

"On the Head of a Pin." *Supernatural: The Complete Fourth Season*, written by Ben Edlund, directed by Mike Rohl, Warner Home Video, 2009.

"Pilot." *Supernatural: The Complete First Season*, written by Eric Kripke, directed by David Nutter, Warner Home Video, 2006.

"Playthings." *Supernatural: The Complete Second Season*, written by Matt Whitten, directed by Charles Beeson, Warner Home Video, 2007.

"Red Sky at Morning." *Supernatural: The Complete Third Season*, written by Laurence Andries, directed by Cliff Bole, Warner Home Video, 2008.

"Something Wicked." *Supernatural: The Complete First Season*, written by Daniel Knauf, directed by Whitney Ransick, Warner Home Video, 2006.

"Swan Song." *Supernatural: The Complete Fifth Season*, story by Eric Gewitz, teleplay by Eric Kripke, directed by Steve Boyum, Warner Home Video, 2010.

Swendson, Shanna. "Keepers of the Lore." *In the Hunt: Unauthorized Essays on Supernatural*, edited by Leah Wilson. Benbella, 2013, pp. 349–363.

"Taxi Driver." *Supernatural: The Complete Eighth Season*, written by Eric Kripke, directed by Kim Manners, Warner Home Video, 2013.

"Theef." *X Files: The Complete Seventh Season*, written by Vince Gilligan, John Shiban and Frank Spotnitz, directed by Kim Manners, Fox, 2000.

"Two Minutes to Midnight." *Supernatural: The Complete Fifth Season*, written by Sera Gamble, directed by Phil Sgriccia, Warner Home Video, 2010.

"Wendigo." *Supernatural: The Complete First Season*, written by Eric Kripke, directed by David Nutter, Warner Home Video, 2006.

Zubernis, Lynn S. *Family Don't End with Blood: Cast and Fans on How Supernatural Has Changed Lives*. Smart Pop, 2017.

Resurrection

Death, Resurrection
and the Monstrous Evolution
of the Winchesters

JESSICA GEORGE

It is a truism to say that we all die.

It is also a truism to say that nobody really dies in *Supernatural.*

Certainly, a series whose central conceit revolves around monsters, Heaven, and Hell will inevitably deal with the undead. *Supernatural*'s protagonists, however, return from the dead rather more often than any of the ghosts, vampires, or demons that they hunt. Both Winchester brothers have been resurrected several times over the course of the show's (at the time of writing) thirteen-year run, and many secondary characters have also come back from the dead. The Season Seven episode "Slash Fiction" (7.06) pokes self-conscious fun at this recurring pattern: after a pair of shapeshifting Leviathan who have been impersonating the Winchesters are killed, the remaining monsters consider the possibility of introducing a new duo of impostors, but reject the idea, saying, "These boys coming back from the dead again starts to strain credulity." Season Ten ended with Dean appearing to kill Death himself, literalizing the Winchesters' apparent ability to triumph over death, and Mary Winchester—whose death kickstarted her sons' life of monster-hunting—is resurrected and plays a central role in Season Twelve.

Death in *Supernatural* may, then, be circumvented, but it is not meaningless. Rather, mortality defines the shape of a "natural" human life, and the capacity to defy death offers a disconcerting challenge to notions of what is human.

The first section of my essay explores some connections between immortality, undeath, and the monstrous in Gothic and horror fiction. From the titular character of Mary Shelley's *Frankenstein* to the immortality-seeking business moguls of Ridley Scott's *Prometheus*, the human being who overreaches his or her bounds by seeking power over death is a recurring figure. *Supernatural* has repeatedly invoked such figures, from the undead spirits and vampires who attack the living to the murderous Sue Ann LeGrange ("Faith"), Doc Benton ("Time is on My Side"), and the Styne family ("Dark Dynasty"; "The Prisoner"). What makes these characters monstrous is not simply their unethical behavior, but that they blur the boundaries of humanity-defining categories—in this case, "living" and "dead." As Jeffrey Jerome Cohen points out, the monster is dangerous because it is a liminal being, one which "threatens to smash distinctions" and "resists [...] classification" (6–7). That which refuses to remain dead is perhaps by definition monstrous.

Monsters blur boundaries; and in the world of *Supernatural*, the borders between human and supernatural beings, heroes and villains, are unstable. It is not only monsters who come back from the dead. Or, if returning from the dead is in itself monstrous, then perhaps Sam and Dean are rather more monstrous, or less human, than they once were. Of course, other major characters—Bobby Singer, Mary Winchester, Castiel, Crowley, and Rowena, for example—have also returned from the dead in various ways, but for reasons of space, I will concentrate here upon the Winchester brothers.

After discussing the links between immortality and monstrosity, I will go on to look at the ways in which *Supernatural* destabilizes the humanity of its protagonists. It confronts them with their own monstrous doubles and with the threat of monstrous contamination—but their departure from humanity is most obvious in their repeated returns from beyond the grave. Margrit Shildrick has argued that monsters disturb us precisely because they foreground our own vulnerabilities (17; 51–52). Immortality may seem to be the opposite of vulnerability, but in Gothic fictions, it opens up the human subject to potential contamination. As nineteenth-century Gothic fiction came to grips with evolutionary theory, it anticipated the horrific possibilities of post-human or superhuman evolution, a dark flipside to the Utopian imaginings of science fiction. Twentieth-century and contemporary Gothic fictions have continued to mine this vein, and I go on to read the Winchesters' resurrections and transformations as stages in a process of monstrous evolution. I argue that this evolution away from human mortality makes clear the characters' similarities to the monsters they hunt, but that this is also complicated by the close relationship between resurrection and familial love, which is perhaps the defining characteristic of humanity in *Supernatural*.

Souls in Heaven and Hell

Supernatural often figures death as a literal descent into an inhuman realm, one during which our protagonists undergo a painful process of transformation.

We see travels through Heaven, Hell, and Purgatory, and learn that demons are former humans turned monstrous after their descent into Hell ("Malleus Maleficarum"). Though human souls are not destroyed when their owners die, Heaven seems to be the most complete of these possible deaths: souls in Heaven remain in a kind of stasis, reliving their old memories and unable to contact the human world. Demons, in contrast, remain conscious of their situation, and may refuse to accept it. These descents into Hell affect Sam and Dean most noticeably.

It is interesting to note that in *Supernatural*'s mythology, humans who go to Heaven after death do not become angels; they are a separate species. An ascent into Heaven does not offer a possibility for angelic transformation the way that a descent into Hell holds a possibility for monstrous degeneration—perhaps because Heaven is considerably less easy to escape. Season Eleven raised the possibility of another realm of the afterlife, the Empty, from which there was no possible return ("Form and Void"), and which seemed to offer the redemptive possibility of a natural death, though this was later disproved when Castiel was able to persuade the unnamed ruler of the realm to return him to the mortal world ("The Big Empty"). I will discuss the way these descents and their effects manifest in the storylines of both Winchester brothers, often seeming to affirm human exceptionalism through the idea that it is more important to stay human than to survive. But it is not always this simple. The intimate way in which the show intertwines resurrection with the theme of family—a defining human trait—suggests a relationship rather more complex than can be contained in simple oppositions between life and death, or human and monster.

The Monstrous and the Undead

Many of *Supernatural*'s monsters are in the literal sense undead. That is, they are once-living humans who have returned to the world of the living in malign form, as vengeful spirits (as, for example, in "Dead in the Water"), zombies ("Children Shouldn't Play with Dead Things"), or vampires ("Dead Man's Blood"). The vampire is perhaps the most famous of undead monsters, but for Timothy K. Beal, "[not] just Dracula but all monsters are undead" (10), while Mark Neocleous argues that "the definition of monster must include [...] its nature as a *once-living* and yet *not fully dead* being" (20–21). As regular viewers of *Supernatural* know, however, not all of its monsters are dead in any literal sense. Some are humans who have been transformed without undergoing physical death; some are completely different species; and some are human beings cast beyond the moral pale by their murderous actions. What, then, is so particularly monstrous about the undead?

Richard Kearney touches upon the answer (or, at least, *an* answer) when he points out that monsters "reveal the undecidable character of many of our neat divisions and borders" (120). That is, they cannot be clearly categorized. They may shapeshift, shedding identities and displaying both human and animalistic characteristics, or exhibit behaviors incongruent with the appearance of ordinariness they present to the world. For Heather L. Duda, humanity itself is "a homogenizing term that separates people into two categories: those who are human—who follow a society's rules and regulations and demonstrate that society's 'humane' qualities—and those who are inhuman, or monstrous—who go against the grain and act in ways that are opposite to society's homogenizing apparatuses like law, education, and religion" (7). This should not be taken to mean that monstrosity is a simple matter of rebellion. Rather, the monster displays characteristics of both the human *and* its horrific, animalistic, or mechanical Others.

Because to be human is to be homogenized, those who will not or cannot conform with the "homogenizing apparatuses" of their society, excluded on the grounds of race, gender, sexuality, disability, or class, may find themselves regarded as hybrid, as only partially human—in other words, as monstrous. The monster is not, however, reducible to an anxious reflection of the foreigner, the lower classes, or the sexually independent woman. It defies these "divisions and borders" in ways that call their very naturalness into question. Jeffrey Jerome Cohen has argued that the existence of the monster constitutes a "refusal to participate in the classificatory 'order of things,'" and this is what makes it "dangerous, a form" suspended between forms that threatens to smash distinctions" (6). The monster both attracts and repels: rather than simply embodying what we know to be bad, it draws "horrid attention to the borders that cannot—*must* not—be crossed" (13), and invites us to imagine what possibilities might exist on the other side.

If there is any border that "cannot [...] be crossed," it is surely that between life and death. Elisabeth Bronfen and Sarah Webster Goodwin have suggested that death itself is a "disordering force," a "challenge to all our systems of meaning, order, governance, and civilization" (4). Death itself is utterly Other, utterly inhuman—but at the same time, a challenge to the ways we make sense of the world, and therefore a little monstrous. Many of these "systems of meaning, order, governance, and civilization" assume the inevitability and naturalness of a particular type of death, however. As S. C. Humphreys argues, "many cultures have some idea of the 'right' shape for a satisfactory life, and make judgments that some deaths are untimely while other people have lived too long" (263). It is death out of place—and perhaps death defied—that challenges order.

For the political philosopher Jean Baudrillard, the imposition of a strict border between the living and the dead is "the primary source of social control"

(130). All other divisions and exclusions take their form from this initial boundary: the dead are "the first restricted area [...] the principle separation is between life and death" (130). The correct shape of a human life is one that ends with "[an] ideal or standard form of death, 'natural' death, [corresponding] to the biological definition of death and the rational logical will. This death is 'normal' since it comes 'at life's proper term'" (162). Baudrillard argues that the morbid fascination exerted by suicides and car crashes derives from the fact that they are manifestly not "natural" deaths, ending lives before their "proper term" is up.

Stories of undead monsters dramatize a similar violation of this fundamental separation. (Indeed, they often connect the two, since it is rarely those who have died "naturally" who return from beyond the grave.) If the boundary between life and death underlies all others, then all monsters who trouble categories are haunted by the specter of the undead. Similarly, the human being who seeks to achieve power over death by gaining immortality may not appear physically monstrous, or even have returned from beyond the grave, but nonetheless exceeds the bounds of this initial category by refusing his or her "*duty* [...] to natural death" (Baudrillard 162). Julia Kristeva views the corpse as "the utmost of abjection," rejected in order to allow the self to exist (4).[1] A dead body that returns to life, or a body that should die but refuses to do so, blurs the boundaries between living self and dead Other, and is therefore monstrous.

Returns from beyond the grave are a staple of Gothic fiction, in literature, film, and TV. Since the latter half of the nineteenth century, these fictions have also grappled with the anxieties engendered by evolutionary theory. In the wake of Darwinism, human beings were confronted with the possibility that we were not the perfect finished products of an act of divine creation, but one stage in an unfinished process of evolution. Humanity was, in the words of Kelly Hurley, "continually in danger of becoming not-itself, becoming other" (3). Boundaries could blur in both directions, and humans could not be clearly separated from our animal ancestors, or from the unknown future beings we might become. Evolutionary development was bound up with fitness to survive, and so the possibility of future human evolution gave cause to rethink the human relationship with death.

As Gothic fiction engaged with the implications of evolution, figures such as Stoker's Dracula and H. Rider Haggard's Ayesha shed their humanity along with their mortality. As Andrew Smith puts it, the possibility of resurrection embodied in these figures is an "evolutionary possibility" that is "demonized" because it is "associated with amoral occult forces"—with that which is not natural (167). Death-defying monsters such as the Great Race of H. P. Lovecraft's "The Shadow Out of Time" would continue the theme into the twentieth century, and similar concerns persist today, as nineteenth-

century concerns with human evolution encounter the transhuman possibilities of technological augmentation. As Donna Lee Brien and Lorna Piatti-
Farnell point out, bodies that refuse to die can "[unveil] underlying concerns
about the current state of humanity"—or what it might become (1).

"*He who fights with monsters...*"

While *Supernatural* has its fair share of monsters who are both villainous
and undead, the relationships between humanity and monstrosity, and
between life and death, are rarely simple. Not every supernatural creature
who returns from the dead comes back evil. Sympathetic vampires such as
Lenore and Benny Lafitte refrain from feeding off the living. Molly McNamara—a ghost who haunts the highway where she was killed—is confused
and lonely rather than murderous, and the prophet Kevin Tran, who is killed
and becomes a ghost in Season Nine, retains his original personality instead
of becoming dangerous.[2]

Significantly, though, these characters all ultimately reaffirm the boundary between life and death. Lenore requests a true end to her life after losing
her ability to resist human blood ("Mommy Dearest"). Benny initially asks
Dean's help to escape the monster afterlife of Purgatory and return to the
world of the living ("We Need to Talk About Kevin"), but life among humans
proves more difficult than he anticipates. His story ends with him willingly
staying in Purgatory to ensure that Sam, a living human, can return to earth,
as Benny accepts that he "was never any good up there anyway" ("Taxi
Driver"). Molly is eventually persuaded to move on when the Winchesters
show her that her husband has continued his life and found love again. In
accepting that she is irrevocably separated from him by death, Molly finds a
measure of peace and, presumably, ascends to Heaven ("Roadkill"). Kevin
also goes willingly to Heaven when given the chance ("All in the Family").
More significantly here, *Supernatural*'s living protagonists also blur any clear
boundary between life and death—and, as the center of its story, they cannot
be allowed to die complete, 'natural' deaths while the show continues.

Both Sam and Dean Winchester have been resurrected on a number of
occasions, and the show's twelfth season deals with their mother Mary's struggle to reintegrate with the living world after she is brought back from the dead.
The Winchesters cross, re-cross, and linger on the border between life and
death repeatedly; it might be accurate to say that this interstitial zone is where
they live. Their deaths and resurrections are often the result of familial love,
which on *Supernatural* functions as a defining feature of humanity. Sam and
Dean's fraternal bond allows them to "keep each other human" ("The End"),
and Castiel becomes more fully humanized as he becomes more deeply

entwined in the Winchesters' lives, eventually being accepted by them as a "brother" ("Alpha and Omega"). At the end of Season Five, when Sam has been possessed by Lucifer—who intends to fight his brother, the archangel Michael, and destroy humanity—it is his connection with Dean which allows him to break Lucifer's hold. This leads directly to Sam's figurative death as he opens a portal to Hell and descends into it, trapping Lucifer and preserving humanity.

We might assume that there is a contradiction here. The Winchesters' familial love is emblematic of humanity, but it is also intimately bound up with their returns from the dead, which blur the boundaries of this humanity. This is brought up directly in the Season Two finale, after Dean has traded his own soul to bring Sam back from the dead. The demon Azazel, aware that Sam has been resurrected, asks Dean, "How certain are you that what you brought back is 100% pure Sam?" ("All Hell Breaks Loose: Part 2"). The simple fact of resurrection is destabilizing, calling Sam's identity into question, and it stems from the same fraternal bond that elsewhere serves to bolster humanity.

In *Supernatural*, the human is always unstable. As Shannon B. Ford points out, "as the series progresses black-and-white distinctions quickly turn grey" (28). The Winchesters are repeatedly confronted with real or potential monstrous doubles of themselves—from the Season One episode "Skin" (1.06), in which a shapeshifter takes on Dean's appearance and frames him for its crimes, to the Leviathans who imitate the brothers during Season Seven ("Slash Fiction"). The fear that a monster may pass for human and thereby destabilize human identity from the inside is not a new one: the monstrous double, as Linda Dryden has discussed (38–43), is a recurring motif in Gothic fictions. Margrit Shildrick conceives of the monster as a double or "mirror of humanity […] a sign of the vulnerability of all men and women to a loss of humanity," and a figure that inspires both "denial *and* recognition […] exclusion *and* identification" (17). Shildrick argues that our fear of monsters is precisely because of this recognition, and not any "external threat"; rather, the monster inspires "a sense of our openness and vulnerability that western discourse insists on covering over" (81).

Central to Shildrick's argument is this notion of "vulnerability," and it may seem at first glance to have little to do with the theme of resurrection. After all, a person who can come back from the dead is surely less vulnerable than the rest of us. Shildrick is not simply talking about vulnerability to harm, however. Rather, her concept of "vulnerability" refers to the vulnerability of our sense of identity and humanity. What is under threat is "not just the singular self, but a normative category as a whole" (71).

When the Winchesters cross from life into death and then back again, they escape permanent physical harm, but they exceed the boundaries of a "natural" human life, and in the process, their humanity itself becomes open to potential contamination. Vulnerability to death and vulnerability to the inhuman are not the same thing, and may even be diametrically opposed. As Jessica Seymour points out, when inhuman characters such as Gabriel, Balthazar, and Meg achieve redemption by aligning themselves with humanity, they do so at the cost of their own lives (141). They must sacrifice their preternatural longevity to prove their commitment to the human; to purge their monstrosity.

"Inside, You're Already Dead": Dean and the Drive Toward Natural Death

Dean hears the above from Famine, one of the Four Horsemen of the Apocalypse, in the Season Five episode "My Bloody Valentine" (5.14). Famine's presence causes most other characters to become overwhelmed by hunger or desire, but Dean remains immune, largely because he is too depressed to want anything. Famine's conflation of Dean's "broken" state with death is a common turn of phrase, but significant in context, grounding Dean's psychological state in the story of his death and resurrection. Famine identifies Dean as inhabiting a liminal space between life and death: he is human, but has a "deep, dark nothing" in his soul; he is alive, but lacks basic desires for food and sex. In this interstitial zone, Dean gains a measure of power—he cannot be controlled by Famine—but his identity, and his humanity, are vulnerable.

This process of monstrous evolution is set in motion at the start of Season Two, when Dean is snatched out of the veil and returned to life by the intervention of Azazel ("In My Time of Dying"). For viewers, Dean's narrow escape from death comes as a relief, but it is suspect, unnatural. Tessa, the reaper sent to collect Dean's soul, reassures him that his reluctance to leave his family is normal—but that it is, nonetheless, right for him to die. "You're not the first soldier I've plucked from the field," she points out. "They all feel the same. […] But they're wrong. The battle goes on without them" ("In My Time of Dying"). This, Tessa suggests, is a 'natural' death.

When Dean escapes "natural" death, he violates a boundary fundamental to the maintenance of the human. Upon returning to life, he is immediately thrown into conflict with one of the pillars of his human identity. His brotherly love for Sam is a foundational part of his personality, but his father suggests that if Dean is unable to stop Sam from turning into a monster, he will have to kill his brother ("Born Under a Bad Sign"). Throughout the season, Dean struggles with the guilt that accompanies his resurrection, fearing that his family would be "better off" if he had died ("Born Under a Bad Sign"). When Dean makes the decision to trade his own life for Sam's in the season finale, it seems to stem as much from discomfort with his own survival as love for his brother. By outliving his family members, he has, he suggests, "let down the people [he loves]"; significantly, he asks, "How am I supposed to live with that?" ("All Hell Breaks Loose: Part 2").

Dean's next resurrection comes at the hands of an angel, not a demon. He is rescued from Hell by Castiel, and Season Four begins with him struggling out of his own grave. The atmosphere in these scenes is tense rather than celebratory, and the sequence in which Dean searches an empty gas station is reminiscent of zombie movies where survivors pick through the abandoned remnants of human civilization ("Lazarus Rising"). Visually and intertextually, this scene serves to separate Dean, via his miraculous survival, from the rest of the human world. The possibility of his being something other than human is emphasized when he visits Bobby, who tests him to ensure he is not a shapeshifter or a demon. Even after he accepts that Dean really is back from the dead, Bobby protests that his return "don't make a lick of sense" ("Lazarus Rising"). Though well aware of the supernatural, Bobby cannot incorporate resurrection into his view of the human world.

As the season progresses, we continue to see Dean caught between monstrous and superhuman spheres. He must play an important part in averting the upcoming Apocalypse, suggesting a more-than-human role, but fears he will be unequal to the task, protesting that it is "too big" ("On the Head of a Pin"). We also learn that Dean has, under duress, transgressed his own moral code while in Hell. After thirty years of torture, he agreed to help the demon Alastair torture other human souls—an act which has, it is suggested, dented Dean's humanity. Alastair insists, "You left part of yourself back in the Pit." In other words, Dean's self is divided between the worlds of the living and the dead, the human and the inhuman ("On the Head of a Pin"). Like a supernatural Doctor Moreau, Alastair has "carved" Dean not into a new man, but "a new animal" ("On the Head of a Pin"). Worse, Alastair reveals that, in agreeing to torture, Dean has assisted the demons in their project of starting the Apocalypse, fulfilling the first part of a prophecy that will end with Lucifer being freed from Hell. Boundaries between angel, demon, animal, and human are thoroughly blurred, and, despite his good intentions, Dean often finds himself occupying the position of monster.

Aware of his compromised human status, and that the persistence of his consciousness after death led to the possibility of the Apocalypse, Dean leans inexorably toward death. Ultimately, it is only his willingness to place himself in danger of death once more that averts the Apocalypse. In the Season Five finale, Dean appears at the site of the intended battle between Michael and Lucifer, who has since possessed Sam. Though Lucifer attempts to kill Dean, Dean refuses to stop trying to get through to his brother. His persistence allows Sam to break Lucifer's hold on him and put an end to the Apocalypse, leaving Dean to live an ordinary, human "apple pie life" ("Swan Song"). Bobby and Castiel, who have also been killed in the confrontation, are miraculously restored in a rare instance of resurrection without monstrous results. Dean's willingness to die a "natural" death, bringing the monstrosity of his initial resurrection to an end, is redemptive for them all.

Of course, this is not in fact the end. *Supernatural* persists past the end of the season, and so must its protagonists. Lorna Jowett and Stacey Abbott have discussed the cyclical nature of *Supernatural*'s storylines—the way in which they "[continue] beyond one lifespan" (53)—and their assertion is borne out here. The process of monstrous evolution is paused rather than halted for good, and plays out again in later seasons. Season Nine begins with Sam in a coma, his soul about to be collected by Death, and Dean once more makes a deal with a supernatural creature to bring him back to life. Sam's experience of resurrection will be explored in more detail in the next section of my essay; what is important here is that interfering in the process of death will place Dean on the path to another death and monstrous resurrection of his own. After an argument with Sam, who feels violated by his actions, Dean heads out alone and takes on the Mark of Cain, a necessary condition to kill the demon Abaddon. The Mark of Cain, like all monstrous bargains, comes with side-effects. Its bearer will die if he does not kill ("Do You Believe in Miracles?"), and acquires a kind of immortality. Cain, we learn from Crowley, was once "willing to accept death, rather than becoming the killer the Mark wanted him to be. So he took his own life [...]. Except, as rumor has it, the Mark never quite let go" ("Do You Believe in Miracles?"). When Dean is killed during a confrontation with the angel Metatron, the Mark transmutes his death into "a new kind of life" and he is resurrected as a demon ("Do You Believe in Miracles?").

As a demon, Dean views himself as a new, improved model: "lean, mean Dean" ("Soul Survivor"). This is borne out by the physical abilities he gains. He is able to heal quickly from injuries and easily outmatches Cole Trenton, a human ex-Marine who seeks Dean out in order to avenge his father's death ("Reichenbach"). At the same time, Dean recognizes that his "new model" self is incompatible with his family ties and attempts to erase the last vestiges of his humanity by killing Sam, telling him, "your very existence sucked the life out of my life" ("Soul Survivor"). This connection, emblematic of Dean's humanity, is here associated with death, and is the one remaining weakness that this highly-evolved monster seeks to eradicate. Sam and Castiel are able to return Dean's humanity relatively quickly ("Soul Survivor"), but the Mark of Cain retains its hold on him, and the possibility that he will return to a monstrous state continues to haunt him.

Dean eventually concludes that he is too dangerous to be allowed to live. Aware that the Mark of Cain will not allow him to die, he summons Death to ask for help ("Brother's Keeper"). Death offers to remove Dean from

Earth so that he will be unable to hurt anybody else, but his price is Sam's life. Sam is willing to die, but at the last moment, Dean changes his mind and kills Death himself. At the same time, a spell that Sam, Castiel, Crowley, and Rowena have been working on takes effect and removes the Mark of Cain from Dean, unleashing a primeval force called the Darkness on the world ("Brother's Keeper"). Lisa Schmidt reads this as a moment where Sam and Dean "both survive and evade monstrosity because of each other" (179), but Dean remains haunted by the monstrous.

The Darkness is eventually revealed to be God's sister, Amara, who claims a special connection to Dean and wishes to destroy her brother's creation. Though her escape is not a direct result of Dean destroying Death, Amara insists that she is free because of him, and their connection works to intertwine the two events in the narrative. Amara feeds on human souls, aligning her with other monsters such as vampires, werewolves, and soul eaters ("Safe House"). Dean is "bound" to her ("Out of the Darkness into the Fire"), and their connection, like the Mark of Cain, keeps him in a liminal zone. At the end of the season, after it becomes clear that Amara cannot be subdued, Dean agrees to act as a supernatural suicide bomber in order to destroy her ("Alpha and Omega").

The introduction of Billie, a reaper who effectively replaces Death in the narrative, becomes significant here. In her first appearance, Billie informed Sam that the next time he or Dean died, she would ensure they were unable to return from the dead by throwing their souls into "the Empty" ("Form and Void"). In the season finale, she returns, and is introduced by Dean as, "reaper. Wants us dead" ("Alpha and Omega"). In fact, Billie wants to ensure that the Winchesters adhere to the conventions of 'natural' death, putting a stop to the cycle of resurrections. It is she who supplies the human souls that will fuel the "soul bomb" intended to destroy Amara, and here she agrees to help because she is "about an hour away from reaping God himself" ("Alpha and Omega"). For humans to survive God would be profoundly unnatural. By agreeing to act as a suicide bomber, Dean effectively accepts his own death—one from which there will be no possibility of return. It is only after he affirms the natural order in this way that he is able to talk Amara out of her plan to destroy the Earth, and put a halt—for now, at least—to his cycle of monstrous evolution.

"Maybe He Came Back Different": Resurrection, the Superhuman and Sam Winchester

We looked earlier at the aftermath of Sam's first resurrection in Season Two, with the demon Azazel questioning whether he is still truly himself after returning from the dead. His identity, Azazel suggests, may be contaminated. It's common knowledge on *Supernatural* that "demons lie," but it isn't only monsters who question the integrity of Sam's resurrected self. A few episodes later, Dean notes the "cold" manner in which Sam dispatches a demon and wonders whether Azazel may have been telling the truth. He suggests that Sam may have "[come] back different," and asks Bobby, "You think [...] something's wrong with my brother?" ("Sin City"). The question of whether Sam has been somehow altered by his death is not clearly resolved, but the chain of events set in motion by his resurrection and Dean's demon deal certainly affects his behavior in ways that tend toward the monstrous.

This manifests clearly in the Season Three episode "Mystery Spot," during which Sam is trapped in a time-loop where he attempts to save Dean, who dies in increasingly unlikely ways with each repetition of the day.[3] The time-loop is revealed as a trick by the archangel Gabriel (at this point known to Sam and Dean only as the Trickster), who claims he is trying to teach Sam that "[s]ometimes you just gotta let people go." After being identified by Sam, Gabriel appears to end the time-loop—but on the following day, Dean is shot by a mugger and dies again, apparently for good. Sam's reaction is cold indeed. A montage shows him hunting alone, having cut ties with Bobby. Sam's behavior is mechanical: he hunts and stitches his own wounds with little expression, and we do not hear him speak. Though he has not been physically transformed here, Sam's lack of affect, his refusal of social ties, and his silence work to dehumanize him. He is on the path to monstrosity, and comes close to reaching it when—gambling on the likelihood that this is actually Gabriel in disguise—he appears to murder Bobby. This prefigures the journey toward monstrosity that Sam will take after Dean's death in the Season Three finale.

After Dean's resurrection at the beginning of Season Four, we learn that Bobby has not spoken to Sam in months. Repeating his behavior from "Mystery Spot," Sam is "real quiet," refuses to answer Bobby's phone calls, and apparently "[doesn't] want to be found" ("Lazarus Rising"). Dean initially assumes that Sam has made a deal with a demon, or used some other "bad mojo," to resurrect him. This is not the case, but Sam's humanity is called into question in other ways. We learn early on in Season Four that Sam's psychic powers are a result of the demon blood that Azazel fed to him as a baby ("In the Beginning"). While Dean has been in Hell, Sam has been developing his powers—which enable him to exorcise and kill demons—with the intention of killing Lilith, whom he holds responsible for Dean's death. It eventually transpires that his increased abilities are the result of his drinking demon blood provided by Ruby ("On the Head of a Pin").

Blood as a vector of monstrous contagion is a common Gothic trope, used most famously in Bram Stoker's *Dracula*, and Sam's blood drinking both raises the potential for contamination—vulnerability in Shildrick's sense—and aligns him with that most famous of undead monsters, the vampire. The vulnerability of his humanity in relation to his powers is brought up early on in Season Four when Dean, on learning of Sam's new ability to exorcise demons with his mind, demands, "Do you even know how far off the reservation you've gone? How far from normal? From human?" ("Metamorphosis"). Toward the end of the season, Dean and Bobby lock Sam up to cure his blood addiction, and when Bobby voices his concern that they may be more likely to kill than cure him, Dean responds, "Then at least he dies human!" ("When the Levee Breaks"). The message is clear: a dead human is better than an undead monster.

Under the influence of Ruby and the demon blood, Sam kills Lilith and inadvertently completes the prophecy, releasing Lucifer from Hell. In the aftermath of this, he is cured of his demon blood addiction by mysterious supernatural means, and spends much of Season Five struggling to atone for his actions and to remain demon-blood free and therefore human ("Good God, Y'All"; "My Bloody Valentine"). In a mid-season episode, the rogue angel Anna Milton suggests that there is a simple solution to the Lucifer problem: "Sam Winchester has to die" ("The Song Remains the Same"). This is the same conclusion to which Sam eventually comes, and the season ends with a confrontation between his human aspect and his monstrous side—personified by Lucifer, who identifies strongly with Sam, and who has himself undergone a kind of resurrection in being raised from Hell. The only way to prevent the Apocalypse, Sam concludes, is for him to undergo a symbolic, if not literal, death, allowing himself to be possessed by Lucifer and then jumping into Hell, trapping them both ("Swan Song").

An archangel, Lucifer is one of the most powerful supernatural beings in existence, and there is a trade-off when Sam agrees to the possession. He temporarily loses control of his body, but as a combined being, they are enormously powerful. There is a suggestion that Sam even subconsciously enjoys this aspect of the possession. Lucifer insists, "You have to admit, you can feel it […] [the] exhilaration," and says that Sam's human family were "foster care at best. I'm your real family" (Swan Song"). The possession is a kind of liminal space, where Sam is trapped between his desire to stop the Apocalypse and save his human family, and the welcome to a community of superhuman monsters that Lucifer offers. In both the case of demon blood and that of possession, Sam's potential to become a monster is tied to the offer of superhuman power. Angels are immortal; demon blood allows him to kill; and Robert Jeschonek reads his use of his psychic powers as a "step up the evolutionary ladder" (73). Yet at the same time, his identity is subsumed. To seek superhuman abilities is monstrous, and it is only in sacrificing his life that Sam regains his human identity and personal agency.

Sam's return from Hell may not be a literal resurrection, but it is certainly a metaphorical one, and once again, he comes back more powerful but less human, lacking a soul and therefore a moral compass. (Interestingly Darwin viewed the moral sense as an evolutionary adaptation (124–125).) Sam makes tactical decisions that put Dean at risk, allowing Dean to be temporarily turned into a vampire in order to locate the Alpha, or first, vampire ("Live Free or Twihard"). He does not need to sleep ("Family Matters") and insists that he is "a better hunter than I've ever been. Nothing scares me anymore, 'cause I can't feel it" ("You Can't Handle the Truth"). A soul is "a liability," and without one he is "sharp, strong" ("The Man Who Knew Too Much"). Despite— or perhaps because of—these apparently superhuman attributes, Sam's identity and humanity are once again called into question. Dean repeatedly insists that Sam is "not my brother" ("You Can't Handle the Truth"), and when Castiel tells him that Sam's soul is missing, his immediate reaction is to ask, "So, is he even still Sam?" ("Family Matters"). It is in the process of resurrection that Sam's soul has been separated from his body, and once more, his ability to transcend the human limitation of a "natural" death is cast as monstrous.

Eventually, Sam appears to come around to a similar view of resurrection and monstrosity to that held by Dean, exhibiting the apparent desire to seek a "natural" death and thereby purge his humanity of the contamination to which his resurrections have opened it. During Season Eight, Sam undertakes a series of Trials intended to permanently close the gates of Hell. It is hinted early on that the Trials may require the death of the person who completes them ("Trial and Error"), and Sam soon becomes seriously ill. As his symptoms worsen and he grows closer to death, Sam insists that he has never been "clean" because of the demon blood in his system, but that the trials are "purifying" him, effectively restoring his humanity in his journey toward death ("The Great Escapist").

Like Dean at the beginning of Season Two, Sam is snatched back from the brink of death by a deal with a supernatural creature—in this case, the angel Gadreel, who inhabits Sam's body without his knowledge ("I Think I'm Gonna Like It Here"). Sam gradually becomes aware that there is something different about him, his suspicions raised when another character tells him, "I want to know what you are" after Gadreel takes over his body to heal an otherwise fatal injury ("Dog Dean Afternoon"). Once again, superhuman abilities and the escape from death accompany a slide away from the human. Sam's monstrous suspicions are confirmed when Gadreel allies himself with the season's major villain, the angel Metatron, and kills the human prophet Kevin Tran before taking over Sam's body entirely ("Holy Terror"). The realization that Dean—who assisted Gadreel in possessing him—was prepared to let him become monstrous rather than die is deeply distressing to Sam, and he asks, "what is the upside of me being alive?" ("The Purge"). Once again, a "natural," human death is preferable to survival via monstrous, superhuman means. This is affirmed once more at the end of Season Ten, when Sam is willing to let Dean kill him if this helps Dean eventually "find [his] way back" to humanity ("Brother's Keeper"). Indeed, Dean's willingness to die to defeat Amara suggest that this has, at last, happened, and might be read as a final affirmation of humanity.

A Family of Monsters?

As we have seen, however, the themes of resurrection and monstrosity are intimately intertwined with those of humanity and family, seen as a defining human trait. For some viewers, such as Gregory Stevenson, this is the Winchesters' "greatest strength" (45). Stevenson writes that "it is precisely that ability to act in the interests of others, to sacrifice oneself for another, that defines the human potential for good. [...] It is what makes one human" (45). The Winchesters, though, sacrifice their lives to resurrect one another, value one another's humanity, and call that humanity into question when they ward off death. The relationship between monstrosity and resurrection is problematized and rendered more complex than a simple human/monster dichotomy.

Immediately after Dean seems to humanize Amara by persuading her to reconcile with her brother, she blurs the boundary once more by resurrecting another member of the Winchester family, the brothers' mother, Mary ("Alpha and Omega"), who will spend Season Twelve struggling with her return to the living and at one point losing her identity as she becomes a living weapon for the season's antagonists, the British Men of Letters ("Who We Are"). Even defining human traits, it seems, can become monstrous when exhibited in excess—particularly when that excess threatens to overspill the boundary of mortality. In this way, the show refuses any clear-cut boundary between the human and the monstrous, for there is monstrous potential already present within human characteristics. For the Winchesters, the specter of monstrosity is never far away.

NOTES

1. The term "abjection" refers to the process by which individuals exclude those qualities we do not wish to include in our ideas of ourselves by attributing them to a rejected Other (Kristeva 1–2).

2. See Rebecca Stone Gordon's essay "Got Salt? Human Remains and Haunting in *Supernatural*" for more discussion of ghosts.

3. For more on the episode "Mystery Spot," see Michail-Chrysovalantis Markodimitrakis' essay titled "Dean's Groundhog Day: Negotiating the Inevitability of Death via *Supernatural*."

WORKS CITED

"All Hell Breaks Loose: Part 2." *Supernatural: The Complete Second Season*, story by Eric Kripke and Michael T. Moore, teleplay by Eric Kripke, directed by Kim Manners, Warner Home Video, 2007.
"All in the Family." *Supernatural: The Complete Eleventh Season*, written by Eugenie Ross-Leming and Brad Buckner, directed by Thomas J. Wright, Warner Home Video, 2016.
"Alpha and Omega." *Supernatural: The Complete Eleventh Season*, written by Andrew Dabb, directed by Phil Sgriccia, Warner Home Video, 2016.
Asma, Stephen T. *On Monsters: An Unnatural History of Our Worst Fears*. Oxford UP, 2009.
Baudrillard, Jean. *Symbolic Exchange and Death*. Translated by Iain Hamilton Grant. SAGE, 1993.
Beal, Timothy K. *Religion and Its Monsters*. Routledge, 2002.
"The Big Empty." *Supernatural: The Complete Thirteenth Season*, written by Meredith Glynn, directed by John Badham, Warner Home Video, 2018.
"Born Under a Bad Sign." *Supernatural: The Complete Second Season*, written by Cathryn Humphris, directed by J. Miller Tobin, Warner Home Video, 2007.
Brien, Donna Lee, and Lorna Piatti-Farnell. "Writing Death and the Gothic." *TEXT*, vol. 35, 2016, http://www.textjournal.com.au/speciss/issue35/Brien&PiattiFarnell.pdf. Accessed 23 March 2018.
Bronfen, Elisabeth, and Sarah Webster Goodwin. "Introduction." *Death and Representation*, edited by Sarah Webster Goodwin and Elisabeth Bronfen. Johns Hopkins UP, 1993, pp. 3–25.
"Brother's Keeper." *Supernatural: The Complete Tenth Season,* Written by Jeremy Carver, directed by Phil Sgriccia, Warner Home Video, 2015.
"Children Shouldn't Play with Dead Things." *Supernatural: The Complete Second Season*, written by Raelle Tucker, directed by Kim Manners, Warner Home Video, 2007.
Cohen, Jeffrey Jerome. "Monster Culture (Seven Theses)." *Monster Theory: Reading Culture*, edited by Jeffrey Jerome Cohen. U of Minnesota P, 1996, pp. 3–25.
"Dark Dynasty." *Supernatural: The Complete Tenth Season*, written by Eugenie Ross-Leming and Brad Buckner, directed by Robert Singer, Warner Home Video, 2015.
Darwin, Charles. *The Descent of Man and Selection in Relation to Sex*. John Murray, 1883.
"Dead in the Water." *Supernatural: The Complete First Season*, written by Sera Gamble and Raelle Tucker, directed by Kim Manners, Warner Home Video, 2006.
"Dead Man's Blood." *Supernatural: The Complete First Season*, written by Cathryn Humphris and John Shiban, directed by Tony Wharmby, Warner Home Video, 2006.
"Do You Believe in Miracles?" *Supernatural: The Complete Ninth Season*, written by Jeremy Carver, directed by Thomas J. Wright, Warner Home Video, 2014.
"Dog Dean Afternoon." *Supernatural: The Complete Ninth Season*, written by Eric Charmelo and Nicole Snyder, directed by Tim Andrew, Warner Home Video, 2014.
Dryden, Linda. *The Modern Gothic and Literary Doubles: Stevenson, Wilde and Wells*. Palgrave Macmillan, 2003.
Duda, Heather L. *The Monster Hunter in Modern Popular Culture*. McFarland, 2008.
"The End." *Supernatural: The Complete Fifth Season*, written by Ben Edlund, directed by Steve Boyum, Warner Home Video, 2010.
"Faith." *Supernatural: The Complete First Season*, written by Raelle Tucker and Sera Gamble, directed by Allan Kroeker, Warner Home Video, 2006.
"Family Matters." *Supernatural: The Complete Sixth Season*, written by Andrew Dabb and Daniel Loflin, directed by Guy Norman Bee, Warner Home Video, 2011.
Ford, Shannon B. "Hunters, Warriors, Monsters." *Supernatural and Philosophy: Metaphysics and Monsters ... for Idjits*, edited by Galen A. Foresman. Wiley-Blackwell, 2013, pp. 26–36.
"Form and Void." *Supernatural: The Complete Eleventh Season*, written by Andrew Dabb, directed by Phil Sgriccia, Warner Home Video, 2016.
"Good God, Y'all." *Supernatural: The Complete Fifth Season*, written by Sera Gamble, directed by Phil Sgriccia, Warner Home Video, 2010.

"The Great Escapist." *Supernatural: The Complete Eighth Season*, written by Ben Edlund, directed by Robert Duncan McNeill, Warner Home Video, 2013.

Haggard, H. Rider. *She*. 1886–1887. Oxford UP, 1998.

"Holy Terror." *Supernatural: The Complete Ninth Season*, written by Eugenie Ross-Leming and Brad Buckner, directed by Thomas J. Wright, Warner Home Video, 2014.

Humphreys, S.C. "Death and Time." *Mortality and Immortality: The Anthropology and Archaeology of Death*, edited by S.C. Humphreys and Helen King. Academic, 1981, pp. 261–283.

Hurley, Kelly. *The Gothic Body: Sexuality, Materialism, and Degeneration at the* Fin de Siècle. Cambridge UP, 1996.

"I Think I'm Gonna Like It Here." *Supernatural: The Complete Ninth Season*, written by Jeremy Carver, directed by John Showalter, Warner Home Video, 2014.

"In My Time of Dying." *Supernatural: The Complete Second Season*, written by Eric Kripke, directed by Kim Manners, Warner Home Video, 2007.

"In the Beginning." *Supernatural: The Complete Fourth Season*, written by Jeremy Carver, directed by Steve Boyum, Warner Home Video, 2009.

Jeschonek, Robert T. "Sympathy for the Devils." *In the Hunt: Unauthorized Essays on Supernatural*, edited by Supernatural.tv with Leah Wilson. BenBella, 2009.

Jowett, Lorna, and Stacey Abbott. *TV Horror: Investigating the Dark Side of the Small Screen*. I.B. Tauris, 2013.

Kearney, Richard. *Strangers, Gods and Monsters: Interpreting Otherness*. Routledge, 2003.

Kristeva, Julia. *Powers of Horror: An Essay on Abjection*. Trans. Leon S. Roudiez. Columbia UP, 1982.

"Lazarus Rising." *Supernatural: The Complete Fourth Season*, written by Eric Kripke, directed by Kim Manners, Warner Home Video, 2009.

"Live Free or Twihard." *Supernatural: The Complete Sixth Season*, written by Brett Matthews, directed by Rod Hardy, Warner Home Video, 2011.

Lovecraft, H.P. "The Shadow Out of Time." 1936. *The Dreams in the Witch House and Other Weird Stories*, edited by S.T. Joshi. Penguin, 2005, pp. 335–395.

"Malleus Maleficarum." *Supernatural: The Complete Third Season*, written by Ben Edlund, directed by Robert Singer, Warner Home Video, 2007.

"The Man Who Knew Too Much." *Supernatural: The Complete Sixth Season*, written by Eric Kripke, directed by Robert Singer, Warner Home Video, 2011.

"Metamorphosis." *Supernatural: The Complete Fourth Season*, written by Cathryn Humphris, directed by Kim Manners, Warner Home Video, 2009.

"Mommy Dearest." *Supernatural: The Complete Sixth Season*, written by Adam Glass, directed by John F. Showalter, Warner Home Video, 2011.

"My Bloody Valentine." *Supernatural: The Complete Fifth Season*, written by Ben Edlund, directed by Mike Rohl, Warner Home Video, 2010.

"Mystery Spot." *Supernatural: The Complete Third Season*, written by Jeremy Carver and Emily McLaughlin, directed by Kim Manners, Warner Home Video, 2007.

Neocleous, Mark. *The Monstrous and the Dead: Burke, Marx, Fascism*. U of Wales P, 2005.

"On the Head of a Pin." *Supernatural: The Complete Fourth Season*, written by Ben Edlund, directed by Mike Rohl, Warner Home Video, 2009.

"Out of the Darkness, Into the Fire." *Supernatural: The Complete Eleventh Season*, written by Jeremy Carver, directed by Robert Singer, Warner Home Video, 2016.

"The Prisoner." *Supernatural: The Complete Tenth Season*, written by Andrew Dabb, directed by Thomas J. Wright, Warner Home Video, 2015.

Prometheus. Directed by Ridley Scott, 20th Century–Fox, 2012.

"The Purge." *Supernatural: The Complete Ninth Season*, written by Eric Charmelo and Nicole Snyder, directed by Phil Sgriccia, Warner Home Video, 2014.

"Reichenbach." *Supernatural: The Complete Tenth Season*, written by Andrew Dabb, directed by Thomas J. Wright, Warner Home Video, 2015.

"Roadkill." *Supernatural: The Complete Second Season*, written by Raelle Tucker, directed by Charles Beeson, Warner Home Video, 2007.

"Sacrifice." *Supernatural: The Complete Eighth Season*, written by Jeremy Carver, directed by Phil Sgriccia, Warner Home Video, 2013.

"Safe House." *Supernatural: The Complete Eleventh Season*, written by Robbie Thompson, directed by Stefan Pleszczynski, Warner Home Video, 2016.

Schmidt, Lisa. "We All Have a Little Monster in Us: Dean Winchester, the Mark of Cain, and the New Monster Paradigm." *The Gothic Tradition in Supernatural: Essays on the Television Series*, edited by Melissa Edmundson. McFarland, 2016, pp. 167–182.

Seymour, Jessica. "'We've all been demons': Postmodern Gothic and the Fragmented Self." *The Gothic Tradition in Supernatural: Essays on the Television Series*, edited by Melissa Edmundson. McFarland, 2016, pp. 129–142.

Shelley, Mary Wollstonecraft. *Frankenstein, Or, the Modern Prometheus*. Penguin, 2003.

Shildrick, Margrit. *Embodying the Monster: Encounters with the Vulnerable Self*. SAGE, 2002.

"Sin City." *Supernatural: The Complete Third Season*, written by Robert Singer and Jeremy Carver, directed by Charles Beeson, Warner Home Video, 2008.

"Skin." *Supernatural: The Complete First Season*, written by John Shiban, directed by Robert Duncan McNeill, Warner Home Video, 2006.

"Slash Fiction." *Supernatural: The Complete Seventh Season*, written by Robbie Thompson, directed by John F. Showalter, Warner Home Video, 2012.

Smith, Andrew. "Victorian Gothic Death." *The Victorian Gothic: An Edinburgh Companion*, edited by Andrew Smith and William Hughes. Edinburgh UP, 2012, pp. 156–169.

"The Song Remains the Same." *Supernatural: The Complete Fifth Season*, written by Sera Gamble and Nancy Weiner, directed by Steve Boyum, Warner Home Video, 2010.

"Soul Survivor." *Supernatural: The Complete Tenth Season*, written by Eugenie Ross-Leming and Brad Buckner, directed by Jensen Ackles, Warner Home Video, 2015.

Stevenson, Gregory. "Horror, Humanity, and the Demon in the Mirror." *In the Hunt: Unauthorized Essays on* Supernatural, edited by Supernatural.tv with Leah Wilson. BenBella, 2009, pp. 39–52.

Stoker, Bram. *Dracula*. 1897. Wordsworth, 1993.

"Swan Song." *Supernatural: The Complete Fifth Season*, story by Eric Gerwitz, teleplay by Eric Kripke, directed by Steve Boyum, Warner Home Video, 2010.

"Taxi Driver." *Supernatural: The Complete Eighth Season*, written by Eugenie Ross-Leming and Brad Buckner, directed by Guy Norman Bee, Warner Home Video, 2013.

"Time Is on My Side." *Supernatural: The Complete Third Season*, written by Sera Gamble, directed by Charles Beeson, Warner Home Video, 2007.

"Trial and Error." *Supernatural: The Complete Eighth Season*, written by Andrew Dabb, directed by Kevin Parks, Warner Home Video, 2013.

"We Need to Talk About Kevin." *Supernatural: The Complete Eighth Season*, written by Jeremy Carver, directed by Robert Singer, Warner Home Video, 2013.

"When the Levee Breaks." *Supernatural: The Complete Fourth Season*, written by Sera Gamble, directed by Robert Singer, Warner Home Video, 2009.

"Who We Are." *Supernatural: The Complete Twelfth Season*, written by Robert Berens, directed by John F. Showalter, Warner Home Video, 2017.

"You Can't Handle the Truth." *Supernatural: The Complete Sixth Season*, written by Eric Charmelo, Nicole Snyder and David Reed, directed by Jan Eliasberg, Warner Home Video, 2011.

"When I come back, I'm gonna be pissed"

Signaling Narrative and Character Shifts Through Death in Supernatural

Erin M. Giannini

When *Supernatural* was renewed for a twelfth season, it officially became the longest-running science-fiction/fantasy series in U.S. television history. Unlike a series such as *Doctor Who*,[1] which allows for a physical "regeneration" (i.e., bringing in a new actor to play the role) of the main character of the Doctor, *Supernatural* has always been built on the trials and travails of its dual leads: Sam and Dean Winchester. Their "family business," as any long-time viewer knows, is hunting monsters, the stakes of which are always high: loss of family and friends ("Pilot," "In My Time of Dying," "Death's Door," "Dark Dynasty"); loss of opportunities outside the "hunting" life for the brothers; the end of the world ("Swan Song": "Alpha and Omega"); and the end of their own lives.

Physical regeneration, however, is not really built into the premise of *Supernatural*. While the brothers may die and come back numerous times, they do not do so with new faces and bodies.[2] Indeed, the later seasons of the series have been characterized by numerous references to the fact the brothers are aging. Dean in particular has been called "old man" more than once. The burden of hunting and the traumatic memories it has caused lay heavily on the brothers and on the narrative itself. This is vital, as both on a textual and production level, the longer a series runs, the greater the risk of a kind of creative death if the characters do not grow, change, or develop significantly over time (Ramaswamy).

How then does the series cheat this creative death after thirteen seasons and more than 250 episodes? It is a question the series has asked itself, most

122

notably in Season Seven's "How to Win Friends and Influence Monsters" (7.09), in which Dean asks, "We're on our third 'the world is screwed' issue in what, three years? And we've steered the bus away from the cliff twice already…. What if the bus wants to go over the cliff?" Given the serial nature of the program, the events of the series must leave their marks on both its narrative and its characters in order to avoid redundant plot or character beats, move the characters and story forward, and keep audiences engaged, while simultaneously deferring narrative closure.

Viewing the series as a whole, it is clear that death, stalking the Winchester family since the pilot episode, operates as a signal indicating significant shifts in either character or narrative. Throughout thirteen seasons, Sam and Dean have been shot, stabbed, ripped apart by hellhounds, and fallen into Hell or Purgatory, to name a few iterations of a trope that has become so common on the series that Death himself has purportedly died ("Brother's Keeper").[3] On the surface, one could look at the brothers' cheating of death (and Death) as a sign of narrative exhaustion for a series that has run too long. *Supernatural*, however, is a series aware of its production and broadcast context (Garcia 146–160), whether it is the reference to the rainy weather of "Los Angeles" (aka Vancouver) in "Hollywood Babylon" (2.19) or the meta-madness of "The French Mistake" (6.15), with "Bob Singer's" (Brian Doyle-Murray) constant comments on the challenges of following up the epic fifth season of the series.

On a deeper level, however, Sam and Dean's numerous deaths represent narrative and character opportunities and are related to the longevity of the series itself (Petruska 219–29). Focusing on particular deaths and their aftermaths, I will analyze the ways in which the "significant" Sam and Dean deaths in *Supernatural*—Sam in "All Hell Breaks Loose: Part 1" (2.21), "Dark Side of the Moon" (5.17), and "Swan Song (5.22)"; Dean in "No Rest for the Wicked" (3.16), "Dark Side of the Moon (5.16)," "Survival of the Fittest" (7.23), and "Do You Believe in Miracles?" (9.23)[4]—represent particular facets of character growth and upheavals in the boys' strongly held beliefs, including their responses to violence, faith, and the things they hunt.

In that respect, rather than serving as narrative emotional shorthand to elicit viewer/fan reactions, these deaths are used purposefully to push the Winchesters into new—and occasionally terrifying—directions. On *Supernatural*, death represents both an end and a beginning, not unlike the alpha and omega embodied in God and Amara in Season Eleven. The darkness of death (the end) and the illumination of continued life (a new beginning) are as necessary to one another as were God and his sister. Given the lack of narrative closure following the fifth season's apocalyptic battle and end of a seasons-long narrative arc, death has become one of the strategies *Supernatural* uses to breathe new life into narrative and character development that has no fixed end point. Both the traumas these deaths elicit and the deaths themselves operate as both character development/narrative momentum and a way to help the series itself avoid its own "creative" death.

"Nothing lasts forever. Well, I do": The Meaning of All This Death

The episode "Twigs and Twine and Tasha Banes" (12.20) focuses on the Banes twins, Alicia and Max, first introduced early in Season Twelve. Alicia calls the brothers for help; their mother has not returned from a hunt, and Alicia is concerned. Sam tells Dean that "Their mom's on a hunting trip and hasn't been home in a week." This moment is a pointed reference to the very first episode of the series, in which Dean brings Sam back into the hunting life by telling him "Dad's on a hunting trip, and he hasn't been home in a few days" ("Pilot").[5]

This self-reflexive reference allows both the characters and the series to reflect on its own long narrative life in a more subtle way than the series' numerous meta-textual episodes. Further, the resolution of the episode, in which Tasha and Alicia are both killed, and Max makes a demon deal to save his sister, mirrors the brothers' similar narrative trajectory early in the series. In particular, it is Alicia's death that changes both Alicia herself and her brother Max, who sold his soul in exchange for the power to resurrect her, much as Dean does for Sam ("All Hell Breaks Loose: Part 2"). It also allows the series itself to reflect on the character development that death has provided to both Sam and Dean by reminding the audience of the choices and consequences of the brothers' experiences.

This mirroring helps the series to avoid retreading familiar ground— allowing the viewer to connect Max's choice to earlier choices made by Sam and Dean—and highlighting the brothers' growth and development. Karen Petruska, in her analysis of the first five seasons of *Supernatural*, attributes its longevity to three particular factors: its position on the (then) fledgling CW network, technological advances such as the DVR and DVD, and the commitment of its fans (Petruska 229), all of which remain applicable from an industrial perspective in Season Thirteen. From a narrative perspective, however, the question remains as to how to manage the constantly deferred closure of Sam and Dean's story arc. If one marries the production considerations with the narrative ones—neither Sam nor Dean can "stay dead" until the series itself is completed, yet, the stakes must remain high in order to retain audience interest—the situation becomes even more complicated.

Suzette Chan's analysis of the bodily effects of the hunting life on Sam and Dean (both in the series itself and in fanfiction) offers a partial answer.

Chan points out the ways in which the various bodily traumas the brothers experience, due to the exigencies of what she calls the "tension between marketability and storytelling" (para 1.4), render such traumas "invisible" so as not to disturb television's "expectations of beauty." Instead, these physical effects are "internal and internalized" (Chan para 1.4). In this respect, the traumas of the numerous deaths of both Sam and Dean, including being shot ("Dark Side of the Moon"[6]), stabbed ("All Hell Breaks Loose: Part 1"); "Do You Believe in Miracles?"), or ripped apart ("No Rest for the Wicked") are by necessity shown as psychological damage rather than through permanent physical wounding or scarring.[7]

Viewing these numerous deaths in the light of sustained, if physically invisible, trauma and subsequent growth offers a different meaning to a storytelling choice that could easily be viewed as an overused trope to artificially raise narrative stakes. However, it is not just the deaths, but the subsequent resurrections that provide the opportunity to develop both narrative and character. In Cathy Caruth's analysis of trauma through the lenses of psychoanalysis, literature, and literary theory, she writes:

> Is the trauma the encounter with death or the ongoing experience of having survived it? At the core of these stories … is thus a kind of double telling, the oscillation between a crisis of death and the correlative crisis of life: between the story of the unbearable nature of an event and the story of the unbearable nature of its survival [7–8].

This "double telling" is at the heart of the narrative and character shifts Sam and Dean experience through death. It is important to return to the aforementioned concept of both character and narrative memory. In "Dark Side of the Moon" (5.16), Joshua tells the brothers they have been to Heaven before, although their memories of it have been wiped. This time, however, they are allowed to retain the memory of the trip in order to understand why God will not be stopping the Apocalypse. In essence, if they do not recall what occurred, they are unable to learn from the experience and move forward. While this particular forward movement takes the form of despair in the moment, it is nonetheless an affirmation of their mission in Season Five: stopping the Apocalypse through the exercise of free will.

In that respect, when both Sam and Dean are brought back to life at the end of the episode, the gunshot wounds that killed them have disappeared, but the experience itself left its mark on them as well as on the narrative. This is true of each death the brothers experience; with the exception of the angel Castiel's handprint on Dean and Sam's missing soul, any physical injuries that lead to said death—most notably Dean's shredded body in "No Rest for the Wicked" (3.16)—are absent upon resurrection. The trauma and resulting shifts in ideas, narratives, or characterizations exist only within Sam's and Dean's own memories and the narrative memory of the series itself. These traumas bear testimony to both the "unbearable … event[s]" and (at times) equally "unbearable … survival" (Caruth 8).

As Jim Corder writes, "each of us is a narrative … of all the choices we've made, accidentally or on purpose" that are "the evidence we have of ourselves and of our convictions" (Corder 18, qtd. in Torrey 54). These numerous deaths operate as a "double telling" in another respect: the plot of the series and the character trajectories of the brothers. As I will address in the next section, these deaths signpost these shifts, whether from resentment to revenge, or from rigidity to nuance, even if the marks of such are not readily apparent.

"Are you sure what you brought back was 100% pure Sam?" The Pain of Change

Reluctance was a defining characteristic of Sam Winchester during the first two seasons of the series. While subsequent seasons would introduce other hunters who either longed to, or eventually do, leave the hunting life behind, Sam, having grown up in the hunting life, eventually abandons it in favor of college and law school.[8] It is only Dean's reappearance, to inform him their father has not returned from a hunt, that draws Sam back into the hunting life ("Pilot"). The death of his fiancée Jessica at the end of the first episode and the subsequent revelation that even his non-hunting life was micromanaged by the demon Azazel ("Swan Song") ensures that there is little in his post-hunting life worth returning to that holds the same pull as avenging her death.

Yet, conflict and resentment still exist in the triangle between Sam, Dean, and their father John, particularly around the ways in which Sam perceives Dean as unquestioningly following both their father's orders as "loyal little soldiers" ("Scarecrow") and John's single-minded quest for vengeance. The Sam of Seasons One and Two still seemingly believes that there is a life for him that does not include hunting. While Dean may mock him for that, there are hints that Sam's independence and desire for a different path was, at least, something Dean could rely upon ("What Is and What Should Never Be"), and possibly admire ("Wishful Thinking").

The first significant shift in Sam's outlook occurs in the final episode of Season Two. Previous to this, the goal was first to find their missing father; after John's death ("In My Time of Dying"), it was to track down Azazel, the demon responsible for both Mary and John Winchester and Jessica's deaths. In "All Hell Breaks Loose: Part 1" (2.21), Sam is kidnapped by Azazel, who dosed Sam and others with demon blood as infants; this group is forced to battle for supremacy. Sam refuses to fight, which leads to his death. Unable to reach Sam in time to save him, Dean makes a deal to exchange his own soul for Sam's life, and Sam is brought back from the dead, with little (initial) realization that he had died ("All Hell Breaks Loose, Part 2").

"All Hell Breaks Loose: Part 2," along with Azazel himself, asks the question about whether the resurrected Sam is still the same. This question remains pertinent until Sam's third death at the end of Season Five, when he jumps into Hell ("Swan Song"). The Sam that refused to fight the last survivor, Jake, in "All Hell Breaks Loose: Part 1," coldly shoots him several times in the season finale. It becomes increasingly clear, between Seasons Three to Five, that the post-resurrection Sam is a colder Sam. In "Sin City" (3.04) and "Fresh Blood" (3.07), Dean is clearly disturbed by the ruthless nature of Sam's actions.

When Dean returns after his sojourn in Hell ("Lazarus Rising"), he discovers Sam has isolated himself from other hunters, including the brothers' father figure Bobby Singer. Dean soon finds out that Sam is using his demon-granted powers to exorcise demons ("Metamorphosis"); however, it is not until near the end of the fourth season that Dean realizes Sam's powers are tied to the consumption of demon blood ("The Rapture"). Season Five reveals that all of this was part of a plan to create the perfect vessel for Lucifer to return in Sam's body and jumpstart the Apocalypse ("Free to Be You and Me").

This shift, from reluctance to isolation and demon blood-drinking, is only the first step in Sam's character trajectory. It is arguably brought about in part by Sam's lack of memory of his brief sojourn into the afterlife; as Joshua indicates in "Dark Side of the Moon" (5.16), the brothers' previous trips to Heaven are erased when they are resurrected. That is, something is "taken" from Sam upon his resurrection in "All Hell Breaks Loose: Part 2"; he cannot use any insight or knowledge gained during that particular journey. Season Six's resurrection also initially requires a removal: Sam returns from Hell soulless, then is re-ensouled with the traumas of his time in Hell blocked ("Appointment in Samarra"). This "wall," erected by Death himself to keep Sam sane, fails ("The Man Who Knew Too Much"), leaving Sam to deal with the overwhelming trauma of endless torture until the angel Castiel takes them into himself as recompense for destroying said wall ("The Born-Again Identity"). Yet, this failure actually facilitates Sam's character growth. The Sam of Seasons Six through Eight is closer to that of the Sam of the first two seasons; when Dean is blasted into Purgatory at the end of the seventh season ("Survival of the Fittest"), Sam abandons hunting and develops a relationship with a local veterinarian, Amelia. He is once again reluctant to take up the hunting life and is drawn back in by the reappearance of his brother.

The storyline around Amelia purposefully echoes Sam's earlier desire for a life outside of demons and angels in order to elucidate its eventual impossibility. It also serves as an analogue to Dean's earlier foray into a non-hunting suburban life with girlfriend Lisa in Season Six ("Exile on Main

Street"), which ended with Lisa and her son Ben's memories being wiped of Dean's existence for their own safety ("Let It Bleed"), an instance of these characters' growth and development being sacrificed to facilitate Dean's.[9] The brothers' inability to live a normal life exists within the narrative for both diegetic and non-diegetic reasons. The most obvious, of course, is that without "saving people, hunting things," there is no series.[10]

That being said, while Sam's first death shifted reluctance to vengeance, his third death and subsequent (soulless) resurrection at the end of Season Five ("Swan Song") provides the opportunity to combine these seemingly disparate characterizations in a particularly interesting way. Splitting Sam's resurrection into two parts—his body in "Swan Song" (5.22) and his soul in "Appointment in Samarra" (6.11)—offers a tidy metaphor for the characterization that would remain fairly steady in subsequent seasons. With Sam, the "double telling" of both the traumatic event and the survival is literalized. Sam's deaths allow him, having lived both lives—reluctant hunter turned vengeance-seeking human/empty, cold-blooded vessel, and a "normal" non-hunting life—to blend these disparate elements of his experience and finally be at peace with them following Season Eight.

This is perhaps made most clear by Sam's decision to accept death (and Death) at the start of Season Nine ("I Think I'm Going to Like It Here"). The toll on Sam's body of trying to close the gates of Hell leaves him fatally injured, and when Death appears to reap him personally, he accepts it, asking that, "nobody can reverse it, nobody can deal it away … and nobody else can get hurt because of me" (9.01). Sam's particular request indicates a level of peace with not only the inevitability of death, but with his own actions throughout the series. This is not the same Sam who questioned whether he belonged in Heaven, given his role in starting the Apocalypse, nor the one who abandoned everything in a single-minded quest for vengeance, but rather a manifestation of an integrated individual. That his brother could not accept this ("There ain't no me if there ain't no you," is Dean's plea to his brother) means that this final (near) death of Sam's actually provides greater insight into Dean's narrative arc.

Dean

Dean's narrative journey throughout the series is less clear-cut than Sam's, although equally signified by the numerous deaths he experienced throughout the course of twelve seasons. If Sam initially represents reluctance, Dean's particular quality is loyalty, often unquestioning. His loyalty to and willingness to obey their father leads to the first on-screen rupture between Sam and Dean, when John insists they not try to find him or the demon that killed their mother, but rather focus on a case in Indiana ("Scarecrow"). That this argument and separation occurs right after the events of "Asylum," in which a possessed Sam tells Dean: "I have a mind of my own; I'm not pathetic like you" (1.10), is not surprising. While Dean knows Sam was possessed, it is clear Sam's words had both a positive and negative effect on Dean. Subsequent episodes (and seasons) make it clear that Dean struggles with self-esteem issues, considering himself the "lesser" of the two brothers; witness his aforementioned inability to accept Sam's death at the start of Season Nine. Yet, Dean also stands up to their father and insists he and Sam be treated as adults and partners in their father's revenge quest, rather than accepting John's orders that the boys are safer without him ("Dead Man's Blood").

Unfortunately, John's sacrifice of his life for Dean's in "In My Time of Dying" (2.01) erases some of this growth. John's decision leaves Dean with an overwhelming sense of both guilt for John's sacrifice and the responsibility of his father's last instructions: either save or kill Sam ("Hunted").[11] In particular, it is the burden John places on Dean to be the sole arbiter of whether Sam is worth saving that creates the first real crack in Dean's willingness to be, in Sam's words, "a good little soldier." Dean's solution is to make his own deal (his life for Sam's) at the end of season two ("All Hell Breaks Loose: Part 2"), which seems to indicate it was one he was not prepared to carry. Dean's unquestioning loyalty to John and John's mission, and the onus to take care of Sam, undermine Dean's ability to trust his instincts. On both an emotional and psychological level, it is easier for Dean to sacrifice his own life than take Sam's.

In monomythic fashion, Dean, having endured Hell, returns in "Lazarus Rising" (4.01) with the "gift" of a growing disdain and rage for the ways in which their father raised them. When they finally meet their half-brother Adam and Sam starts training him like a hunter, telling him that "hunting is life" and personal connections are weaknesses, Dean is furious: "You hated Dad for saying that stuff, and now you're quoting him?" ("Jump the Shark"). The insight Dean gains from his experience in Hell—experiencing torture, and torturing in return ("Heaven and Hell")—and numerous instances of problematic behavior from the denizens of Heaven shift both Dean's sense of loyalty to family and his black-and-white perspective on questions of morality.

The nefarious nature of the angels' plan for the brothers is not entirely revealed until the end of Season Four and the beginning of Season Five. "Lucifer Rising" (4.22) exposes that the angels never had any desire to prevent the Apocalypse, and "Sympathy for the Devil" (5.01) shows they plan to use Dean's body to fight their war. This is not a surprising outcome; Season Four offers numerous examples of the angels' callous disregard for the brothers' personal autonomy. This includes wiping their memories and putting them in a hunting situation with no previous knowledge of the supernatural ("It's a Terrible Life"); forcing an emotionally fragile Dean to use the torturing skills he gained in Hell, despite both Dean's guilt and horror over what he had done ("Wishful Thinking") and his desire to forget and move past that experience ("On the Head of a Pin"); and revealing the brothers' adventures and thoughts for public consumption without their permission ("The Monster at the End of This Book").

The positive outcome of these actions is the formation of what Dean terms "Team Free Will" (Bobby, Castiel, Sam, and Dean), indicating a shift in Dean's perception that he can trust anyone outside of his blood or chosen family. This perspective change is underscored in three separate instances of Dean's death: when both brothers are shot by fellow hunters angry that Sam released Lucifer ("Dark Side of the Moon"), when Dean and Castiel are thrust into Purgatory as a consequence of their destruction of the Leviathan Dick Roman ("Survival of the Fittest"), and when Dean is killed by the angel Metatron and is resurrected as a demon ("Do You Believe in Miracles?").

Each of these instances offers an opportunity for change. While Dean is disappointed and discontented with the aforementioned machinations of the angels, both he and Castiel still rely on divine intervention (that is, God), to put a stop to it. Instead, Dean and Sam's (remembered) trip to Heaven reveals that God knows what is going on, but "doesn't think it's his problem" ("Dark Side of the Moon"). This revelation clearly causes a despair Dean struggles to overcome; however, this despair is not solely caused by God's nonchalance in the face of potential cosmic destruction. Dean's heavenly journey is yoked with Sam's, which means Dean is unable to deny the chasm between Sam's experiences and point-of-view and Dean's own. The importance of family is Dean's guiding principle; family is primarily defined as Sam at this point in the narrative. The brothers' heavenly journey, however, indicates that independence and choice are more important values for Sam. While Dean experiences memories of their former home or his best times with Sam, Sam's "happiest times" are when he was allowed to choose either his associates, such as sharing a Thanksgiving with a pre-teen girlfriend's family or striking out on his own by running away to Flagstaff.

This disparity in values Dean assumed he shared with his brother serves as the subtextual goad that leads Dean to seriously consider giving in to the angels' plan and allowing his body to be used as a vessel. While the stark contrast between the brothers' perspectives could have offered an opportunity for Dean to form his own independence and embrace a different or looser definition of family and responsibility, this particular "death" does not quite translate into shifting Dean's perspective as much as earlier or later deaths manage. As late as Season Nine, Dean intervenes with a dying Sam, who is ready to accept death as a permanent state; he tricks Sam into becoming yet another angelic vessel in order to heal Sam's fatal injuries ("I Think I'm Gonna

Like It Here"). As Sam rightly points out, this was less for Sam and more about Dean's inability to be alone ("Road Trip"). Further, as indicated earlier, Dean grapples with defining himself as anything beyond "hunter" and "Sam's brother" and is still convinced that he is an empty vessel without those defining characteristics. The combination of this existential emptiness and the subsequent rift between the brothers is likely a reason why in the next episode, Dean accepts the Mark of Cain as a tool to kill both of the season's villains: angelic scribe Metatron and Knight of Hell Abaddon ("First Born"). He is literally "marked" with a purpose that cannot be removed regardless of the actions of Dean or anyone around him.

The biggest character development death offers Dean is within his viewpoint regarding demons. Leaving aside questions of morality for the moment, Dean's "death" in Purgatory finds him making common cause with Benny, the spirit of a vampire also trapped in Purgatory. Their alliance was initially based on survival, as well as Benny's promise to find Dean a way out. The rest of the season, however, made it clear that the two of them shared a stronger bond than Dean felt with Sam, particularly when it is revealed that Sam had made no effort to locate his missing brother during the year Dean had spent in Purgatory ("We Need to Talk About Kevin").

While the fourth season featured Sam's alliance with the demon Ruby to Dean's disgust, and the seventh a rift between the brothers when Dean kills an old friend of Sam's who was a creature known as a kitsune ("The Girl Next Door"), Season Eight turns the narrative tables. In this instance, it is Sam who does not trust Dean's alliance with a creature they have been trained to hunt. While there are significant differences in the nature of these alliances—Ruby was manipulating Sam into releasing Lucifer, while Benny fought with Dean and helped him survive Purgatory—there are equally significant correlations between the two if viewed from an addiction/recovery model. In basic terms, Ruby appealed to Sam's desire to be both strong and effective in fighting demons, providing him with the unnatural means in which to increase his strength (not unlike steroids) and downplayed the negative effects that said means would have on Sam both physically and psychologically. The interaction between Benny and Dean, however, hews closer to the concept of addict (Benny) and sponsor (Dean), underscored by the number of times Benny contacts Dean to share his struggles of adjustment ("We Need To Talk About Kevin") or relapse ("Torn and Frayed"). The brothers' shared history, however, eventually forces Dean to choose between hunting with Sam and remaining friends with Benny ("Torn and Frayed").[12]

This type of alliance with creatures the brothers have been trained to fight takes a more significant turn when Dean dies at the end of Season Nine. He is resurrected as a demon, and runs off with Crowley, the King of Hell ("Black"). Much as soulless Sam was still Sam, minus the warmth and the understanding of consequences for his behavior, demon Dean still possesses elements, such as rage, that are part of non-demon Dean, while deleting other qualities, such as compassion.[13] While Dean is eventually cured of his demonness ("Soul Survivor") and the Mark of Cain that continued to negatively affect his behavior is removed ("Brother's Keeper"), the viewpoint with which he was brought up—demons are bad and must be destroyed—is no longer followed with any degree of fidelity. This is most obvious, perhaps, in Dean's relationship with Crowley, both previous to and following his death in "Do You Believe in Miracles?" (9.23).

Unlike his previous deaths, Dean's "death" in "Do You Believe in Miracles?" leaves both his body intact and his "soul" un-departed. Mirroring Sam's earlier journey in Seasons Two through Five, Dean becomes what he has always hunted, an outcome manipulated by Crowley throughout the ninth season. Unlike Benny, Crowley neither sought redemption nor discontinued perpetrating evil and/or violent acts despite serving as an (occasional) ally to the Winchesters. Particularly in Season Eight, Crowley's acts are unrepentant, including killing all potential prophets ("A Little Slice of Kevin") and individuals the brothers had saved in the past ("Clip Show"). In the final episode of Season Eight ("Sacrifice"), however, Sam's attempt to close the gates of Hell required "curing" a demon by dosing them with human blood (among other rituals). While this cure was unfinished, it had enough of an effect on Crowley to, if not express remorse, at least make him aware of his own loneliness. Crowley thus sets into motion a plan that will not only rid him of his enemy (Abaddon) but create a friend and companion in the Winchester with whom he feels a connection: Dean.

Crowley thus acts as both killer (of Dean) and mother (to "demon Dean") with little apparent understanding of the effects of the triple traumas of Dean's "unbearable" death at the hand of Metatron, his "unbearable" survival through his rebirth as a demon, and his equally "unbearable" resurrection as human through Sam's intervention in Season Ten. Yet, the trauma of Dean being forced to carry the memories of his actions as Crowley's protégé provides an opportunity to broaden his perspective on both his own nature (as killer) and that of the demons he hunts. Further, Crowley's willing self-sacrifice in "All Along the Watchtower" (12.23) to trap Lucifer in an alternate dimension could be read as a testament to the wisdom of Dean's death-induced change in perspective that kept him from killing the King of Hell.

Perhaps most important is the ways in which these numerous deaths have consequently freed Dean to develop his own identity. Writing in 2010, Chan reads the persistence of Castiel's handprint on Dean as "indicating that the ownership of Dean's body has passed from John (his biological father) and Alastair (his father-figure in Hell) to the agents of God" (para 2.4). This view is underscored by KT Torrey's analysis of the ways in which Castiel undermined the brothers' agency in Season Six, including bringing Sam back soulless, thrusting them into an alternate reality ("The French Mistake"), and demanding they worship him as their new God when he ingests all the souls of Purgatory ("The Man Who Knew Too Much"). Torrey reads this as Castiel buying into the very system of patriarchal control "Team Free Will" had fought against in Seasons Four and Five.

Dean's lack of both narrative and bodily agency also applies, as Rhonda Nicol argues, to Dean's (brief) transformation into a vampire in the episode "Live Free or Twihard" (6.5). Nicol's analysis indicates that both the initial "turning" and the subsequent transformation put Dean into a feminized subject position followed by desires and behaviors that are hypermasculine. This cycle—subjection followed by hypermasculine behavior—is repeated when Dean becomes a demon. He is the object of Crowley's desire for companionship and is manipulated into "turning" into a demon, yet his behavior as a demon is frequently shown in terms of hypermasculine behavior: casual sex, drinking, and brawling. Yet, the earlier "turning" of Dean facilitated his character's development by allowing Dean the ability for "touring the margins and discovering empathy for the Other, sometimes by experiencing Otherness himself" (Nicol 165). His Season Six transformation into a vampire foreshadows both his brotherly relationship with Benny in Season Eight and his transformation into Demon Dean in Season Ten. This is facilitated through Season Six's constant undermining of both Dean's and Sam's physical and psychological autonomy by forces beyond their control. Despite the trauma of these experiences, it is arguable that they allow the brothers (particularly Dean) to experience the empathy for the Other that Nicol suggests.

It is perhaps this empathy-through-transformation that, despite either Castiel's mark or Crowley's role in creating "demon" Dean, keeps either from exerting the type of control over Dean's actions that either his father or Alastair managed when he was younger. The fact that Castiel's mark on Dean has not been seen in several seasons may be one indication that his numerous deaths may have finally rendered Dean's body—and potentially his soul—as his own.

Conclusion

A series with as long a life as *Supernatural* requires periodic narrative resets in order to continue moving the story and character arcs forward. This becomes increasingly important as the series continues to air, given that it lacks the narrative closure suggested by its initial five-year story arc: Dean's first death ("No Rest for the Wicked") and resurrection ("Lazarus Rising"), and the angels attempting to use the brothers to start the apocalypse ("Lucifer

Rising"; "Sympathy for the Devil"). Without the fixed narrative endpoint envisioned by series' creator Eric Kripke, *Supernatural*'s narrative must continually find ways to extend the brothers' stories without lowering the narrative stakes. The physical renewals of the brothers upon resurrection thus offer a tidy metaphor for the narrative renewals these deaths represent. Just as the marks of their deaths may not be present on their bodies but remain (and resonate) on a psychological level, so too do these events make an impact on the narrative.

The numerous deaths of Sam and Dean represent a necessary component of the series' longevity and continued momentum. Rather than death operating as a sign of narrative exhaustion, it instead signals plot and character shifts of an unfolding text with no clear end point. That is, the constantly deferred closure inherent in such a long-running series is ameliorated by the ways in which Sam and Dean's deaths both close certain narrative and character beats while simultaneously creating or resurrecting new or additional possibilities or perspectives for the brothers. Like the surprise appearance of Mary Winchester at the end of the eleventh season, death in *Supernatural* is often a new beginning in disguise.

NOTES

1. *Doctor Who*, which celebrated its fiftieth anniversary in 2013, is actually the longest-running science fiction/fantasy series ever.

2. One slight exception: Dean, when rescued from Hell at the start of Season Four, points out to Sam that his body has been physically renewed; "No bullet wounds, knife cuts, none of the off-angled fingers from all the breaks" ("Monster Movie" 4.5).

3. Death's death persisted for two seasons; a new Death, former reaper Billie was introduced in Season Thirteen's "Advanced Thanatology" (13.05).

4. For this analysis, I have chosen not to examine a few episodes in which either Sam or Dean have died, as said deaths were of short duration and did not have the same significance on a character or narrative level: Sam's death via lightning strike in "Wishful Thinking" (4.08); Dean's 100+ deaths in "Mystery Spot" (3.11), which had more of an effect on Sam than Dean, who did not remember them; Anna Milton's killing of Sam in 1978 to prevent the Apocalypse, reversed by the archangel Michael possessing a young John Winchester in "The Song Remains the Same" (5.13); Dean's death via injection by Dr. Robert (Robert Englund) in order to contact Death in "Appointment in Samarra" (6.11); Dean's barbiturate overdose to contact Billie the reaper in "Red Meat" (11.17); and Sam and Dean's temporary deaths in order to escape federal custody in "First Blood" (12.11). While these deaths do have narrative significance, all of them last only minutes.

5. This callback is used again in Season Thirteen's "Wayward Sisters" (13.10) as a way to signal its status as a backdoor pilot.

6. Given that Heaven is presented, both in this episode and in "The Man Who Would Be King" (6.20) (which has a scene that takes place in deceased Enron CEO Kenneth Lay's Heaven) as a particular individual's best memories or happiest times—a never-ending concert at the Meadowlands, as per Pamela Barnes, or a fireworks display Dean put together for a young Sam; in other words, a kind of Disneyland afterlife—it is an amusing little meta-moment that the hunters that shoot Sam and Dean are named Roy and Walt. Both Roy and Walt reappear, after a seven-year absence from the series, in "Who We Are" (12.22).

7. The Promethean nature of the brothers' frequent deaths/resurrections is suggested in the episode "Remember the Titans" (8.16). A man, known as Shane (John Reardon) but

in fact the Greek of the myth, is cursed to die and be reborn each day fully healed. The positioning of this particular episode within the eighth season allows the series itself to offer a subtle metatextual commentary on both Sam and Dean's ability to consistently cheat death.

8. The hunting couple Jesse and Cesar are among the few within the series who chose to leave the hunting life after completing their avowed, initial mission, without one or the other dying ("The Chitters").

9. It's arguable that this mindwipe of Lisa and Ben serves as a less physically brutal example of "fridging"; their development through knowledge of the supernatural is erased in order to both save their lives and motivate Dean to return to hunting.

10. It is also arguable that, given the longevity of the series itself and Sam and Dean's investment in the "family business," they lack the anonymity of many of the other hunters seen within the world of the series; that is, the brothers are too recognizable to the demonic underworld to not put others at risk by association.

11. An amusing sidenote: Rachel Talalay, who directed "Hunted," went on to direct several recent episodes of *Doctor Who*, which, as stated earlier, is the only other fantasy series to surpass *Supernatural* in longevity.

12. Sam also affirmatively decides to end things with Amelia, so both can focus on closing the gates of Hell.

13. The different reactions to soullessness are explored in greater depth throughout Season Eleven of the series, most prominently in "Thin Lizzie" (11.05). For Len, a Lizzie Borden superfan, his soulless state is akin to a living death: he feels "cold" and takes no pleasure in anything. Sidney describes the loss of her soul as "blissful," freeing her from the memories of her painful and abusive childhood.

WORKS CITED

"Advanced Thanatology." *Supernatural: The Complete Thirteenth Season,* written by Andrew Dabb, directed by Phil Sgriccia, Warner Home Video, 2018.

"All Along the Watchtower." *Supernatural: The Complete Twelfth Season,* written by Andrew Dabb, directed by Robert Singer, Warner Home Video, 2017.

"All Hell Breaks Loose: Part 1." *Supernatural: The Complete Second Season,* written by Sera Gamble, directed by Robert Singer, Warner Home Video, 2007.

"All Hell Breaks Loose: Part 2." *Supernatural: The Complete Second Season,* written by Eric Kripke, directed by Kim Manners, Warner Home Video, 2007.

"Alpha and Omega." *Supernatural: The Complete Eleventh Season,* written by Andrew Dabb, directed by Phil Sgriccia, Warner Home Video, 2016.

"Appointment in Samarra." *Supernatural: The Complete Sixth Season,* written by Sera Gamble and Robert Singer, directed by Mike Rohl, Warner Home Video, 2011.

"Asylum." *Supernatural: The Complete First Season,* written by Richard Hatem, directed by Guy Bee, Warner Home Video, 2006.

"Black." *Supernatural: The Complete Tenth Season,* written by Jeremy Carver, directed by Robert Singer, Warner Home Video, 2015.

"The Born-Again Identity." *Supernatural: The Complete Seventh Season,* written by Sera Gamble, directed by Robert Singer, Warner Home Video, 2012.

"Brother's Keeper." *Supernatural: The Complete Tenth Season,* written by Jeremy Carver, directed by Phil Sgriccia, Warner Home Video, 2015.

Caruth, Cathy. *Unclaimed Experience: Trauma, Narrative, and History, 20th Anniversary Edition.* Johns Hopkins UP, 2016.

Chan, Suzette. "Supernatural Bodies: Writing Subjugation and Resistance Onto Sam and Dean Winchester." *"Saving People, Hunting Things,"* special issue of *Transformative Works and Culture,* vol. 4, no. 1, 2010, http://journal.transformativeworks.org/index.php/twc/article/view/179/160. Accessed 20 March 2017.

"The Chitters." *Supernatural: The Complete Eleventh Season,* written by Nancy Won, directed by Eduardo Sanchez, Warner Home Video, 2016.

"Clip Show." *Supernatural: The Complete Eighth Season,* written by Andrew Dabb, directed by Thomas J. Wright, Warner Home Video, 2013. DVD.

Corder, Jim. "Argument as Emergence, Rhetoric as Love." *Rhetoric Review*, volume 4, no. 1, 1985, pp. 16–32.

"Dark Dynasty." *Supernatural: The Complete Tenth Season*, written by Eugenie Ross-Leming and Brad Buckner, directed by Robert Singer, Warner Home Video, 2015.

"Dark Side of the Moon." *Supernatural: The Complete Fifth Season*, written by Andrew Dabb and Daniel Loflin, directed by Jeff Woolnough, Warner Home Video, 2010.

"Dead Man's Blood." *Supernatural: The Complete First Season*, written by Cathryn Humphris and John Shiban, directed by Tony Wharmby, Warner Home Video, 2006.

"Death's Door." *Supernatural: The Complete Seventh Season*, written by Sera Gamble, directed by Robert Singer, Warner Home Video, 2012.

"Do You Believe in Miracles?" *Supernatural: The Complete Ninth Season*, written by Jeremy Carver, directed by Thomas J. Wright, Warner Home Video, 2014.

"Exile on Main Street." *Supernatural: The Complete Sixth Season*, written by Sera Gamble, directed by Phil Sgriccia, Warner Home Video, 2011.

"First Blood." *Supernatural: The Complete Twelfth Season*, written by Andrew Dabb, directed by Robert Singer, Warner Home Video, 2017.

"First Born." *Supernatural: The Complete Ninth Season*, written by Robbie Thompson, directed by John Badham, Warner Home Video, 2014.

"Free to Be You and Me." *Supernatural: The Complete Fifth Season*, written by Jeremy Carver, directed by J. Miller Tobin, Warner Home Video, 2010.

"The French Mistake." *Supernatural: The Complete Sixth Season*, written by Ben Edlund, directed by Charles Beeson, Warner Home Video, 2011.

"Fresh Blood." *Supernatural: The Complete Third Season*, written by Sera Gamble, directed by Kim Manners, Warner Home Video, 2008.

Garcia, Alberto N. "Breaking the Mirror: Metafictional Strategies in *Supernatural*." *TV Goes to Hell: An Unofficial Road Map of* Supernatural, edited by Stacey Abbott and David Lavery. ECW, 2011, pp. 146–160.

"The Girl Next Door." *Supernatural: The Complete Seventh Season*, written by Andrew Dabb and Daniel Loflin, directed by Jensen Ackles, Warner Home Video, 2012.

"Heaven and Hell." *Supernatural: The Complete Fourth Season*, written by Trevor Sands and Eric Kripke, directed by J. Miller Tobin, Warner Home Video, 2009.

"Hollywood Babylon." *Supernatural: The Complete Second Season*, written by Ben Edlund, directed by Phil Sgriccia, Warner Home Video, 2007.

"How to Win Friends and Influence Monsters." *Supernatural: The Complete Seventh Season*, written by Ben Edlund, directed by Guy Bee. Warner Home Video, 2012.

"Hunted." *Supernatural: The Complete Second Season*, written by Raelle Tucker, directed by Rachel Talalay, Warner Home Video, 2007.

"I Think I'm Gonna Like It Here." *Supernatural: The Complete Ninth Season*, written by Jeremy Carver, directed by John Showalter, Warner Home Video, 2014.

"In My Time of Dying." *Supernatural: The Complete Second Season*, written by Eric Kripke, directed by Kim Manners, Warner Home Video, 2007.

"It's a Terrible Life." *Supernatural: The Complete Fourth Season*, written by Sera Gamble, directed by James L. Conway, Warner Home Video, 2009.

"Jump the Shark." *Supernatural: The Complete Fourth Season*, written by Andrew Dabb and Daniel Loflin, directed by Phil Sgriccia, Warner Home Video, 2009.

"Lazarus Rising." *Supernatural: The Complete Fourth Season*, written by Eric Kripke, directed by Kim Manners, Warner Home Video, 2009.

"Let It Bleed." *Supernatural: The Complete Sixth Season*, written by Sera Gamble, directed by John Showalter, Warner Home Video, 2011.

"A Little Slice of Kevin." *Supernatural: The Complete Eighth Season*, written by Brad Buckner and Eugenie Ross-Leming, directed by Charlie Carner, Warner Home Video, 2013.

"Live Free or Twihard." *Supernatural: The Complete Sixth Season*, written by Brett Matthews, directed by Rod Hardy, Warner Home Video, 2011.

"Lucifer Rising." *Supernatural: The Complete Fourth Season*, written by Eric Kripke, directed by Eric Kripke, Warner Home Video, 2009.

"The Man Who Knew Too Much." *Supernatural: The Complete Sixth Season,* written by Eric Kripke, directed by Robert Singer, Warner Home Video, 2011.

"The Man Who Would Be King." *Supernatural: The Complete Sixth Season,* written and directed by Ben Edlund, Warner Home Video, 2011.

"Metamorphosis." *Supernatural: The Complete Fourth Season,* written by Cathryn Humphris, directed by Kim Manners, Warner Home Video, 2009.

"The Monster at the End of This Book." *Supernatural: The Complete Fourth Season,* written by Julie Siege and Nancy Weiner, directed by Mike Rohl, Warner Home Video, 2009.

"Monster Movie." *Supernatural: The Complete Fourth Season,* written by Ben Edlund, directed by Robert Singer, Warner Home Video, 2009.

"Mystery Spot." *Supernatural: The Complete Third Season,* written by Jeremy Carver and Emily McLaughlin, directed by Kim Manners, Warner Home Video, 2008.

Nicol, Rhonda. "'How is that not rape-y?': Dean as Anti-Bella and Feminism Without Women in *Supernatural.*" Supernatural, *Humanity, and the Soul: On the Highway to Hell and Back,* edited by Susan A. George and Regina M. Hansen. Palgrave MacMillan, 2014, pp. 155–67.

"No Rest for the Wicked." *Supernatural: The Complete Third Season,* written by Eric Kripke, directed by Kim Manners, Warner Home Video, 2008.

"On the Head of a Pin." *Supernatural: The Complete Fourth Season,* written by Ben Edlund, directed by Mike Rohl, Warner Home Video, 2009.

Petruska, Karen. "Crossing Over: Network Transition, Critical Reception, and *Supernatural* Longevity." *TV Goes to Hell: An Unofficial Road Map of* Supernatural, edited by Stacey Abbott and David Lavery. ECW, 2011, pp. 219–229.

"Pilot." *Supernatural: The Complete First Season,* written by Eric Kripke, directed by David Nutter, Warner Home Video, 2006.

Ramaswamy, Chitra. "When Good TV Goes Bad: How the Simpsons Ended Up Gorging on Itself." *The Guardian,* 24 April 2017, https://www.theguardian.com/tv-and-radio/2017/apr/24/jump-the-shark-when-good-tv-goes-bad-the-simpsons. Accessed 30 April 2017.

"The Rapture." *Supernatural: The Complete Fourth Season,* written by Jeremy Carver, directed by Charles Beeson, Warner Home Video, 2009.

"Red Meat." *Supernatural: The Complete Eleventh Season,* written by Robert Berens and Andrew Dabb, directed by Nina Lopez-Corrado, Warner Home Video, 2016.

"Remember the Titans." *Supernatural: The Complete Eighth Season,* written by Daniel Loflin, directed by Steve Boyum, Warner Home Video, 2013.

"Road Trip." *Supernatural: The Complete Ninth Season,* written by Andrew Dabb, directed by Robert Singer, Warner Home Video, 2014.

"Sacrifice." *Supernatural: The Complete Eighth Season,* written by Jeremy Carver, directed by Phil Sgriccia, Warner Home Video, 2013. DVD.

"Scarecrow." *Supernatural: The Complete First Season,* written by Patrick Sean Smith and John Shiban, directed by Kim Manners, Warner Home Video, 2006.

"Sin City." *Supernatural: The Complete Third Season,* written by Robert Singer and Jeremy Carver, directed by Charles Beeson, Warner Home Video, 2008.

"The Song Remains the Same." *Supernatural: The Complete Fifth Season,* written by Sera Gamble and Nancy Weiner, directed by Steve Boyum, Warner Home Video, 2010.

"Soul Survivor." *Supernatural: The Complete Tenth Season,* written by Brad Buckner and Eugenie Ross-Leming, directed by Jensen Ackles, Warner Home Video, 2015.

"Survival of the Fittest." *Supernatural: The Complete Seventh Season,* written by Sera Gamble, directed by Robert Singer, Warner Home Video, 2012.

"Swan Song." *Supernatural: The Complete Fifth Season,* written by Eric Kripke, directed by Steve Boyum, Warner Home Video, 2010.

"Sympathy for the Devil." *Supernatural: The Complete Fifth Season,* written by Eric Kripke, directed by Robert Singer, Warner Home Video, 2010.

"Thin Lizzie." *Supernatural: The Complete Eleventh Season,* written by Nancy Won, directed by Rashaad Ernesto Green, Warner Home Video, 2016.

"Torn and Frayed." *Supernatural: The Complete Eighth Season,* written by Jenny Klein, directed by Robert Singer, Warner Home Video, 2013.

Torrey, KT. "'We're just food … and perverse entertainment': *Supernatural*'s New God and the Narrative Objectification of Sam and Dean." Supernatural, *Humanity, and the Soul: On the Highway to Hell and Back*, edited by Susan A. George and Regina M. Hansen. Palgrave MacMillan, 2014, pp. 53–65.

"Twigs and Twine and Tasha Banes." *Supernatural: The Complete Twelfth Season,* written by Steve Yockey, directed by Richard Speight, Jr., Warner Home Video, 2017.

"Wayward Sisters." *Supernatural: The Complete Thirteenth Season,* written by Robert Berens and Andrew Dabb, directed by Phil Sgriccia, Warner Home Video, 2018.

"We Need to Talk About Kevin." *Supernatural: The Complete Eighth Season,* written by Jeremy Carver, directed by Robert Singer, Warner Home Video, 2013.

"What Is and What Should Never Be." *Supernatural: The Complete Second Season,* written by Raelle Tucker, directed by Eric Kripke, Warner Home Video, 2007.

"Wishful Thinking." *Supernatural: The Complete Fourth Season,* written by Ben Edlund, directed by Robert Singer, Warner Home Video, 2009.

"Who We Are." *Supernatural: The Complete Twelfth Season,* written by Robert Berens, directed by John Showalter, Warner Home Video, 2017.

When Women Die

"The (Dead) Girl with the Dungeons and Dragons Tattoo"

Supernatural *and the Disposable Other*

Anastasia Salter

The CW's *Supernatural* stands out on a network that increasingly values diversity in its cast. Unlike its action-counterparts *Flash* (2014–) and *Arrow* (2012–), the show doesn't build a supportive group of women and non-white characters around its (ostensibly) straight white male leads. The show's early arc was firmly fixated on the brotherly relationship and family business of the two Winchester brothers, Sam and Dean, and even opened with the death of Sam's fiancée at the hands of a demon in a moment that both recalled the fate of the boys' mother and telegraphed the future fate of most women characters who would venture into the Winchesters' macho world.

The main cast has occasionally expanded but primarily to include other white men. Bobby Singer, the boys' substitute father figure, joined center stage for several seasons before his own death, while angel Castiel and crossroads demon turned King of Hell Crowley more recently fill major roles. All of these characters display different patterns of white masculinity and are defined primarily in relationship to one another. While women occasionally pass through the Winchesters' world, they rarely become fixtures, and even love interests and fellow hunters typically leave the show through death rather than arcs of growth or moving forward. Bronwen Calvert notes that such women are often seen as interruptions, used primarily "to motivate and drive the plot of this show from its pilot" (90). The introduction of Charlie Bradbury, an intelligent and proactive queer woman with her own life and goals outside the Winchesters, seemed like an opportunity to address some of this imbalance—making it all the more dramatic and heartbreaking when her character arc was abruptly ended.

Charlie Bradbury's journey began as one entry in a series of *Supernatural* sidekicks, but quickly grew to be more than that despite only eight total episodes. Charlie grew significantly over these few appearances in her own version of a hero's journey, yet the progression of that arc was betrayed in her as-of-2017 final appearance on the show in "Dark Dynasty" (10.21.)[1] In a series where death isn't permanent, Charlie's death as both iconic fangirl and visible lesbian character was even more biting. The lack of a magical resurrection where a show's lesbian characters are concerned is not a new problem, holding echoes of Willow and Tara's fate on *Buffy the Vampire Slayer* (Anders). The "Bury your Gays" (McConnaughy) and "Dead or Evil Lesbian" ("The Death of Tara...") tropes have haunted science fiction and fantasy television particularly over the past decade. *Supernatural*, with its already limited representation of women and history of using women's deaths as motivation for the main characters, is no exception.

I critique and contextualize fan responses to this betrayal, particularly in the form of fanfiction addressing or remedying Charlie's demise through means readily available to main characters on the show. I will examine the ramifications and aftermaths of Charlie Bradbury's death through conversations on Tumblr, "fix-it" fics and other fan revisions and rejections of the canon, and recaps responding to the episode in the larger context of the challenges of representation and diversity in current media. Through this contrast of canon and fanfiction interpretations of Charlie's fate, her significance as a lesbian woman agent in a show of heterosexual, hypermasculine heroism becomes clear, and the impact of her death on the fandom can be better understood.

"The Girl with the Dungeons and Dragons Tattoo"

Charlie Bradbury is introduced in "The Girl with the Dungeons and Dragons Tattoo" (7.20). The Winchester boys (and Bobby, now a ghost) find out a hard drive with compromising information about their aliases and location is currently, as Dean describes it, "in the middle of the Death Star" of Leviathan corporate headquarters. We first see Charlie's face as the hacker trying to decrypt the drive, but following the opening credits, her role in the narrative is clarified with a parallel *Star Wars* reference. We see her hopping off a yellow Vespa, listening to Katrina and The Waves' "Walking on Sunshine," and wearing a Princess Leia shirt that says "Rebel." Her desk is covered in a merchandise display straight out of ThinkGeek: a Legolas bust, Star Wars comic cover, Wonder Woman action figure, and Hermione Granger bobblehead all occupy places of honor. She even exchanges a Star Wars quote with her cubicle neighbor ("I love you" / "I know") before being summoned into the office to meet the season's very own Darth Vader, head Leviathan Dick Roman. Charlie Bradbury's geek cred is thus immediately and undeniably established.

The Geekgirl (or Geekboy) character continually occupies the position of marginalized sidekick in media. One of the most iconic examples, Willow, added a depth of knowledge and computer skills to the *Buffy the Vampire Slayer* crew but was for years cast in the role of poorly-dressed, perpetually single social misfit. Willow's transformation into powerful, sexually confident, techno-witch is dramatic. Jes Battis notes that Willow's "relationship with Tara, and consequent abandonment of Oz as a romantic interest, is probably the most dramatic character shift experienced by any of the Scoobies" (23). This type of character arc, by contrast, is typically denied to women characters on *Supernatural* with a few exceptions. Sheriffs Jody and Donna, who have attracted their own fan base among calls for a *Supernatural* spin-off,[2] have both been allowed this type of growth, thanks in part to their completely non-romantic relationships with the central cast (Rachel-A).

Charlie's identity and character is mostly credited to writer Robbie Thompson, who is responsible for the Charlie Bradbury episodes of the show. Thompson credited actress Felicia Day's significant influence on her character (@rthompson1138). Charlie at first appears to have a lot in common with early Willow, and is less immediately a fit for the physically violent world of *Supernatural* than Jody or Donna. But it quickly becomes apparent that Charlie is a hero in search of a story.

While she might not comfortably and immediately occupy the Winchesters' more physical world of violence, she is both integral to their efforts against the Leviathans and outside of the Winchesters' usual sphere of women love interests. Her identity as a lesbian is established in a sequence played for humor in her first episode. At a moment of indecision facing the prospect of infiltrating Dick Roman's office, Sam spurs Charlie back to action by asking her to name her favorite Harry Potter character, then urging her to imitate Hermione in the face of danger. Both Charlie and Hermione share a common trope of playing girl sidekick (and occasionally rescuer) to a pair of boys, developing a sibling-like relationship with one while becoming romantically involved with the other. Charlie even comments on the connections between herself and Hermione when she starts describing Hermione's strategies and notes "and then, she ends up with the wrong person..." ("The Girl with the Dungeons and Dragons Tattoo"). However, only a few minutes after the parallels are reinforced in a way that suggests Charlie's future romantic connection with one of the brothers, she encounters a security guard and is stopped in her tracks. Dean suggests that she needs to "flirt her way past," but is surprised when Charlie says "he's not my type ... as in, he's not a girl" ("The Girl with..."). This moment is played comically, but serves to immediately remove Charlie from potential consideration as a romantic interest of the brothers.

Charlie's potential presence as a sexual interest and object is thus immediately removed from the equation, emphasizing this sibling positioning. In many ways, Charlie occupies a nonsexual sidekick role usually assigned to male characters, explicitly referencing those roles through her language and interactions, which "allows Charlie to be the one with the power and confidence in the exchange, rather than the damsel in distress, the bystander, or the passive object" (Walton 118). Megan Genovese argues that "Charlie has an extraordinary affinity for masculinity. Unfortunately, this is only possible in *Supernatural* through the sublimation of her femaleness into symbolic maleness through her sexuality" (114). As one of the few women allowed to occupy this position, she is elevated both in fan perception and in the show's own lore.

Her status as a lesbian makes this positioning even more exceptional, as no other canonically queer character occupies a lasting role on the show. *Supernatural* has included several representations of gay characters: notably, the Dean and Sam modeled duo in "The Real Ghostbusters" (5.09) and hunting team Jesse and Cesar in "The Chitters" (11.19), who are an interracial married gay couple who even have a happy ending because, as minor characters, they fade away without further resolution. Macklem suggests that "female characters are not acceptable when they pose any kind of a challenge to the male characters' prowess or the relationship between the two brothers" (231). Macklem was writing before Charlie's death, and noted that "fan reception for Charlie has been very strong, in part because she is played by Felicia Day, but [to] a large extent because the character is self-identified as gay" and thus no threat to any existing relationships (236). However, it is even more significant that Charlie is allowed to have meaningful connections to the main characters that are non-romantic, making her a powerful self-projection and identification character for queer fans.

Fan discussion following the character's introduction noted how her sexuality (and thus lack of "love interest" status) could be her salvation in the Winchester universe's rules. Suzette Chan commented that she had hopes for Charlie as a recurring character because "as a lesbian, Charlie is safe from having her mind wiped or dying as the result of becoming sexually involved with Dean or Sam. Hopefully, she can survive the Leviathans, too." Fans and scholars alike had noted Charlie's resilience and characterization as an exception to the previous pattern: all major female characters must die (Walton 119). This hopefulness of Charlie as an exception surrounded her with an aura of presumed resilience—one soon to come crashing down as a result of her abrupt demise.

Charlie Bradbury's iconic role on the show as a representation of a fangirl (through everything from her wardrobe to her interactions with the LARP community as queen) made her emblematic to the *Supernatural* Family. Mary Frances Casper defines the *Supernatural* Family as a fan culture tied together by the shared myth of the Winchester family as one that doesn't end with blood (77). Charlie Bradbury cosplays, gifs, and memes circulated rapidly on Tumblr following the character's first appearance. She serves as a counterpoint to the show's previous representation of the fangirl: Becky, a super-fan who abducts Sam Winchester with the aid of a love potion. Lisa Macklem noted that Becky was "over the top," with poor social skills, and seemed to be particularly an attack on the passions of "Samgirls" with her eventually violent need to possess Sam Winchester ("I See What You Did There" 40).

The "fangirl" as an archetype already has an uncomfortable and complex relationship with the *Supernatural* universe. Fan labor is simultaneously relied upon to support the show's ratings, and mocked within the text of the show (Busse). Fangirls are continually aware of the rhetoric aimed at us, as Katherine Larsen and Lynn S. Zubernis discuss in *Fangasm*: "fans—especially female fans—are so accustomed to accusations of insanity and prohibitions against being out of control that we have become hypervigilant for any evidence of these sorts of behaviors" (31). Francesca Coppa describes the hated position such women fans occupy: "One of the most derided figures in Western culture is the woman in sweatpants watching television and eating ice cream out of the carton, and I've often thought about why that woman is so detested" (x). Coppa concludes that it is because the fan resists the male gaze, and instead is active in observing, in "feasting her eyes" (x).

Charlie is that woman, despite her portrayal by conventionally attractive actress Felicia Day. She wears t-shirts with references that are frequently obscure, drawing on feminist comics such as *Lumberjanes,* and is far more interested in the gaze of other women than that of any man. She continuously references popular culture. In her presence, other characters seem more likely to join in and, like Sam, embrace their inner "Dumble-dork" ("Dead Girl with…"). Her presence on the show as a hero with her own narrative arc suggested a radical change in the showrunners' relationship with their own fan girls, making her coming abrupt demise resonate on a deeper level: her death is the death of the fan girl personified.

Charlie's Quest

Charlie Bradbury is powerful and knowledgeable in her own right, recalling the superhero women and counterparts who occupy other shows on the CW network. Macklem observes that this is a trend with the women who last on *Supernatural*: "Interestingly, while one would not immediately think of many of the female characters on *Supernatural* as *super*women, many of them do fit these criteria" (Macklem 227). Charlie is a prime example. Her technical sidekick role is one women are only beginning to occupy on television. Her CW network counterpart, Felicity Smoak on *Arrow,* is cast in a similar vein but with the added burden of a love interest, which, as discussed, Charlie's lesbian identity allows her to escape. Charlie seems to occupy the position of an archetypal survivor, recalling the horror concept of the "final girl," who is "boyish, in a word … her smartness, gravity, competence in mechanical and other practical matters, and sexual reluctance set her apart from other girls and ally her, ironically, with the very boys she fears or rejects" (Clover 204). Charlie's relationships with other characters on the show do not fit this simple model of including the girl within masculine discourse. Her sisterly, playful interactions with Dean remind us that, like Charlie, he is more complicated than his signifiers: muscle car and rock music aside, he is "more than a one-dimensional representation of hard, violent, white masculinity resurrected from the 1970s and the 1980s" (George 152).

Charlie and Dean's relationship (and the corresponding play with masculinity) is emblematic of the show's own transition towards more complex relationships with gender and narrative. Charlie's episodes are particularly progressive in their representations of gender, and Charlie is typically able to break out of the stereotypical mold of the "final girl" in part thanks to her refusal to accept the limitations expected within the genre (Leddy). In her second appearance, "LARP and the Real Girl," Charlie is shown escaping the "real" supernatural through a fantasy setting where she has established herself as queen. Even this pseudo-fantastical environment presents us with a Charlie who is more in her element, even as the narrative of the episode accommodates a story of a captured fairy awaiting Charlie's rescue.

This an exception to the typically masculine-focused episodic structure of the show. "Lore and narrative can involve female characters, but the performance itself may not be particularly feminine since the characters … conform to pertinent behaviors and cultural markers of masculinity" (Rozario 127). Charlie occupies a complicated position on this spectrum, reintroduced as the sword-wielding LARP queen through a hair-tossing "exaggerated performance of the feminine" (Rozario 136). During the episode, her banter with Dean establishes their shared interest in the maidens of the fantasy world. "I notice a lot of these maidens checking you out," Dean comments, to which Charlie replies, "I can't shut this down. It's good to be queen" ("LARP and the Real Girl"). These connections and the willingness to place Charlie's gaze, as a queer woman, on the same "objects" as Dean as the show's iconic man further emphasize Charlie's exceptional status among the women who have populated the show, drawing the fan's attention to her as an agent.

Charlie's recurring appearances build on that sense of agency as they establish her interest in a heroic journey of her own, which she achieves off-screen following the introduction of Dorothy (of *Wizard of Oz* fame). Charlie leaves on a journey to save Oz in "Slumber Party" (9.04), after explaining to Sam her desire for her own adventure: "Saving people, hunting things, the family business? I am down. But … I was raised on Tolkien, man. I mean, where is all *this*? Where are my White Walkers and my volcano and magic ring to throw in the damn thing?" She disappears for an entire season, which inspired a pairing with 144 listed works in *Archive of Our Own*, a fan-run repository of fan fiction, as of 4/21/17: Dorothy Baum/Charlie Bradbury.

Some of these stories center on Dorothy and Charlie's adventures (and, usually, romance) while in others they are joined by *Supernatural* mainstays and are enlisted to follow the yellow brick road. BiJane's "Friend of Dorothy" sequence, which includes "Over the Rainbow" and "Saviors of Oz," focuses exclusively on Dorothy and Charlie's developing romance alongside encounters with Oz mainstays such as Glinda the Good and the Munchkins (BiJane). These crossover works draw upon both the transformative version of Oz established within the *Supernatural* text (in which Dorothy is a daughter of Men of Letters member Frank Baum) and in the original books, although frequently they include nods to other adaptations such as Gregory Maguire's book-turned-musical *Wicked*.

The choice of Oz for Charlie's journey is appropriate given the original work's feminist overtones, which Linda Rohrer describes as a woman-centric quest: "the fabulous Wizard seems the object of Dorothy's quest; however, on another level, our heroine's true search is for the power within herself, the power of the female imagination—that which patriarchy, the Wizard, denies women. The Wizard of Oz represents the voice of patriarchy—the authority behind the curtain—hidden, but loudly demanding that women fulfill its prescriptions" (149). Charlie's escape into Oz is similarly a refusal to fit her quest and desires into the patriarchal, violent model of *Supernatural*. Her fantasy is different, and her presence in *Supernatural* is a nod to the value of these fantasies, even as her death is a closing of the door on that same disruption.

When Charlie reemerges into the *Supernatural* universe, her journey appears to have changed her significantly. The version of Charlie who appears in "There's No Place Like Home" (10.11) is reminiscent of Vampire Willow, the first time Willow's character development was foreshadowed on *Buffy the Vampire Slayer*. Good Charlie sums up the difference between herself and her split counterpart:

> "We're still connected physically, if you hurt her, you hurt me. But bottom line, she's bad and I'm good. And let me just tell you being good is really annoying. Normally at a place like this, I'd be pounding Harvey Wallbangers and checking out the bartender's ass. Now all I wanna do is sip club sodas and send her to college" ["There's No Place Like Home"].

These complex Charlies present a duality of fan girl identity not present in any previous representation on the show: Charlie, like *Supernatural*'s own fan girls, has a dark side and a complex relationship with the show's characters and ideologies.

In an interview on her character's reappearance, Felicia Day commented on the importance of the character to her while noting the significance of this complex projection of the fan girl she embodies:

> I really enjoy that they haven't killed me because that means I can come back. I mean they have killed me. Technically in the last Oz episode I did die. But you know I come from a world of fandom. I live on the internet. That's where ... my whole career has been grown by fans one by one, versus from the top-down and I wouldn't have it any other way. So it's really the fans' approval that I want more than anything. And I really think that Charlie is an authentic projection of the kind of person who loves Supernatural [Clarissa].

These words illustrate the connection between Charlie and the fans, and suggest Charlie's death can also be seen in terms of the conflict between fans and showrunners: "to the authors and producers of *Supernatural,* fans can legitimately be seen as a form of adversary. Whether the *Supernatural* writers are laughing with or at the fans, there seems to be a basic distrust of the fan's motives" (Coker and Benefiel 98). Charlie returned from Oz an apparent hero, having faced the true difficulty and violence of a fantasy universe. Yet, rather than a quest attempted on her own terms, it is the violence of Dean and Sam's world that ends her arc, adding to the (perceived) senselessness of her death and fueling fans' outrage.

#CharlieDeservedBetter

I watched "Dark Dynasty" air on May 6, 2015, with Twitter open and an increasing sense of dread as the minutes passed. This episode marked a turning point in the tenth season of *Supernatural*, with an opening that featured the (mostly) human season villains, the Stynes, harvesting organs from victims as part of a Frankenstein-esque practice of self-renewal. During Season Ten, the Winchester brothers are primarily motivated by trying to find a spell in The Book of the Damned to remove The Mark of Cain from Dean's arm. Or, at least, that's what Sam is doing, as Dean deemed the effort too risky and believed the book had been burned. Instead, Sam enlisted the unlikely help of witch-extraordinaire Rowena (best known as Crowley's mother), Castiel, and Charlie Bradbury, code-breaker and hacker. The team isn't exactly compatible. Charlie finally loses her temper and runs off to a motel for some peace and quiet. Unsurprisingly, the Stynes track her down. Her last act is to send Sam the information he needs to decode the book of spells, even as she refuses to give her notes to the Stynes and potentially save her own life:

DEAN: (Dean takes the phone away from Sam) Charlie, I don't know what the hell is going on, but you need to listen to me. Give whoever that is whatever they want. You understand? Charlie?!
CHARLIE: I can't do that, Dean [sends her notes in an email to Sam].

In a recap, Charlie Jane Anders sums up some of the greatest problems with this moment: "she dies in an idiot plot. Charlie, who's always been shown to be quite resourceful, gets herself killed really stupidly." She knows the threats are real. She has proven herself battle-ready before, with escapades ranging from fighting the evil Wizard of Oz to lying directly to evil world-eating Leviathans. Yet, she goes out poorly armed and unprotected to meet her death. Ashley Walton observed that the most unsettling part of Charlie's death is how it betrays her progressive narrative as one of the show's heroes. Charlie dies "losing her wits and regressing to the stereotypical female horror victim and not unlike nineteenth-century Gothic heroines, playing second-fiddle in a patriarchal narrative" (124). She is no longer the "final girl" of Clover's slasher films. She is instead one of the first victims, naively going off alone after a minor conflict.

Why?

Many of those watching in horror took to Twitter with hashtags such as #CharlieDeservedBetter, reflecting the frustration at the death of a character who, as a queer woman and a fan, served as a point of connection and identification for many of us (Uve). Charlie's death was thus more than just another escalation of the darkness of *Supernatural*. It was a summary ending to Charlie's arc as a successful Other in the Winchester's straight white male universe of macho heroism and women victims. Alena Karkanias points out that *Supernatural*'s creative team must be understood as a changing collective. Charlie Bradbury's own creator Robbie Thompson was one of many who argued against Charlie's death, "knowing how much she meant to the fan community, even if they did not understand all the reasons exactly why she was so symbolically important to them" (18). Killing off Charlie Bradbury was not only disappointing to fans who identified with the character, but also felt like a betrayal of her journey. This significance explains the strong reaction to Charlie's death, with fans reacting through many mechanisms, including the authoring of fanfiction.

Examining Fanfiction: If Charlie Bradbury Lives...

In the introduction to *The Fanfiction Reader*, Francesca Coppa observes that the capitalist structures of mass media storytelling are what create the ecosystem of the fanfiction writer: "The average person is—in the Marxist sense—alienated from the process of storytelling" (7). Charlie Bradbury's death may have been a point of contention in the writer's room, but the character's many fans were powerless to enter that room or to direct the narrative. Fanfiction is one outlet for their alternative narratives.

In *Archive of Our Own* as of December 30, 2016, there are thirteen works explicitly tagged "Charlie Bradbury Lives," with one of them adding the modifier "Charlie is alive because I'm in love with her (2016)." Several other tags also address the event: "Charlie Lives," "Episode: s10e21 Dark Dynasty," and several others include both fix-it fic and revisions of the narrative. Only some of these stories actually address the death and/or alter its events, including RickyPine's "Blackbird" (2015), Aini_NuFire's "In the Shelter of Your Wings" (2016), SabbyStarlight's "Heaven" (2016), Yalu's "Single Candle" (2015), and twiceshy's "Never Have to Go to War No More" (2015). These narratives include both examples of the "fix-it" fic genre and broader reactions to the mistreatment of women characters on *Supernatural*. On a show where every major character's death is apparently the beginning of a negotiation, with even Mary Winchester herself back from the dead as of Season Eleven, why are so many of the strong women of *Supernatural* permanently six feet under?

The impermanence of death has been such a fixture in *Supernatural* as to be the subject of several meta episodes, including one where Sam and Dean go to Heaven and learn that they have made that journey through death and back many times ("Dark Side of the Moon"). Some of the fanfiction reimagines Charlie's fate could have been avoided through a similar type of luck. In RickyPine's "Blackbird," the disaster is averted through literal angelic intervention:

> "Who … who are you?" I ask. "Some kind of guardian angel?"
> "If you wanna get super-technical about it," Angel-Me says. "For now, though, just consider me a concerned third party from a Second Universe."
> I watch as the door—which had been blown shut in the wind fight—swings open by itself. "I … I…" I don't know how to thank you. The words bounce around my brain but refuse to let themselves be coherently spoken out loud.
> "Like I said, no worries." Angel-Me becomes visible for a second and smiles at me. "You don't have to thank me." With that, she vanishes from sight once again, leaving me for good.

Given *Supernatural*'s narrative, this sort of transformative work includes elements of both the meta-fiction of the show and the main story's reliance on angelic guardians and foes. However, it also works on another level, serving as a reminder of how Charlie's death is unnecessary and preventable given the existing rules of the universe. In this case, Angel-Me is an insertion of the author (or even the reader, who presumably is also unimpressed by Charlie's inelegant demise), but could just as easily serve as a critique of the writer. The character is a clear expression of frustration, and, through use of the "she" pronoun, can be identified as an embodiment of every fan girl who watched the episode wishing for the power to intervene.

Aini NuFire's story makes use of an existing angel for an intervention. Castiel, receiving a call from Charlie instead of the call she made in canon to Dean, flies to her rescue and finds Charlie still alive: "Castiel quickly turned and hurried back to Charlie. Her entire body was trembling, hands shaking too much to apply pressure to her wound. Tears were streaming down her cheeks and her breaths hiccuped [sic] in her chest." The two bond over Castiel's exertion and their mutual affection of Dean, and return to the bunker relatively intact. The story ends with Charlie reassured by her angelic protector: "Charlie smiled. And when she later dozed off to the sound of screeching steel and clashing swords, stretched out on the bed next to Castiel, if she half-dreamed one giant wing was curled around her, well, it kept the nightmares at bay." The story has an accusatory tone: unlike "Angel-Me," Castiel is canonical, and easily available as an intervening force to the show's writers: yet, while Dean and Sam warrant endless rescues from Castiel, Charlie is left abandoned.

Other authors turn to different potential sources of supernatural intervention. Yalu's "Single Candle" includes a succinct description from the author: "We all know ep 10x21 never happened, doesn't exist, etc.—but if it had, this is how it should have gone." Dean, receiving Charlie's call, realizes that there is no way for him or Castiel to make it in time. So, he makes a phone call to Crowley: "Dean clutched the phone as he drove one-handed, trusting his baby not to hydroplane because there wasn't a hope in hell he could concentrate enough right now. He felt his heart hammering his [sic] his throat. 'Please, I'm begging you. We'll owe you. Anything.'" Dean's passion and love is the focus: "Dean's heart only had room for Charlie right now." This use of demonic intervention is a further indictment of the showrunner's callousness with regards to Charlie: characters for whom Heaven and Hell are a phone call away are apparently incapable of interrupting her authorially mandated end.

In a larger indictment of the showrunner's similar callousness towards women of significance throughout the many seasons of *Supernatural,* SabbyStarlight's "Heaven" doesn't attempt to fix the ending of "Dark Dynasty." Instead, it connects Charlie's arc and fate with two women characters who also died in the name of the Winchesters: Jo Harvelle and Ellen Harvelle. The story opens with Charlie's realization of her own death and a feeling of peace: "she remembered the exact moment she knew it was over, when she closed her eyes and gave in and, despite everything, smiled. Because she had solved the encryption. Now Sam could save Dean. They would be okay. Her boys would be okay. And her job was done" (SabbyStarlight). Jo, initially introduced as an apparent love interest for Dean, was eventually relegated to a role closer to younger sister, a position Charlie also filled. This fanfiction revision builds on the concept of Heaven already established within *Supernatural*, but it also acknowledges the apparently utilitarian role of both Jo and Charlie in the Winchester brothers' lives: once they've advanced the plot, they are no longer necessary.

As the women get to know one another, Charlie sums up the fate of women on the show with a simple explanation: "How do you think I ended up dead? Loving those boys is a death sentence. You of all people should know that." Charlie and Jo bond over their continuing love of the Winchesters, and as Charlie explains:

> "Because we love them. Because they stumbled into our lives, battered and broken, and we tried our best to help them even when it seemed hopeless and somehow along the way we fell in love with them. Romantic love, family love, it doesn't matter. Love is love" [SabbyStarlight].

These words (not so dissimilar from the passionate defenses of the show and its main characters found on recaps, Tumblr, and similar spaces across the internet) encapsulate the shared positioning occupied by character and fan.

twiceshy's "Never Have to Go To War No More" adds something fundamentally missing from Charlie's death: an acknowledgment of her journey to the afterlife, and in doing so critiques the showrunner's decision to silence Charlie immediately after her death. Several times one of the major characters (Sam, Dean, and Bobby) has come close to death or died, the viewers have seen their interactions with the reapers who inhabit *Supernatural* and take the dead to their destination. twiceshy imagines Charlie's encounter with a reaper dressed in cloak and mail:

> "I'm flattered—really—I just wasn't expecting my reaper to be so—dramatic. Don't you guys go for the suit and tie look, usually? Because I have to say, the chain mail babe thing—"
> "I was called Valkyrie."
> "Valkyrie. Right. Of course." Charlie sighed, "Because I get the only reaper in the fleet with a twisted sense of humor. Please could you just—tone it down ... a bit?"
> "Celeste. We truly do not have time for this prattle."

The Winchesters have been continually warned by the reapers and Death himself of the risks of reversing and cheating death. Charlie's reaper gives a similar warning, and adds to it the suggestion that Sam and Dean will try to save her: "The demons willfully perverted mortals for their own ends while the angels stood by, and now these men, these Winchesters, make a game of mortality. There has been too much meddling, my charge, and each interference joins with the rest and comes crashing back over the world in waves of destruction." (twiceshy). This description plays with the narrative tropes of the show, passing judgment on the writers' excessive use of *deus ex machina*.

Though not a typical fix-it fic, twiceshy's additions explain some of the inconsistencies of Charlie's experience to that of the Winchesters and their companions more broadly, while also highlighting the extent to which women are denied agency even in their own death by the show's canonical narrative choices. Collectively, these works serve as part of a larger rejection of canon by the show's fans, with Charlie Bradbury alive and well in fanfiction. As of April 25, 2017, Charlie Bradbury is tagged on 8,458 works of fanfiction on *Archive of Our Own* ("Charlie Bradbury"). Prominent tags in stories within the search include Fluff, Alternative Universe, Angst, Alternative Universe–High School, and Alternative Universe–College/University. Alternative Universe narratives, like fix-it fics, are a category where fanfiction authors not only address any undesirable elements of canon but usually rewrite the rules of the universe entirely.

Conclusion, or, The Undead Girl with the Dungeons and Dragons Tattoo

In a slasher film, the "final girl" may find herself cornered, but fights back, using any resources at her disposal. Charlie fought back against her death, but the narrative had already firmly established that her enemy—a white man, symbolic himself of a patriarchal family accustomed to exploiting the supernatural to their own benefit—was beyond her power. However, the very decision to place herself within his easy reach undermined both the strength of mind and physical prowess that her multi-season arc had apparently endowed. Thus, the death of Charlie Bradbury is beyond the hope of any fix-it fic. It is a repudiation of her quest, and a reduction of one of the show's most complete women heroes to a plot device in the Winchesters' brotherly struggles. Her death on-screen even goes without any real attempt at resurrection. Unlike Bobby, she is not even granted a return visit as a ghost, as her body is immediately given a hunter's funeral and her spirit apparently consigned to the afterlife. While the churning rules of *Supernatural*'s universe certainly leave room for a surprise reappearance by the character, even a future resurrection cannot rewrite the decision of the writers to reinforce the instrumental role of women in the narrative through Charlie's fate.

As I am writing, *Supernatural* is again renewed and heading towards the end of a thirteenth season that brings with it the promise of more visible women occupying new spaces in the *Supernatural* universe. The planned "Wayward Sisters" spinoff (aired as a pilot on January 18, 2018) places underserved women characters Jody and Donna at the helm of their own narrative arc, serving to raise a generation of women heroes in a tradition splintering from the patriarchal models embedded in both the lore of hunters and Men of Letters.[3] However, even in a moment of hope, there is reason for caution: as fans of Charlie Bradbury will not soon forget, the fate of the fangirl in the universe of *Supernatural* remains that of object and instrument, not of agent. The primary heroic journeys of such women seem destined to continue as off-screen footnotes, not unlike Charlie's mostly-unknown journey into the depths of Oz.

While encounters and relationships such as the powerful sisterly bond of Dean and Charlie seem to probe both at the show's portrayal of masculinity and values, ultimately there is only room in the Impala for two brothers who, in the words of another on-screen fangirl, must remain "Out on the road. Just the two of us. The two of us against the world" ("Fan Fiction"). That scene—occurring at the start of Season Ten, and featuring several young women as authors and actors crafting their own "transformative work" around Sam and Dean with plenty of subtext—raised the hopes of many fans that *Supernatural* was demonstrating more love and respect for the women of its fanbase. However, it was quickly bookended by Charlie's death at the end of the same season, reaffirming the show's focus and willingness to disregard the growth of women to serve the narrative of brotherly love.

NOTES

1. Season Thirteen offers us an Alternate Universe Charlie Bradbury, but she is not exactly the same Charlie we knew in earlier seasons.
2. In Season Thirteen, the backdoor pilot episode "Wayward Sisters" teased the possible fruition of this fan movement with the seeds for an upcoming spinoff. At the time of writing, "Wayward Sisters" has not been picked up on any network.
3. As this text was being edited, the news came that the CW network declined to pick up the backdoor pilot "Wayward Sisters."

WORKS CITED

@rthompson1138 (Robbie Thompson). "I Did My Part, but @Feliciaday Deserves Credit Too." *Twitter,* 2 May 2013, 4:29 p.m., twitter.com/rthompson1138/status/330056505409798144.
Aini_NuFire. "In the Shelter of Your Wings." *Archive of Our Own.* 15 June 2015. archiveof ourown.org/works/7211555.
Anders, Charlie Jane. "Ugh, Supernatural. You Really Didn't Have to Go There." *Io9.* 7 May 2015. io9.gizmodo.com/ugh-supernatural-you-really-didnt-have-to-go-there-1702983980.
Battis, Jes. "'She's not all grown yet': Willow as Hybrid/Hero in Buffy the Vampire Slayer." *Slayage: The Online International Journal of Buffy Studies,* vol. 8, no. 10, 2003.
BiJane. "Friend of Dorothy," *Archive of Our Own,* 13 Nov. 2013, archiveofourown.org/series/60864.
Busse, Kristina. "Fan Labor and Feminism: Capitalizing on the Fannish Labor of Love." *Cinema Journal,* vol. 54, no. 3, 2015, pp. 110–115.
Calvert, Brownen. "The Representation of Women in Supernatural." In *TV Goes to Hell: An Unofficial Road Map of Supernatural,* edited by Stacey Abbott and David Lavery. ECW 2011, pp. 90–102.
Casper, Mary Frances. "Family Don't End with Blood: Building the *Supernatural* Family." In *Fan Phenomena: Supernatural,* edited by Lynn Zubernis and Katherine Larsen. Intellect, 2014, pp. 76–87.
Chan, Suzette. "Supernatural Talk: Tarts Talk About 7.20." *Sequential Tart.* 11 June 2012. www.sequentialtart.com/article.php?id=2254.

"Charlie Bradbury." *Archive of Our Own,* keyword search, 27 April 2017, archiveofourown. org/works/search?utf8=%E2%9C%93&work_search%5Bquery%5D=charlie+bradbury.

"Charlie Bradbury Lives Tag." *Archive of Our Own.* December 30, 2016. archiveofourown. org/tags/Charlie%20Bradbury%20Lives/works.

Clarissa. "Supernatural: Felicia Day Talks Charlie's Return from Oz," *ScreenFad,* January 23, 2015, www.screenfad.com/supernatural/supernatural-interview-felicia-day-season-10-30785.

Clover, Carol J. "Her Body, Himself: Gender in the Slasher Film," *Representations,* no. 20, 1987, pp. 187–228.

Coker, Cait, and Candace Benefiel. "The Hunter Hunted: The Portrayal of the Fan as Predator in Supernatural." In *Supernatural, Humanity, and the Soul: On the Highway to Hell and Back,* edited by Susan A. George and Regina M. Hansen. Palgrave Macmillan, 2014, pp. 97–110.

Coppa, Francesca. *The Fanfiction Reader: Folk Tales for the Digital Age.* U of Michigan P, 2017.

"Dark Dynasty." *Supernatural: The Complete Tenth Season,* written by Eugenie Ross-Leming and Brad Buckner, directed by Robert Singer, Warner Home Video, 2015.

"Dark Side of the Moon." *Supernatural: The Complete Fifth Season,* written by Andrew Dabb and Daniel Loflin, directed by Jeff Wellnough, Warner Home Video, 2010.

"Fan Fiction." *Supernatural: The Complete Tenth Season,* written by Robbie Thompson, directed by Phil Sgriccia, Warner Home Video, 2014.

Genovese, Megan. *Boys, Girls, and Monsters: Regulation of Normative Gender in Supernatural.* Dissertation, 2015.

George, Susan A. "A Man and His 1967 Impala." In *Supernatural, Humanity, and the Soul: On the Highway to Hell and Back,* edited by Susan A. George and Regina M. Hansen. Palgrave Macmillan, 2014, pp. 141–154.

Karkanias, Alena. "And the (Fourth) Wall Came Tumbling Down: The Impact of Renegotiating Fan-Creator Relationships on Supernatural." *Summer Research,* 2015, pp. 248.

"LARP and the Real Girl." *Supernatural: The Complete Eighth Season,* written by Robbie Thompson, directed by Jeannot Szwarc, Warner Home Video, 2013.

Larsen, Katherine, and Lynn S. Zubernis. *Fangasm: Supernatural Fangirls.* U of Iowa P, 2013.

Leddy, Miranda B. "The Women of Supernatural: More than Stereotypes." Thesis, Baylor U, 2014.

Łuksza, Agata. "Boy Melodrama: Genre Negotiations and Gender-Bending in the Supernatural Series." *Text Matters,* vol. 6, no. 1, 2016, pp. 177–194.

Macklem, Lisa. "From Monstrous Mommies to Hunting Heroines: The Evolution of Women on Supernatural." *The Canadian Fantastic in Focus: New Perspectives,* 2014, pp. 224.

_____. "I See What You Did There: *SPN* and the Fourth Wall." In *Fan Phenomena: Supernatural,* edited by Lynn Zubernis and Katherine Larsen. Intellect, 2014, pp. 34–45.

McConnaughy, James. "What Led to Lexa: A Look at the History of Media Burying Its Gays." 29 March 2016. www.themarysue.com/lexa-bury-your-gays/

Members of "The Kitten, the Witches, and the Bad Wardrobe" forum, "The Death of Tara, the Fall of Willow, and the Dead/Evil Lesbian Cliché FAQ." 8 Nov. 2005. www.stephenbooth.org/lesbiancliche.html.

Paige, Linda Rohrer. "Wearing the Red Shoes: Dorothy and the Power of the Female Imagination in the Wizard of Oz." *Journal of Popular Film and Television,* vol. 23, no. 4, 1996, pp. 146–153.

Rachel-A. "Supernatural Fans Want 'Wayward Daughters.'" *The Daily Fandom,* 2 May 2015, thedailyfandom.com/supernatural-fans-want-wayward-daughters/

RickyPine. "Blackbird." *Archive of Our Own.* 30 June 2015. archiveofourown.org/works/4242501.

Rozario, Rebbeca-Anne C. Do. "All That Glitters: The Winchester Boys and Fairy Tales." In *Supernatural, Humanity, and the Soul: On the Highway to Hell and Back,* edited by Susan A. George and Regina M. Hansen. Palgrave Macmillan, 2014, pp. 125–140.

SabbyStarlight. "Heaven." *Archive of Our Own.* 4 May 2016. archiveofourown.org/works/6748108.

"Slumber Party." *Supernatural: The Complete Ninth Season,* written by Robbie Thompson, directed by Robert Singer, Warner Home Video, 2014.

"There's No Place Like Home," *Supernatural: The Complete Tenth Season*, written by Robbie Thompson, directed by Phil Sgriccia, Warner Home Video, 2015.

twiceshy. "Never Have to Go to War No More." *Archive of Our Own*. 13 July 2015. archiveofourown.org/works/4336253.

Uve. "Supernatural: 'Dark Dynasty' Review and Thoughts." *The Daily Fandom*. May 7, 2015. thedailyfandom.com/supernatural-dark-dynasty-review-and-thoughts/.

Walton, Ashley. "'What's up, bitches?' Charlie Bradbury as Gothic Heroine." *The Gothic Tradition in Supernatural: Essays on the Television Series*, edited by Melissa Edmundson. McFarland, 2016, pp. 114–127.

Yalu. "Single Candle." *Archive of Our Own*. 4 Sept. 2015. archiveofourown.org/works/4724573.

"I prefer ladies with more experience"

Virgins, Whores and Post-Feminine Death in Supernatural

FREDDIE HARRIS RAMSBY

CHUCK *(answering phone)*: Mistress Magda?
DEAN: "Who's Mistress Magda?"
CHUCK: "Just, uh ... a close friend,"
DEAN: What happened to Becky?
CHUCK: "Yeh, that didn't work out. I had too much respect for her."
DEAN: "Boy, you really got a whole virgin/hooker thing going, don't you?"[1]

In the blood-drenched world of *Supernatural*, death is a given. And, in the show's hyper-masculine landscape whereby Sam and Dean Winchester relentlessly hew and hack their way through a variety of otherworldly entities, it is disturbingly typical for many male characters—humans, angels, and demons—to die grisly deaths. This is perhaps reflective of a culture that normalizes male violence as well as behaviors and values that de-privilege men's health and wellbeing. Asbjørn Grønstad states that media violence must be scrutinized via theories of "visuality, viewing, and film aesthetics"; nonetheless he implies the social nature of cinematic violence—that is, film violence often reflects culture (2). It is therefore not much of a leap to suggest that male violence and death in *Supernatural* reflects attitudes toward male violence and death that are status quo. We have normalized violent male death.

To clarify, Will H. Courtenay indicates that "Men in the United States are more likely than women to adopt beliefs and behaviors that increase their risks, and are less likely to engage in behaviors that are linked with health and longevity" (1385). While Courtenay focuses broadly on risk behaviors in term of health, he claims that "males of all ages are more likely than females to engage in over 30 behaviors that increase the risk of disease, injury and death" (1386). In all, Courtenay takes the constructionist view that many men believe it is "manlier" to engage in habits and behaviors that may increase their potential for loss of life. Similarly, Susan B. Sorenson concludes that, compared to females, male risk-taking practices contributes to their increased deaths from injury. One cannot help but conjure Virginia Woolf here, when she states, "to fight has always been the man's habit, not the woman's" (9).

Supernatural, however, takes a grisly turn away from the status quo when it comes to gender, violence, and death. In fact, women die in droves. And, while they perhaps don't suffer repeated deaths or after life torment in Hell or Purgatory as Sam and Dean Winchester do, their deaths are guaranteed to be violent. A quick Google search on the most gruesome deaths in *Supernatural* attests to this. In fact, Google's first offering from Hollywood.com presents a 50/50 split between male and female deaths, with Charlie Bradbury, sliced up in the bathtub in a seedy motel in "Dark Dynasty" (10.21), making the number one spot ("The 13 Most...").

The ease with which *Supernatural* has normalized violence against women was not always the case in TV and film media. Writing in 1987, David H. J. Morgan states, "Where women have engaged in or been associated with violent activities, this involvement has been carefully circumscribed and indeed often stigmatized as unnatural or abnormal" (180). Times, it seems, have changed. In *Supernatural,* the signature blood spatter at the start of most episodes knows no gendered bounds; the show spares no mercy when it kills off its women. In fact, in its opening episode, the Winchesters' mother, Mary, and Sam's girlfriend, Jessica, suffer deep gashes to the stomach as they are pinned to the ceiling and set ablaze by the demon, Azazel. The audience is thus prepped for countless acts of violence towards women.

The way in which women die in *Supernatural* is shaped by a hyper-masculine landscape.[2] However, the hyper-masculinity in the show reveals another pattern of status quo gender roles. We can discern this pattern by examining the intensity of brutal female deaths. As academic conversations about the show are rapidly becoming more prolific, many (Brace, Calvert, Nielsen, Walter) have commented on the show's treatment of women. However, I am specifically concerned with *which* women die and *how* and *why* they die. Which women die and how they die is shaped by what psychologists call the virgin/whore binary. Thus, as suggested by the epigraph, I take into account the effects of the virgin/whore binary in *Supernatural* and how it shapes the progression of brutality in terms of feminine death.[3]

In my epigraph above, Dean Winchester defines the virgin/whore binary when he questions the then prophet Chuck about dumping Becky—Chuck's superfan—in favor of Mistress Magda, a call girl who Chuck seemingly prefers to his former admirer. More generally however, the virgin/whore binary—

the trope of lumping women into either the slut or virgin category—is reiterated in the way women in *Supernatural* die. While all feminine deaths in *Supernatural* are violent, slutty behavior warrants a determined and finite death, often bolstered by protracted torture. Also, though some characters are given an afterlife, notably women who fit the heterosexual mold, once the "sluts" are dead, they're not coming back.

So what are we to make of the way these women die, and the role the virgin/whore binary plays in their deaths? I argue that the show kills off more violently—with little hope for resurrection and with prolonged beating and torture—the female characters that characterize the post-feminine.[4] In *Supernatural*, these women are most clearly represented by the demons who occupy the "whore" side of the binary. As for their post-femininity, which I discuss in detail later, *Supernatural*'s post-feminine demons are single, sexual, self-sufficient, and ambitious in their demonic "careers." They are often hybrid characters who blur the line between good and evil, and they ooze wit and irony. And, despite their fluid nature and their seeming capacity to collapse the divide between women who reflect virgin-esque characteristics and those who reflect whorish characteristics, the show really doesn't want them to do it. Instead, the female characters who exhibit traits associated with my reading of post-femininity—despite their demonic stature—are almost guaranteed the bloodiest adventure in *Supernatural*, capped off with a finite and violent death. In all, the way the demons die, most notably Ruby and Meg, appears to send a subliminal warning to viewers that female independence and sexual adventurousness are *not* positive character traits given that those who enact them are not awarded a quick and humane death.

The Virgin/Whore Binary in Psychology, Literature and Television

Before I discuss feminine demon death, it is helpful to offer some context and definitions for both the virgin/whore binary and post-femininity. While the virgin/whore *binary* has been a literary mainstay for centuries, Sigmund Freud first coined the term the virgin/whore *complex* in the early 1900s. He famously wrote, "Where such men love they have no desire, and where they desire they cannot love" (1925). In other words, men who suffer from this complex are unable to remain sexually aroused while in a loving and committed relationship. However, apparently, like Chuck, they can follow through quite adequately with women they devalue as partner-worthy. In short, the cherished, saintly wife, the "virgin" is left wanting, while her man can quite happily get it together with the "whore," a woman he does not care to enter into a committed relationship with, let alone bring home to meet the family.

The virgin/whore complex differs somewhat from the virgin/whore binary. The complex describes the psychological term. The binary, however, is often used in terms of how the complex, or variations on the theme, manifests in literature. According to Vladimir Tumanov, from writings about the differences between Eve (whore) and Mary (virgin) by early Christians, (such as Tertullian, St Irenaeus, and St Jerome), to depictions of the binary in novels by Dostoyevsky, Thomas Hardy, and Jane Austen, many female characters are lumped into virgin/whore categories (519).[5] The former expresses her sexuality in culturally sanctioned ways, like marriage (and all that entails) and is chaste before that event. The latter then, who are sexually active beyond the limits of culturally sanctioned relationships, are "whores" and considered symbolically debauched or immoral.

The virgin/whore dichotomy persists in contemporary television media, also. Yet, this is often the case when a male protagonist is the focal point of the show, as is the case with *Supernatural* and its main protagonists, Sam and Dean. In an article in *Indie Wire*, Jill Soloway, the showrunner for the show *Transparent,* insists that male-centric media often maintains a limited view of female sexuality. She states that when men are the focus of a TV show, women are often subject to the male gaze—a circumstance where women are objects of male pleasure or sexuality. This creates a conception of femininity narrowly defined by the "slut or the good girl" (Soloway qtd. in Lattanzio). Moreover, Soloway argues in another interview with *Time* that in most stories "women are punished for being sexual." In short, the "sexy girls" are often given the chop. Thus, Soloway calls our attention to *Supernatural* and the ways in which the show's women die. Indeed, while women die in droves, it is the sexually active and the post-feminine female characters, typically characterized by the demons, who die particularly nasty deaths. A seemingly fitting punishment for a "whore" in the *Supernatural* universe. But one that is troubling in reality, given its constraining message about female sexuality.

The Post-feminine in Popular Culture

The literature on post-feminism is vast, so I limit my discussion here to definitions of post-feminism advanced by those who relate it to popular culture. I do so to offer a framework so that we may understand *how* post-femininity plays a role in the grisly deaths of some women in *Supernatural*. In her discussion on the HBO show *Girls*, Rose Weitz asserts that the definition of post-feminism is slippery, but she offers a broad overview of various understandings of the term. She states, "Writers do not even agree whether post-feminism is an anti-feminist stance, a critical stance within feminism, or some combination of the two" (219). In short, some feminists, like Angela

McRobbie, assert that post-feminism as depicted by fictional characters like Bridget Jones is actually anti-feminist, and reflects neo-liberal and capitalist tendencies that undo third-wave feminist work, particularly in terms of female sexuality.[6] Others view post-feminism as another iteration of feminism in the twenty-first century.

Fien Adriaens and Sofie Van Bauwel examine post-feminism through an analysis of the HBO television show, *Sex in the City*. They note that the prefix "post"—despite its "anti" connotations—actually suggests something positive (1). They state that post-feminism is not a backlash against third-wave feminism, but rather an expression of feminism after 2010 (5). They insist that while the third wave was characterized by political activism, post-feminism is not the mediatized, shallow, consumerist arena that some claim it to be. Instead, they state that, particularly through pop culture venues like television and film, post-feminists can continue the feminist cause (4).

In general, Adriaens & Van Bauwel offer a breakdown of progressive post-femininity that provides us with a framework of characteristics and behaviors through which to examine the "slutty" women of *Supernatural*—characteristics that ensure them a brutal and prolonged demise. For Adriaens & Van Bauwel, however, and for many women I suspect, their view of post-femininity is overwhelmingly positive. They claim that, "Post-feminists are sexual activists who use their body and attractiveness as an instrument to achieve societal and personal change" (6). The post-feminist woman is sexually adventurous and insistent on her own sexual pleasure (10). This is certainly true for the demon women in *Supernatural* who rely on their sexuality to further their causes—even if these causes are to resurrect Lucifer. In addition, the post-feminist woman is sharply dressed and hip to the latest fashion and technology (8, 16). Furthermore, her own subjectivity is of utmost importance; she is by no means subject to patriarchal discourses (12). In accordance, Shauna Pomerantz and Rebecca Raby note that post–feminists believe that "power and success [are] as readily available to any girl—regardless of her circumstances or background—as long as she believes in herself and tries hard" (550). Accordingly, the demon women in *Supernatural* are nothing but ambitious.

The post-feminist woman exhibits other characteristics. She is body conscious and self-confident. She perfects her body for her own self-actualization (Adriaens & Van Bauwel 12). In addition, she is ironic and funny. She is not afraid to discuss taboo subjects and it is always with a sense of humor (13). She faces off-limits subjects head on, and doesn't beat around the bush. Also, the post-feminist woman is a hybrid and gender fluid (15). Adriaens & Van Bauwel state that "Hybridism stresses the flexibility of the identity and emphasizes the possibility of change" (15). The hybrid does not occupy fixed roles and rejects male/female, gay/straight dualities (16). For the purposes of my argument, *Supernatural's* demon women are also hybrid in that they straddle the dualism of good and evil. Overall, then, this vision of post-femininity saturates *Supernatural's* demon women. Set within the landscape of virgin/ whore dichotomies, how then does *Supernatural* enact feminine death? And, how does post-femininity play a role in how they die?

"Virgin" Deaths

Dichotomies abound in *Supernatural.* As Ashley Walton notes in her discussion of how the Winchester brothers negotiate good/evil binaries, "Aside from the categories of "good" and "evil," the Winchesters live by other dichotomies, such as straight/queer, male/female, and self/other" (2344). It is hardly surprising, then, that the virgin/whore binary frames the way women die in *Supernatural,* given the show's tendency towards binary thinking.

Now, don't get me wrong. When any woman dies in *Supernatural,* it's far from pretty. Frankly, if one is a woman in the company of Sam and Dean, one is bound, sooner or later, to come to a grisly end. As E. J. Nielsen puts it in her discussion of women in the Gothic tradition, "Throughout the course of the show's run, women involved with the Winchesters have often suffered gruesome fates" (1968). And this is indeed the case for those characters I now characterize here as "the virgins"—Sam and Dean's mom, Mary Winchester, and Sam's girlfriend, Jessica Moore. However, at issue here is *how* these women die and how the virgin/whore framework shapes their deaths before, during, and after they die. A close reading of the scenes that frame their deaths reveals characteristics associated with the virgin trope.

A caveat: I use the term "virgin" here to imply a set of characteristics that are privileged as dominant heteronormative sexual behaviors.[7] While prevailing patterns of sexuality in Western culture are changing, heteronormativity is still privileged. Heteronormativity indexes a worldview where heterosexual relationships that culminate in marriage and children are deemed normal. Both Jessica Moore and Mary Winchester subscribe to this pattern. Yet, both characters I discuss in this section are not strictly virgins; Mary has two children, after all. Nevertheless, in Season One, the show frames them as the epitome of white, middle-class femininity, exhibiting all the signifiers of the "good girl." Both are slim, blonde, and impossibly pretty. And they are involved in monogamous and culturally sanctioned relationships—Mary is the devoted mother of Sam and Dean and the loving wife of John. Jessica, likely a student at Stanford with Sam, lives with him for 18 months before her death, and, as he reveals in the Season One episode "Devil's Trap" (1.22), is about to be his fiancée. These are the girls that boys *do* take home to meet the family.

As we discover from the pilot in Season One, Mary and Jessica die almost identically at the hands of the demon, Azazel. Given that Mary dies at the beginning of the episode, I'll discuss her first. At this point in the show, we have little knowledge of Mary's backstory. We know that her name is appropriate, which needs little explanation in terms of its Judeo-Christian association with the Holy Virgin; recall that we learn from Tumanov that the Madonna emerges in early Christian iterations of the virgin/whore trope. What we do *not* know at this point is that before Mary married John Winchester, she was a hunter, as were her family members. Instead, we encounter in the pilot a cookie-cutter reimagining of the nuclear family: a middle-class husband and wife, who are lovingly putting their children to bed. Mary is part of what Bronwen Calvert calls an "idealized heterosexual pairing" (90).

The scene of Mary's death begins with the subtitle "Lawrence, Kansas, 22 years ago." The Winchester family live in a two-story house with a porch, in a middle-class Midwestern suburb. When we see Mary, she is dressed in a long white nightgown, recognizable attire for the perfect mother. She carries four-year-old Dean in her arms, and tells him, "C'mon let's say goodnight to your brother." The scene reveals baby Sam in his crib when she clicks on the light. Both Dean and his Mom kiss the baby as John Winchester appears in the doorway. The perfect family are all together, saying goodnight.

The perfection is short-lived. In the middle of the night, Mary hurries to investigate a noise from the baby monitor and encounters a figure she thinks is John. Seemingly satisfied, she heads downstairs as the camera cuts to two pictures of happy loving couples—the first of Mary and John; the second of an older couple in wedding attire, the woman decked in white. At this point, we can't help but understand that this portion of the show is pushing heteronormativity. Indeed, as Mary descends the stairs, pictures of heterosexual couples adorn the walls. Moreover, as she arrives downstairs, she encounters John fast asleep in front of a World War II movie, a recognizable display of masculine slumber. Mary realizes that the figure next to Sam's crib is not John and clambers headlong upstairs to her now infamous death.

When John hears Mary scream, he rushes to Sam's room to encounter her crucified to the ceiling, her mouth agape and the lace of her white nightgown framing a gash across her stomach. These images are important in terms of constructing Mary as the Madonna, the "virgin," in our binary, and the mother of two men who will go on to save the world, (which clearly evokes the narrative of Jesus Christ). In death, the seeping wound across her belly iterates Mary's role as a vision of sacrificial motherhood. Calvert states that the scene proffers "an image connecting the female body with blood, pain, and (since the wound is across the stomach) childbirth" (93). Yet, the result is a horrifying assault on motherhood, especially a mother who Dean will later remember in "The Song Remains the Same" (5.13) in terms of her "angelic mothering" (Calvert 92). A mother who made him "tomato-rice soup" when he was ill, sang "Hey, Jude" as a lullaby, and told him "angels were watching over [him]" (92). Mary—the perfect mother, and mother of two messiahs—is then set alight by Azazel.

Symbolically, fire evokes Christian martyrdom—Joan of Arc being the most well known of female martyrs burned at the stake. And, it is Mary's death, her sacrifice, which prompts Dean and later Sam, following Jessica's death, to hunt the supernatural. Patricia Brace cites Jean Bethke Elshtain who states that the good mother is like a good soldier: "Some expectations about soldiering and mothering are shared and out in the (cultural) open, so to speak: the soldier is expected to sacrifice for his country as mothers are expected to sacrifice for their children ... uniting the two experiences are duty and guilt" (85). At this point in the series, Mary's death, and indeed her life, *is* framed as sacrificial. Her duty is to her family, to care for them when they are sick, to sing them lullabies. And to die so that Sam and Dean will have something to hunt. Moreover, we later learn that Mary sacrifices her spirit in "Home" (1.09) when she banishes a poltergeist from Sam and Dean's family home. And, she makes a deal with Azazel in Season Four's "In the Beginning" (4.03), to save John's life.[8] Her death then is in congruence with the narrative of sacrifice, characteristic of the virgin or Madonna trope. Good girls are wives and mothers that *do* for their men.

Mary and Jessica's deaths serve as bookends to *Supernatural's* pilot—Mary dies at the start; Jessica dies at the end—and, as noted, their deaths are identical. As is Jessica's status on the virgin side of the virgin/whore binary. Jessica is the epitome of the marriageable woman as suggested by a traditional hetero-normative framework. As Calvert puts it, "Jessica's character is an uncomplicated, nice, and supportive girlfriend who encourages Sam ("I'm proud of you—you're gonna get that full ride [a scholarship to law school]") and leaves homemade chocolate-chip cookies out for him" (92). She has little backstory and Sam has never told her that he is a hunter. She is thus silenced in the relationship, unknowing and kept in the dark about Sam's life.

Connecting both Mary and Jessica, Calvert claims that "[they both] owe much to the notion of the 'Angel in the House,' a Victorian figuration of the perfect wife and mother that identifies both characters with domestic activities and the home" (92). This connection is forged via their costuming. When Sam returns home to find Jessica pinned to the ceiling in an exact replica of Mary's sacrificial crucifixion, she too is dressed in a white nightgown. The imagery of the nightgown evokes the perpetual "goodness" of both women. Calvert says, "The image of the blonde woman in white plays on the association of white (and of paleness and blondeness) with purity and goodness, and this fits with the presentation of these two women earlier in the episode"

(93). Thus, the white nightgown is a critical accessory in terms of *Supernatural's* reconfiguration of the virgin trope through the dead bodies of both women.

Being a "good" girl, even after one has been crucified by a demon, has its rewards, however. After their deaths, both Mary and Jessica are awarded elevated, indeed almost mythic, status. Leow Hui Min Annabeth insists that their deaths reflect "The misogyny of *Supernatural*" and that these deaths have "a spiritual quality [that] provides the men in their lives with aspirational motivation" to destroy aberrant variations of femininity (1834). Jessica's death has a profound effect on Sam: He feels guilty for it, and consequently has difficulty maintaining other intimate relationships without turmoil. Moreover, Jessica crops up repeatedly over the course of twelve seasons, if not in body, at least in mind—Sam's mind, that is.[9] Not bad innings for a girl a demon kills off twelve years before.

As perhaps a more concentrated iteration of the Madonna trope, Mary fares better in terms of resurrection. Jessica is, after all, only re-embodied in Sam's *memory* of the ideal girl, crystallized in her perfection for twelve seasons. Mary, on the other hand, is *literally* brought back to life. In "Alpha and Omega" (11.23), Dean prepares to sacrifice himself to rid the world of the Darkness, God's sister, Amara. Yet, family prevails—a recurring motif in *Supernatural*. Amara, later reconciled with her brother, rewards Dean with "what he needs the most" ("Alpha and Omega"). What he needs the most, it is revealed, is Mary. And, she appears to him in the same white nightgown she died in.

Concerning Mary's resurrection, Brace slyly points out the inherent self-ishness of Dean's desire in that "Sam and Dean have idealized their short time with their mother, thinking of her love as pure and unconditional" (86). In Dean's mind, Brace suggests, Mary wouldn't think twice about being yanked back to Earth from Heaven, such is her unconditional love for her sons. It is a love that Dean manifests through Amara's power to grant him such, but it is love that comes at the expense of Mary's eternal rest. In the Season Twelve opener, "Keep Calm and Carry On," as Mary and Dean move to embrace each other, the camera settles on the wedding ring on Mary's left hand. The Madonna figure is granted resurrection. But as the season reveals, her resurrection is not entirely happy, and she continues to sacrifice herself for her sons.

"Whorish" Death and the Post-Feminist Demons

The "virgin" half of the virgin/whore dichotomy in *Supernatural* is clearly apparent in Mary and Jessica's characterization and untimely ending.

And, their deaths intensify the dichotomy. That is, in life they are idealized and resurrected—figuratively in Jessica's case—after death. The ways in which the whores die also exaggerate the dichotomy. Certainly, while the "virgins'" deaths are horrific, yet rewarded, the "whores'" deaths are often preceded by violent sexual exhibitionism and torture. And, the "whores" do not come back. Unsurprisingly, the "whores" are demons. It is these demonic women who exhibit, most resonantly, features of the post-feminine that I describe earlier.

This association between demon demise and post-femininity is troubling. In his now iconic "Monster Culture (Seven Theses)," Jeffrey Jerome Cohen suggests that "The monster polices the borders of the possible" (12). He claims, "From its position at the limits of knowing, the monster stands as a warning against exploration of its uncertain demesnes" (12). In other words, the monster patrols both literal and figurative arenas and acts to keep explorers out. Cohen continues to explain in this "thesis" that what we monsterize often reflects behaviors that we should avoid, places we should not explore. To connect this with the demon women in *Supernatural*, one wonders if the demons' deaths constitute a subliminal warning against the exploration and exhibition of the post-feminine. "Young women!" it seems to say; "Curb your sexual independence and career aspirations."

Supernatural features many demonic women, but I discuss here the two that most closely resemble the trope of the whore, yet who also clearly exhibit characteristics congruent with post-femininity: Meg Masters and Ruby. Meg and Ruby appear in Seasons One, Five, Six, Seven, and Eight, and Seasons Three and Four, respectively. Meg is loyal to the demon Azazel, and later Lucifer. Ruby, also loyal to Lucifer, serves the demon Lilith. These two characters are an interesting study given their multifaceted roles as both adversaries and allies to Sam and Dean. As Calvert puts it, "The brothers' reactions to Meg and Ruby, and especially those characters' shifts from villains to damsels and back again, make for complex and often confusing characters" (98). This complexity, however, is congruent with post-femininity, as we shall discover.

But first, how do Meg and Ruby die? During her tenure on the show, Meg, inhabiting the bodies of two beautiful twenty-something women, is tortured on several occasions, and eventually dies at the hands of Crowley, the quick talking, British-accented King of Hell. Two torture scenes are noteworthy. Her first torture scene in "Devil's Trap" (1.22) is unsettling, to say the least. Meg is strapped to a chair, while Sam reads the exorcism and Dean pressures her for information about John Winchester's whereabouts. Calvert notes, "The exorcism makes for a grim and disturbing death scene (see Borsellino 108, 117) as the brothers and Bobby use the ritual to torture demon-Meg for information" (98). Indeed, despite Meg's demonic nature, during this scene she appears vulnerable and pitiful. And, she sheds tears as Dean first suggests he will let her go if she offers them the information they want, but then urges Sam to "finish it" once she reveals John's location. Sam struggles to complete the ritual, given that Meg's meat suit is certain to die.

Meg returns, as a loyalist to Lucifer, in a different female body in Seasons Five and Six. Here, she forms an uneasy alliance with the Winchesters. In a second notable torture scene, Meg is strapped, naked, to a torture table where she is sliced up by Christian, Sam and Dean's third cousin on Mary's side of the family ("Caged Heat"). By the time Christian tortures Meg, he has been possessed by a demon loyal to Crowley for some time. This scene is also extremely unsettling, and unlike Meg's first torture scene, unnervingly sexualized. Christian, rolling up his sleeves in preparation to torture Meg, states that Crowley wants him to "carve information" out of Meg. Meg, resorting to innuendo, responds with "whatever makes you feel like a man." In response to her taunt, Christian runs the blade over Meg's mouth, chin and breasts—the latter covered by leather restraints reminiscent of a BDSM nightmare. Christian's move is sadistically carnal and as he disappears out of the shot to wield the knife, the viewer can assume that the knife is piercing Meg in a manner reminiscent of one of the most horrific scenes in David Fincher's 1995 movie, *Seven*. In said scene, a prostitute dies from multiple stab wounds inflicted on her by a client forced to wear a phallic knife. This suggestion is confirmed when Meg, having been stabbed by Christian, cries, "You know, you're sticking that thing in all the wrong places."

As noted, Meg is eventually killed by Crowley—after more torture—in "Goodbye Stranger" (8.17). As Crowley taunts Meg and Sam, Meg says, "Are you gonna talk us to death, or get down to it already." Crowley retorts, "There's my whore." The exchange is again sexual. In response to Sam's announcement that Crowley won't get his hands on the "stone with funny scribbles on it" (an angel tablet), Crowley shoots back, "I love it when you get all tough. Touches me right where my bathing suit goes." The line is supposed to be funny. In this instance, given Meg's alliance with the Winchesters, as well as her imminent death, the joke falls flat. As Crowley pulls out an angel blade, Meg instructs Sam to leave to "save your brother and my unicorn." Her unicorn is the angel Castiel; Meg clearly expresses her attraction to him. Crowley then thrusts his blade into Meg's stomach. And that is the last we hear of her.

Ruby appears in three meat suits during her time on the show in Seasons Three and Four, although two are significant.[10] Her first choice of meat suit is that of a young blonde played by Katie Cassidy. The dark featured Genevieve Cortese plays the demon's second meat suit. Given that Ruby signals the post-feminine, it is significant that she maintains a sexual relationship with Sam as they fight demons together; their sex scene in "Heaven and Hell" (4.10) is one of the most erotic scenes in a series that doesn't indulge us with romance often. Her tryst with Sam assists her in her cause for Lilith and Lucifer; although she tricks him into thinking they are fighting Lilith until both (Ruby and Lilith) die at the end of Season Four. During this season, their intimacy deepens as Ruby manipulates Sam into drinking her blood so that his power to exorcise demons is strengthened and he takes on demonic features.

In a scene strikingly similar to Meg's torture scene described above, the demon Alastair tortures Ruby with her knife in "Heaven and Hell" (4.10).[11] Like Meg, Ruby is strapped naked to a torture table, yet this time leather restraints *cover* her mouth, while other restraints bind her in the manner of a crucifixion. The sounds of pierced flesh accompany Ruby's muffled screams, and we wonder if Alastair is, like Christian, stabbing her flesh below the belt. The scene is not as blatantly sexual in terms of dialogue as the one between Christian and Meg, although Ruby's nudity and Alastair's comment "Let's relish the moment" point in that direction. Moreover, Ruby's nudity, like Meg's, raises the question: why is it that the demon women in *Supernatural* are tortured nude, while demon men, Alastair for instance, are tortured fully clothed and standing up? Yes, Ruby and Meg are demons, but these scenes unnervingly sexualize the fragility of their female bodies. And, their torture perpetuates an objectifying trope of the suffering and bleeding female body reiterated in torture-porn films like *Hostel* and *Saw*. That these women reflect characteristics of the post feminine, discussed later, render these torture scenes more problematic.

Eventually, Dean kills Ruby in "Lucifer Rising" (4.22). After Sam kills Lilith, the last of 66 seals that must be broken in order to set Lucifer free, Ruby explains that Lilith's death was the plan all along. Sam was an unwitting accomplice, although as Ruby points out in their final exchange, when he accuses her of poisoning him with her blood, "No it wasn't the blood. It was you. It was your choices. I just gave you the options and you chose the right path every time … you had it in you the whole time, Dumbo." Ruby's tenderness for Sam is palpable. She is not cold. She is invested in her cause and implores Sam to stay with her while Lucifer "repays you in ways you can't even imagine." After this brief exchange, Dean crashes through the door. Sam grabs Ruby from behind pinning her arms behind her back. Dean thrusts the blade into her stomach twice, each time twisting the blade so it penetrates her deeply. She falls and her heads slams against the concrete floor.

Both Meg and Ruby's torture scenes and deaths are notable in terms of the virgin/whore binary. As the show's representative "whores"—their sexual behavior attests to this—their deaths and torture scenes are also troublingly sexualized. Their torture scenes reflect sexual vulnerability, evoking the pathos of a snuff film in such a way that one is forgiven if their demonic natures are forgotten for a while. In addition, they are killed by men following either an attempt at *tender* romantic exchange (after all, Ruby and Sam were lovers) or a sexualized exchange (Meg and Crowley). Finally, both are killed by a thrusting knife to the stomach, reflecting a particularly violent sexual act. In addition, the way Ruby's arms are pinned behind her back by Sam signals a twisted coupling, a perverse sexual role reversal, while Dean thrusts the knife into her. Crowley penetrates his knife into Meg in a similar fashion. Both these deaths perform a troubling connection between deadly violence and sex. Certainly, given my observations here, the women who enjoy sex and are more than open about it during their lives, are consistently sexualized during death and torture. Their occupation on the whore side of the binary apparently guarantees this.

However, Meg and Ruby, while indexing what has traditionally been associated with whorishness, slut-like behavior, wantonness, etc., exhibit features of the post-feminine, which *Supernatural* insists on sexualizing, literally, to death. To recap, post-femininity is largely characterized by individualism and independence, a focus on career and causes over marriage and family, an acceptance of hybridity (in a variety of expressions), and rejection of the sort of dualisms that create expectations about women according to patriarchal values. And, perhaps most important in terms of my discussion here, an attitude toward sex that is not bound by traditional ideas of what constitutes appropriate expressions of sexuality (i.e., no sex before marriage). Both Ruby and Meg exhibit post-feminine characteristics, and yet reside very concretely on the whore side of the virgin/whore trope, which is, unsurprisingly, conflated with the demonic.

Both Meg and Ruby are fiercely independent, ambitious and, of course, single—all features of the post-feminine woman. According to Adriaens & Van Bauwel, citing Kristin Gorton, "Independence and autonomy are very important values; post-feminist women are autonomous, financially independent, and have successful careers" (12). Meg and Ruby's ambitions are fueled by their fight for a cause. Meg's cause is to fight for Lucifer. As she exclaims in "Reading is Fundamental" (7.21),

> Look, I'm simpler than you think. I've figured one thing out about this world—just one, pretty much. You find a cause, and you serve it. Give yourself over, and it orders your life. Lucifer and Yellow Eyes—their mission was it for me.

As for Ruby, she describes the depth of her ambition to free Lucifer to Sam moments before her death in "Lucifer Rising" (4.22). As she reveals feverishly,

> You don't even know how hard this was. All these demons out for my head. No one knew. I was the best of those sons of bitches! The most loyal! Not even Alastair knew. Only Lilith. Yeah, I'm sure you're a little angry right now, but, I mean, c'mon Sam, even you have to admit it, I'm … I'm awesome.

Here, moments before death, Ruby reveals the complexity of her plans, the depths to which she was willing to go to fulfill them, the extraordinary lengths she went to, even keeping secrets from those at the top. As she divulges her true self to Sam, Ruby is emphatic, tearful, a true believer, and her admissions are not gloating. She signals an emphatic young woman who will go to all lengths to achieve what she truly believes in.

Like many post-feminist women depicted in popular culture, Meg and Ruby are both funny and forthright. They are not afraid to tackle difficult subjects, often with wry humor. This is very different from our "virgin" Mary Winchester, who in twelve seasons has rarely, if not at all, supplied us with comedy. To illustrate her gallows humor, in "Jus in Bello" (3.12), Ruby announces, "Does anyone have a breath mint? Some guts splattered into my mouth while I was killing my way in here" ("Ruby [Character]"). And, in "The Kids are Alright," (3.02), Ruby's attraction to Sam is wittily framed in the following:

> RUBY: I'm interested in you.
> SAM: Why?
> RUBY: Because you're tall, I love a tall man. And then there's that whole Anti-Christ thing ["Ruby (Character)"].

Meg also displays her comedic side. In "Survival of the Fittest" (7.23), she and Dean have the following exchange about Castiel:

> MEG: You deal with him. I can't anymore.
> DEAN: You might want to be more specific.
> MEG: I was laying low halfway across the world when Emo Boy pops up out of nowhere and zaps me right back here.
> DEAN: Why?
> MEG: Go ask him. He was *your* boyfriend first ["Meg (Character)"].

Unsurprisingly, given their occupation on the "whore" side of the binary, many of Meg and Ruby's jokes are about sex.

Both Ruby and Meg index hybridity, another feature of the post-feminine according to Adriaens & Bauwel. They state, "Hybridism is the idea that everyone has a multiplex of identities. These identities operate as contradictions in someone's concept of self-feeling/self-being" (14). The notion of hybridity in postmodernism, for instance, has been advanced to contradict oppressive societal practices that keep marginalized bodies on the periphery—gay and trans bodies, for instance. Hybridity thus challenges essentialized ideas of gender and sex, for example, and I use this example to illustrate that hybridity involves the concept of the *fluidity of identity*. Indeed, hybrids often exhibit conflicting and contradictory identities—the fragmented self—compared to a modernist sense of a "true" self, whereby one believes that one has an essence. In *Supernatural,* the hybrid characters—angels and demons—

challenge status quo and essentialized structures, structures that have traditionally characterized Heaven and Hell, i.e., all angels are inherently good
and all demons are inherently evil. This is not the case in the show, however,
where angels are often dodgy power mongers, and demons such as Crowley
help the Winchesters, as do Meg and Ruby. Thus, angels and demons reflect
conflicting identities.

Yet, hybridism is often not rewarded, especially in Meg and Ruby's case
as I demonstrate in terms of the way they die, and especially given the vir-
gin/whore binary that frames them in the show. Ruby and Meg display their
hybridity most obviously as they are portrayed by two or three actors per character. This is hardly surprising given that demons walk the Earth as a conflation of human and the black smoke that signals their demonic presence; thus
it is easy to exchange one meat suit for another when an actress' contract
runs out. But Meg and Ruby's hybridity extends beyond their embodiment.
Both characters walk an uneasy line between good and evil, between alliances,
and between helping the Winchesters and betraying them. Ultimately, Ruby
betrays Sam and Dean. Meg, however, gives her life so that they can escape.

Finally, given the overarching framework of this essay, the virgin/whore
binary and how it engenders feminine death in *Supernatural*, it's most pertinent to wrap up with Meg and Ruby's attitudes towards sex. In her impres-
sive overview of the etymology of the term "slut" and its many variants,
including "whore," Feona Attwood notes that traditionally the term took on
a pejorative meaning associated with female sexuality in the fifteenth century
(233). She goes on to say that,

> Later, it became associated exclusively with women and acquired "the negative sexual
> sense of a promiscuous woman." By the twentieth century it had become "a wide-
> spread term of abuse" for women who did not "accept the double standards of soci-
> ety" [233].

Muriel Schulz has argued that this pattern, in which terms associated with
women acquire negative connotations and become a "sexual slur," is a common one (Attwood 233).

As I have shown, both Meg and Ruby are extremely sexual and sexualized, both on and off the torture table and in death. As indicated by Ruby's
remarks to Sam above, she seduces him and the two of them indulge in a sexual relationship for the majority of Season Four. There are not many sex
scenes in the show, but one of the most explicit and erotic, as I note above,
is that between Ruby and Sam in "Heaven and Hell" (4.10), and Ruby makes
the first advance. This is a far cry from the saintly Jessica who leaves Sam
cookies before bedtime.

Similarly, Meg has a hearty sexual appetite, and comes on to her man
first, as illustrated by the following from "Salvation" (1:21): "Well, I've lied …

a lot. I've stolen. I've lusted." Meg is also outright about her attraction to the angel Castiel in "Goodbye Stranger" (8.17):

MEG: We survive this ... [seductively]
MEG: I'm gonna order some pizza and we're gonna move some furniture around, you understand?
CASTIEL: [shaking his head] No, I ... I ...
[pause; Meg raises her brows suggestively]
CASTIEL: Wait, actually ... yes, I...

In this scene, Meg exhibits three traits associated with the post-feminine: her hybridity, (given her cross over to the "good" side), her humor, and her forthright sexuality. Unfortunately, Meg is killed before she and Castiel get to do some damage to the living room.

Post-femininity is very clear about female sexuality. A woman who expresses her sexuality outside the confines of marriage does *not* constitute a slut or any other derogatory term for that matter. As Adriaens & Bauwel put it, "[Post-feminine] women have a fundamental right to sexual freedom and pleasure and are not judged if they use this right" (10). In addition, Attwood views the attitude that women who enjoy sex with multiple partners and are constructed as slutty is merely a reiteration of the virgin/whore binary and a sexual double standard configured by patriarchal values. Yet, she states, "While the term 'slut' has clearly taken on its meaning in the context of a sexual double standard that conceives of women's sexuality in terms of a Madonna-Whore binary, a diverse range of contemporary uses suggests that it need not be understood in this way" (233). She confirms that the post-feminine woman should have the agency to explore her sexuality in whatever ways she deems fit.

Unfortunately, given the way Meg and Ruby die and are tortured in *Supernatural*, the show suggests that an assertive woman who initiates sex— a post-feminine woman—must be dispensed with, especially if she is a whore/demon. Indeed, none of Sam and Dean's idealized women have developed sexual tendencies such as those of Meg and Ruby –at least not the ones with whom they would consider "legitimate" relationships. And, by legitimate, I mean the sort of relationship characterized by the "virgins" I discuss earlier.

Conclusion

In killing off and torturing the women who most clearly resemble the post-feminine—the "whorish" Meg and Ruby—it might be argued that *Supernatural* rejects post-femininity as a positive force.[12] In other words, the way in which they die shows us that feminism has a long way to go. So perhaps the show subliminally reiterates McRobbie's suggestion that post-feminism is a nefarious effort to counter feminist forces. One could argue that the show is, *subtly*, advancing the feminist cause by reiterating the blood-splattered trope of feminine objectification in ways that resemble torture porn. After all, we should be horrified by it. Pomerantz and Raby state that what *seems* like the post-feminine is often revealed as a ruse to hide networks of gendered inequity. In their article about a collection of schoolchildren they interviewed by way of both post-feminist and feminist frameworks, they find that "Through a post-feminist lens, the girls saw their lives as highly individualized projects infused with freedom and personal choice. But through a feminist lens, the girls saw themselves as susceptible in a world where gender inequality is still threateningly real" (561). The ritual torture and killing of post-feminine Ruby and Meg suggests that feminists still have their work cut out for them. But I think this is a generous reading. I suspect, given the show's overwhelming masculinity, as well as its tendency to capitulate to the virgin/whore dichotomy, *Supernatural* undermines both feminism and post-feminism in the way it kills off its independent, single, career focused female demons. Certainly, it seems, the enactment of a feminine agency exhibited by Ruby and Meg must, ultimately, be put down.

NOTES

1. "Swan Song" (5.22).
2. Hyper-masculinity characterizes male behavior that is aggressive, over-sexualized, and emphasizes strength and bravado.
3. This binary is perhaps most broadly referenced as the Madonna/Whore binary, which nods to its Judeo-Christian etymology. The term is often used interchangeably with virgin/whore and the characteristics of each side of the binary are similar.
4. My use of the term is specific in terms of feminine sexual and social independence. Nevertheless, it is a much debated term, but generally speaking, post-feminism is a reaction to third-wave feminism.
5. From Tumanov: "Thus, Tertullian writes, 'For into Eve, as yet a virgin, had crept the word which was the framer of death. Equally into a virgin was to be introduced the Word of God which was the builder-up of life; that, what by that sex had gone into perdition, by the same sex might be brought back to salvation.' St. Irenaeus makes a similar opposition: 'With a fitness, Mary the Virgin is found obedient […] but Eve was disobedient; for she obeyed not, while she was yet a virgin' (Boyce 2001: 210). And St. Jerome sums up the situation succinctly in his 22nd Epistle: 'Death by Eve, life by Mary' (Boyce: 218)" (512).
6. Third-wave feminism involves a period between the early 1990s and approximately 2010. It constituted a movement in reaction to the Clarence Thomas hearings and deepened feminism's focus on issues of diversity. Critiques of post-feminism, in terms of sexuality and third-wave feminism, rest on what is sometimes understood as a sexual regression. That is, some feminists state that post-feminine expressions of sexuality merely mimic sexuality perpetuated by the male gaze and the exploitation of women's bodies through advertising.
7. In a heteronormative society, heterosexual romantic relationships are often conceptualized as default categories that further male/female relationships as normal and natural.
8. Brace sees this move as Mary's objectification of John. In reference to the episode when Dean is sent back in time to Kansas, she states, "John is put in the traditional ingénue position when he is brutally killed and used by the demon to blackmail Mary. Azazel makes her an offer she can't refuse: not only will he bring John back to life, but "You'll be done with

Hunting forever, white picket fence, station wagon with a coupla kids, no more monsters or fear." Mary knows she's alone without John, and he's her ticket out of hunting"(86). Brace goes on to accuse Mary of objectifying John, using him "without his knowledge or consent" (86).

9. Jessica haunts Sam's dreams and psyche in eleven episodes in Season One, three episodes in Season Two, two episodes in Season Four, three episodes in Season Five, one episode in Season Six, one episode in Season Seven, two episodes in Season Eight, and at least once in Season Twelve (12.01). In Season Twelve, Sam sees a vision of Jessica while being tortured by Lady Bevall.

10. Ruby actually appears in the body of a blonde woman in one episode. The encounter is fleeting, however.

11. I should explain that actually the Ruby torture scene occurs *before* the Meg torture scene. However, given Meg's appearance on the show first, even though she is sustained as a character for many more seasons than Ruby, it seems logical to discuss her first.

12. One could argue that Charlie Bradbury's character problematizes the virgin/whore binary in *Supernatural*, given that she is an independent, brilliant woman. And a lesbian. But, then again, she is killed off. (Editor's note: See Anastasia Salter's essay "'The (Dead) Girl with the Dungeons and Dragons Tattoo': *Supernatural* and the Disposable Other" in this collection for more discussion of Charlie's death.)

Works Cited

Adriaens, Fien, and Sofie Van Bauwel. "*Sex and the City*: A Postfeminist Point of View? Or How Popular Culture Functions as a Channel for Feminist Discourses." *The Journal of Popular Culture*, vol. 47, no. 1, 2014, pp. 174–195, https://onlinelibrary.wiley.com/doi/abs/10.1111/j.1540-5931.2011.00869.x. Accessed 8 Mar. 2017.

"Alpha and Omega." *Supernatural: The Complete Eleventh Season*, written by Andrew Dabb, directed by Phil Sgriccia, Warner Home Video, 2016.

Annabeth, Leow Hui Min. "Coloniality and the Chicana Gothic." *The Gothic Tradition In Supernatural: Essays on the Television Series*, edited by Melissa Edmundson. Kindle ed. McFarland, 2016, pp. 1732–1959.

Attwood, Feona. "Sluts and Riot Grrrls: Female Identity and Sexual Agency." *Journal of Gender Studies*, vol. 16, no. 3, 2007, pp. 233–247. www.tandfonline.com/doi/full/10.1080/09589 23070156292. Accessed 12 Jan. 2017.

Brace, Patricia. "Mothers, Lovers, and Other Monsters." *Supernatural and Philosophy: Metaphysics and Monsters … for Idjits*, edited by William Irwin and Galen A. Foresman. Wiley Blackwell, 2013, pp. 83–94.

"Caged Heat." *Supernatural: The Complete Sixth Season*, written by Brett Matthews and Jenny Klein, directed by Robert Singer, Warner Home Video, 2011.

Calvert, Bronwen, "Angels, Demons, and Damsels in Distress: The Representation of Women in *Supernatural*." *TV Goes to Hell: An Unofficial Road Map of Supernatural*, edited by. Stacey Abbott and David Lavery. ECW, 2011, pp. 90–105.

Cohen, Jeffery J., editor. *Monster Theory: Reading Culture*. U of Minnesota P, 1996, p. 12. http://site.ebrary.comlliblbrooklynlDoc?id=10151042&ppg=27. Accessed 21 Apr. 2018.

Courtenay, Will H. "Constructions of Masculinity and Their Influence on Men's Well-Being: A Theory of Gender and Health." *Social Science & Medicine*, vol. 50, no. 10, 2000, pp. 1385–1401. https://www.ncbi.nlm.nih.gov/pubmed/10741575. Accessed 14 Feb. 2017.

"Dark Dynasty." *Supernatural: The Complete Tenth Season*, written by Eugenie Ross-Leming and Brad Buckner, directed by Robert Singer, Warner Home Video, 2015.

"Devil's Trap." *Supernatural: The Complete First Season*, written by Eric Kripke, directed by Kim Manners, Warner Home Video, 2006.

Dockterman, Eliana. "*Transparent* Creator Jill Soloway on Ending the Madonna V. Whore Stereotype." *Time*, 13 May 2015. http://time.com/3857874/transparent-creator-jill-soloway-on-ending-the-madonna-v-whore-stereotype. Accessed 4 March 2017.

Edmundson, Melissa, editor. *The Gothic Tradition in Supernatural: Essays on the Television Series*. Kindle ed. McFarland, 2016.

Giannini, Erin. "'There's nothing more dangerous than some a-hole who thinks he's on a holy mission': Using and (Dis)-Abusing Religious and Economic Authority in *Supernatural.*" *TV Goes to Hell: An Unofficial Road Map of Supernatural*, edited by Stacey Abbott and David Lavery. ECW, 2011, pp. 163–176.

"Goodbye Stranger." *Supernatural: The Complete Eighth Season*, written by Robbie Thompson, directed by Thomas J. Wright, Warner Home Video, 2013.

Gottschall, Jonathan, Elizabeth Allison, Jay De Rosa and Kaia Klockemen. "Can Literary Study Be Scientific?: Results of an Empirical Search for the Virgin/Whore Dichotomy." *Interdisciplinary Literary Studies*, vol. 7, no. 2, 2006, pp.1–17.

Grønstad, Asbjørn. *Transfigurations: Violence, Death and Masculinity in American Cinema* (Film Culture in Transition). Amsterdam University Press, 2008.

"Heaven and Hell." *Supernatural: The Complete Fourth Season*, story by Trevor Sands, teleplay by Eric Kripke, directed by J. Miller Tobin, Warner Home Video, 2009.

"Home." *Supernatural: The Complete First Season*, written by Eric Kripke, directed by Ken Girotti, Warner Home Video, 2006.

"In the Beginning." *Supernatural: The Complete Fourth Season*, written by Jeremy Carver, directed by Steve Boyum, Warner Home Video, 2009.

"Jus in Bello." *Supernatural: The Complete Third Season*, written by Sera Gamble, directed by Phil Sgriccia, Warner Home Video, 2008.

"Keep Calm and Carry On." *Supernatural: The Complete Twelfth Season*, written by Andrew Dabb, directed by Phil Sgriccia, Warner Home Video, 2017.

Lattanzio, Ryan. "Jill Soloway Says 'There is an all out-attack' on Female Filmmakers." *IndieWire.* 27 Jul. 2015. http://www.indiewire.com/2015/07/jill-soloway-says-there-is-an-all-out-attack-on-female-filmmakers-185875. Accessed 29 April 2017.

"Lucifer Rising." *Supernatural: The Complete Fourth Season*, written by Eric Kripke, directed by Eric Kripke, Warner Home Video, 2009.

"Meg (Character)." IMDbwww, www.imdb.com/character/ch0018172/quotes. Accessed 15 May 2017.

McRobbie, Angela. "Post-Feminism and Popular Culture." *Feminist Media Studies,* vol. 4, no. 3 2004, pp. 255–264. www.tandfonline.com/doi/abs/10.1080/1468077042000309937? journalCode=rfms20. Accessed 1 Jan. 2017.

Morgan, David. "Masculinity and Violence." Women, *Violence and Social Control*, edited by Jalnar Hanmer and Mary Maynard. Palgrave, 1987, pp. 180–192.

Nielsen, E.J. "Wearing the Woman in White: The Doomed Lives and Afterlives of Women." *The Gothic Tradition in Supernatural: Essays on the Television Series*, edited by Melissa Edmundson. Kindle ed. McFarland, 2016, pp. 1963–2172.

Palmer, Lorrie. "The Road to Lordsburg: Rural Masculinity in *Supernatural.*" *TV Goes to Hell: An Unofficial Road Map of Supernatural*, edited by Stacey Abbott and David Lavery. ECW, 2011, pp. 77–89.

"Pilot." *Supernatural: The Complete First Season*, written by Eric Kripke, directed by David Nutter, Warner Home Video, 2006.

Pomerantz, Shauna, and Rebecca Raby. "'Oh, she's so smart': Girls' Complex Engagements with Post/Feminist Narratives of Academic Success." *Gender and Education*, vol. 23, no. 5, 2011, pp. 549–564. www.tandfonline.com/doi/abs/10.1080/09540253.2010.538014. Accessed 20 Jan. 2017.

"Reading Is Fundamental." *Supernatural: The Complete Seventh Season*, written by Ben Edlund, directed by Ben Edlund, Warner Home Video, 2012.

"Ruby (Character)." IMDbwww, www.imdb.com/character/ch0029488/quotes. Accessed 15 May 2017.

Seven. Directed by David Fincher, screenplay by Andrew Kevin Walker, New Line Cinema, 1995.

"The Song Remains the Same." *Supernatural: The Complete Fifth Season*, written by Sera Gamble & Nancy Weiner, directed by Steve Boyum, Warner Home Video, 2010.

Sorenson, Susan B. "Gender Disparities in Injury Mortality: Consistent, Persistent, and Larger than You'd Think." *American Journal of Public Health*, vol. 101, no. 1, 2011, pp. S353–S358. www.ncbi.nlm.nih.gov/pubmed/21778511. Accessed 20 Jan. 2017.

"Survival of the Fittest." *Supernatural: The Complete Seventh Season*, written by Sera Gamble, directed by Robert Singer, Warner Home Video, 2012.

"Swan Song." *Supernatural: The Complete Fifth Season*, story by Eric Gewitz, teleplay by Eric Kripke, directed by Steve Boyum, Warner Home Video, 2010.

"The 13 Most Gut-Wrenching Deaths on '*Supernatural*.'" Hollywood.Com. 28 Sept. 2015, http://www.hollywood.com/tv/saddest-deaths-on-supernatural-60405272/. Accessed 4 March 2017.

Tumanov, Vladimir. "Mary Versus Eve: Paternal Uncertainty and the Christian View of Women." *Neophilologus*, vol. 95, 2011, pp. 507–521.

Walton, Ashley. "'What's up, bitches?' Charlie Bradbury as Gothic Heroine." *The Gothic Tradition in Supernatural: Essays on the Television Series*, edited by Melissa Edmundson. Kindle ed. McFarland, 2016, pp. 2175–2422.

Woolf, Virginia. *Three Guineas*. 1938. Harcourt, 2006, pp. 2175–2422.

Grief and Grieving

Dean's Groundhog Day

Negotiating the Inevitability
of Death via Supernatural

MICHAIL-CHRYSOVALANTIS MARKODIMITRAKIS

One of the most commonly discussed issues in *Supernatural*, one that dominates the discussion between Sam and Dean while riding in their Impala or enjoying burgers and beers in bars throughout the continental United States, is that of their (im)possible retirement from the unusual family business of hunting. In the show itself, the viewers do not encounter many sage figures of hunters. Two of the most prominent, Bobby Singer and his best friend Rufus Turner, will often remind the young Winchesters that there is no such thing as retirement for their profession, only death. The nature of death and its inevitability, though, is more often bent in favor of the audience, ratings, network needs, and character popularity. Nonetheless, *Supernatural*, which, quite fittingly if you believe in superstitions, completed its thirteenth season in 2017–2018, has more than its fair share of dead-that-stayed-dead beloved characters: from the Winchesters' father John, Bobby Singer, and Charlie Bradbury, to a long list of others.

What stands out for this show, apart from its longevity, is that death is a multifaceted, multilayered concept, and occasionally personified. Long before audiences are introduced to the cold bitterness and culinary preferences of Death himself, viewers of *Supernatural* had quite a bizarre experience with a rather beloved, albeit weird, villain: the Trickster. While the identity of the "villain" in "Mystery Spot," the episode analyzed in my essay, is not revealed until the last third of the plot, his actions are rather obvious for the audience, though confusing and incomprehensible for the Winchesters. Sam and Dean are stuck in a time loop that only Sam is aware of. While Sam is trying to solve the puzzle of the time loop, for Dean the Tuesday he relives is a never-ending repetition of his final moments.

Death has undergone numerous depictions throughout different times in Western culture. From the mythical journey of Orpheus, who went to Hades to bring back his wife, only to lose her because of her curiosity, to Superman dying at the hands of an extraterrestrial, mindless gym rat, the return of the dead and repressed has been a subject of study and a popular motif in folk myth and literature. However, it is the issue of coming to grips with death that will be the main focus of this essay, in a discussion of how a show such as *Supernatural* offers a fresh take on it, while at the same time involving concepts intrinsically related to the Uncanny, as it was both defined by Sigmund Freud in his homonymous essay and Nicholas Royle's expansion on the concept.

Using the Gothic, Freud, and Royle's discussions of the Uncanny as interpretive frames, I will closely analyze the episode "Mystery Spot" to argue that *Supernatural* helps viewers come to terms with the inevitability of death. The focus question of this essay is not "what is death" but how people become accustomed to it, how the repeated death of a character reveals a ritual, or how pop culture, in this case, forces us to become familiarized with, and ultimately accept, the idea of death, its permanence and unavoidable nature. In this case study, the fact that Dean has no memory of the incidents and Sam walks away with full consciousness of his torment, is strikingly similar to our familiarization with death in news and everyday life incidents and the simultaneous surprise and grieving process when death occurs to those involved in our lives.

The Road So Far...

In "Mystery Spot" (3.11), viewers follow Sam's perspective as he wakes up to the sound of Asia's rock classic "Heat of the Moment." It is Tuesday, and the brothers are in Broward County, Florida, investigating the disappearance of a man at a "mystery spot." The plot follows the brothers as they have breakfast, discuss their plan of action, and ultimately visit the location under investigation, following the procedural nature of the show. That is, until Dean is accidentally shot point blank by the owner of the tourist establishment the Winchesters were investigating, and dies tragically in the arms of his shocked brother. The screen quickly goes dark and the viewers experience their first déjà vu; the episode seems to have just restarted, to the surprise of only one of the Winchester brothers. Sam is the only one that remembers the events of Tuesday. And, as he will immediately come to realize, it is Tuesday again. The brothers will proceed to relive the day, and it will end and reset once more, with Dean's death—only this time he will get hit by a car.

In a *Groundhog Day–like* fashion, Sam will experience the death of his brother an unidentified number of times with all possible (and improbable) ways. Sam will at some point identify the culprit, the Trickster, a familiar foe to the Winchesters and the viewers. After finally cornering the creature that was posing as a diner customer during each repetition of the day, Sam decides to kill it. He confronts the Trickster, who promises to end the time loop. Sam wakes up on Wednesday, only to witness his brother's murder one last time. However, this time, the timeline does not reset.

Dean's seemingly final death will set Sam on a ruthless and violent crusade against all supernatural creatures. While the viewers do not see the moral descent of Sam on screen, we learn through voicemails from Bobby Singer, the father figure of the show, that Sam's condition is exceptionally worrisome. The plot reaches its climax at the end of the episode, when Sam and Bobby argue about a ritual that would destroy the Trickster; Bobby is horrified that the gallon of human blood necessary for the ritual's completion poses no problem for Sam to obtain. Their argument escalates, and Sam stabs Bobby with a wooden stake without hesitation: the familiar character shape-shifts to the Trickster, the day resets, and the characters and viewers return to yet another Wednesday, one when Dean is alive and the whole ordeal never seemed to have happened. Sam is the only person who remembers the whole sequence of events, and the repercussions of this adventure on his character development and his view of their daredevil lifestyle and adventures is hinted to never be the same from that point onwards.

Death Becomes Us

The overarching theme of the third season of *Supernatural* is the brothers' struggle to find a way for Dean to avoid going to Hell after making a deal with a crossroads demon to save Sam's life. Those deals, while typically awarding humans with ten years to live with whatever they desire, in Dean's case took a different turn: he only has one year to live and was provided with no personal merits other than Sam's life. In "Mystery Spot," Dean's death becomes an inescapable fact. The complication for the audience is that Dean's death, no matter how heroic or self-sacrificial it might be, will only lead to the character's soul going to Hell. The first thing Sam says when he experiences his brother's first death is "Not like that." Thus, the first contact the brothers and the viewers have with death in the episode is one that is underwhelming and anticlimactic. The immediacy of Dean's death, without prolonging speeches and heartwarming last words, catches the audience completely unprepared.

One of the reasons "Mystery Spot" has a compelling plot is that, following Sam's perspective, the finality of Dean's death puts both the hero and the audience in a metanarrative posthumous process. Sam and *Supernatural* fans throughout the episode wonder whether Dean deserved a more heroic end, or even an afterlife worthy of his deeds. Galen Foresman, in discussing the depiction and perception of Hell in the show, argues that, while the concept of Hell itself is supposed to deter us from "acting wrongly" (58), ultimately it is inefficient as a discipline mechanism; the brothers know the kind of creatures that inhabit Hell, and yet Dean still chooses to condemn his soul.

The helplessness of Sam and the audience as the day resets an uncountable number of times will put the process of death and grief itself into question. Is it worse to accept a beloved one's death or to relive their last moments for the rest of your life? Sam inarguably lives in his own version of Hell, while Dean is, at the same time, condemned to spend eternity there. The brothers relive Tuesdays that look and feel the same—the only thing that changes is the means of Dean's demise. The eventuality of Dean's impending death is well-known to the viewers of the show by now. What is the purpose then of the repetitive nature of death in this episode? Is there a lesson to be learned? Or is it all inexplicably uncanny?

Freud, the Uncanny and Random (?) Acts

Sigmund Freud's essay "The Uncanny" was first published in 1919, and while many of Freud's theories have been extensively dissected and disproven, this particular work has been a cornerstone of the Gothic mode and literary studies concerning supernatural phenomena. Nicholas Royle in his homonymous study describes the concept of the uncanny as a "flickering sense of something supernatural" (1). While loyal fans of the show know that the Winchesters deal with the supernatural realm on a weekly basis, in this case the inexplicable pertains to the narrative, as the viewers are just as clueless as the characters of the show. The uncanny as a concept is based on a binary, that of comfort that derives from familiar surroundings and discomfort when the same surroundings remain *almost* the same; the slightest change to a familiar setting/situation can trigger an uneasiness in the subject that is having a first or second hand sublime experience. Slavoj Žižek describes it best as "the alteration of a small detail" that changes the whole image (53); the viewers will, even against their own will, start noticing all the small differences between each seemingly identical Tuesday. They will partake in Sam's nightmarish routine and will have an immersive uncanny experience.

Another prominent literary theorist, Tzvetan Todorov, calls the uncanny an "experience of limits" (48). While he refers mainly to literary limits, Todorov's words resonate with *Supernatural* viewers because the inexplicable occurs again and again in front of our eyes, and even the know-it-all monster hunters seem baffled by their experience. The confusion comes from the observation of Sam's attempts to save Dean from his inevitable future. Dean, in the course of recurring Tuesdays, dies from choking on food, a desk crushing him as he's walking down the street (much like a cartoon), a Golden Retriever tearing him apart, a car hitting him, slipping and falling in the bathroom, being electrocuted by his razor, and, in one case, Sam actually kills him by accidentally hitting him with an axe. Sam will admit he has seen his brother die over a hundred times. However, no matter how hard he's tried to avert each incident, while learning from previous experience, Dean's death is inevitable.

The alteration of time observed because of Dean's death, despite being an obviously paranormal incident, is not a new concept. In Western culture, as Aries observes, the death of a man would fundamentally alter the space and the time of the community he inhabited (559). The period of grief would signify a movement of the society forward, as the memory of the deceased, and the wound it created to the society they belonged to, would need to be healed. (559) Sam cannot move forward, though. He suffers in a temporal continuum where there is no room for grief. There is no possibility to move forward; Sam desperately seeks to learn from his repetitive experience in order to protect his brother from fate but fails. Even when Sam subdues the creature responsible for this time alteration, and finally wakes up on a Wednesday free from the time loop, he cannot prevent Dean's unexpected death yet once more. That last death, though, will not reset the timeline, but instead will finally let Sam mourn. Dean's "final" death seems like a lesson from a higher power regarding the acceptance of death as final; but who, exactly, is the Trickster, the messenger of such a cruel test of human spirit?

The image of the Trickster is familiar to most cultures. From Norse mythology and African gods to Native American deities, the creature has had many mythological names. A common denominator, though, is that the Trickster does not act randomly; there is a method to its madness. Hynes and Dotty discuss the archetypal Tricksters and accurately note that, as in Sam's case, the deities appear "primarily at the points of growth and change" (4), when the characters of the story are in need of a transition to advance their fate (and the storyline). As it has been established from the previous season that Dean will die in a year, the Trickster is the divine intervention, a *deus ex machina*, whose purpose is to help Sam prepare for his eventual transition to a life without Dean.

In an era of information, social media, photographs and videos, losing someone does not mean their memory will fade easily. There is an abundance of audiovisual evidence to remind us of them and we tend to cling to the past, significantly extending the grieving process and living in times gone by. The Trickster will use this desire to live in the past to teach a lesson about the repercussions of such feelings. His method of teaching Sam a lesson is described in the next two sections. I will use two different terms related to the concept of the uncanny, the "déjà vu" and the death drive, in order to connect Sam's sublime experience with grief and the depiction of the finality of death. The mythical figure of the Trickster is an agent of the sublime. His limitless powers will show Sam that death is inescapable, even if in Western culture we have chosen to conveniently deny its finality.

Over a Hundred (Gothic) Tuesdays

In *Groundhog Day*, Phil Connors, played by Bill Murray, lives the same day over and over. After realizing this, he engages in a series of disorderly activities, as the consequences are eliminated by the time the day would reset. The déjà vu generated by the repetition of the day thus provides the character of the movie with a "get-out-of-jail-free" card for any actions he undertakes. For Sam, though, the never ending déjà vu is not an opportunity to satisfy his deepest desires and engage in otherwise unlawful activities (for the most part). The main difference between *Groundhog Day* and "Mystery Spot" is that the subject of disarray is the death of a major character: a death that has been foregrounded as the major story arc for *Supernatural,* but seems, at that point, untimely and anticlimactic.

The use of déjà vu in "Mystery Spot" has an uncanny quality that is, by no means, pleasant, as Sam has no agency in his life and, unlike Phil, does not re-live a mundane day. Rather, Sam experiences trauma, which changes every time he attempts to avert it, despite his prior knowledge. Freud defines déjà vu as:

> the peculiar feeling we have, in certain moments and situations, of having had exactly the same experience once before or of having once before been in the same place, though our efforts never succeed in clearly remembering the previous occasion that announces itself in this way.[...] and we must not leave out of account the fact that what is looked for is never remembered [Freud *Psychopathology* 328–329].

The experience of Dean's death for Sam follows what Freud describes in the excerpt above in the most disturbing way. For example, even though Sam will remember all the events that led to Dean's first demise, his brother's death the second time will be at the hands of an elderly driver in the middle of a street, at a different time than what Sam remembers and in an entirely different manner. Thus, there is a discontinuation of the memory, one that is also exemplified in the perception of death as the force majeure that disrupts memory. In the examination of Sam's frustration over the reliving of Dean's death lies one of the fundamental notions of death in Western culture: those left behind wonder what could have prevented their loved one's demise.

The experience of death and that of déjà vu are similar in that they are both offering distorted versions of memory for the living. Sam will continuously fail to save his brother despite attempting to look for a solution, confirming Freud's notion that "what is looked for is never remembered" (329). The way out of the Winchesters' predicament is also traced back to a long tradition of people attempting, through any means necessary, to avoid inevitable events in their lives and communities. For example, remedies to avoid death, even of an anticipated and supernatural manner, have been part of folklore and oral tradition, and showcase how the fear of death at some point in time was transferred from the individual to the loved ones, shifting the focus from the individual to the society to which they belong. Instead of comforting the individual and preparing them for their final journey, Western societies collectively mourn and engage in ritualistic activities to solidify a collective memory. In "Mystery Spot," Dean's experience is reset on a daily basis, and so is his memory. He is a deceased person, unaware of his fate, while Sam is left behind, unable to deal with the consequences of his brother's death. Instead, Sam has to experience it as a conscious memory that is in direct opposition to the reality he lives in. Of all the people in Sam's surroundings, he is the only one aware of the time loop they are all trapped in.

For Freud, one of the most uncanny qualities of déjà vu is that when the subject attempts to touch on the (perceived) previous identical experience, then the conscious recollection becomes impossible because "it has never been conscious" (329). If we are to treat Sam's déjà vu as a fantasy of his brother's already established, waiting-to-happen death, then the continuous deaths become an exercise in dealing with the mortal nature of humanity. As the memory becomes the only way through which we retain a somewhat holistic image of the ones deceased, the memory becomes the only way to tap into the lives of the ones we have lost.[1] The limited point of view of human experience is showcased in Sam's frustration as he is unable to deal with his grief, while the repetition of Tuesdays provides him with an illusion of agency.

As Dean's death becomes part of Sam's daily routine, the feeling of déjà vu becomes the foundation of his analytic experience. Having lived all possible ways his brother could die, Sam experiences death much like Royle defines the phenomenon of déjà vu: "the uncanny figure of that which is irreducible to the physical or the real, an undecidable trembling that phantomizes the possibility of 'belief'" (178). Reality and fantasy are mixed into the mind of the one who suffers from déjà vu, and the subject cannot trust their own mind and memories in order to comprehend and perceive reality. Hence, while Freud uses the experience of déjà vu to describe the psychoanalytic experience of patients, I suggest, in this case, that the concept can be applied to the experience of death, especially in the presence of supernatural occurrences.

For the viewers of *Supernatural*, Sam and Dean are trapped in "Mystery Spot," an embodiment of competing realities they need to figure out. At the same time, as hunters of supernatural entities, the Winchester brothers are familiar with traditional beliefs and often use "the lore" to plan the extermination of their supernatural prey. The possible Tuesdays that Sam lives each time, though, uncanny in their own right, are not terrifying only through their repetition but also their consistency. As Royle argues, Freud had consistently noted the belief of forefathers that possibilities were realities. If something happens in our lives that seems to confirm the "old, distanced belief" (179) a sublime feeling would be generated, a self (and cultural)–fulfilled prophecy. The rational part of our mind would be at conflict with the irrational one as, despite the sensory input, the brain would recognize patterns that would be uncanny.

To bring a practical example into the discussion, let us imagine a person about to cross the street. The person drops the keys they are holding and thus delays the ascension for a split second, right as a car speeds by where the person would otherwise have been standing had they not dropped their keys when they did. This close encounter with death though, according to the forefathers' belief, could have very well ended in a different manner in another time or another (parallel) reality. The uncanniness and random character of the circumstances through which that hypothetical person is still alive would mean that there is a world, similar to ours, where the person would have been run over by the car in question and would have ended up dead. If the person feels that the reason they did not cross the street was of supernatural nature, then, in the same context, it would be explained as a reflexive subconscious movement, a mental "muscle memory" movement that saves this version of the person after learning the possible outcome from the death of the person in another universe.

A Tuesday that would repeat itself would create no problem to our senses. The brain, though, would generate an uneasiness stemming from the perception of a past experience repeated in the present. It is the "fundamental unsettling of the first time of experience" (Royle 180) that throws Sam off every Tuesday that he wakes up, and this exact feeling is magnified when he finally wakes up on a Wednesday but still loses his brother in a new, unexpected, and seemingly final way. The day will not reset, as it had countless times up to that point, and thus the disruption of déjà vu itself becomes uncanny, as the cycle breaks by a familiar action (a repeated death of a beloved one) which, in turn, becomes unfamiliar through its unexpected consequences. Life will seemingly go on for Sam, and Dean's death ceases to affect reality. Sam is finally allowed to grieve. However, his perception of death is permanently affected, both by the hundreds of times he has experienced it occurring to a person he loves, as well as his powerlessness to interfere.

Dean's Death Drive

One of the major impulses that characterizes Gothic protagonists is that of the notorious "death drive," the innate tendency of people towards death and self-destruction. As a term, the death drive was popularized by Sigmund Freud in the early twentieth century. As a literary motif though, the death drive is apparent in Poe's tales with characters like the narrators of "The Tell-Tale Heart" and "The Black Cat." In *Supernatural*, the characters who are immediately affected by the death drive are Dean and Sam—each though for different reasons. The concept itself is pretty self-descriptive; in the hands of the Trickster, the induced to an extreme degree "death drive" becomes a lesson for the Winchesters because their quest throughout the season is to avert Dean's death. If a person's desire to die is unavoidable, then the brothers' race to disrupt it goes against human nature. The race against death itself also becomes ironic, as the Winchesters keep practicing a profession that brings them closer to their demise with each passing day. The didactic character of Sam's experience (repeating on the one hand without obvious purpose the day his brother dies, and on the other hand living six months in a parallel reality where his brother is dead) is presented by the Trickster as a deadly joke. This underlies the paradoxical and impossible nature of keeping Dean alive. The experience was never "about killing Dean" as the deity admits when cornered by the brothers. The object of the Trickster-enhanced death drive is Sam and his denial concerning his brother's eventual fate.

Royle identifies, as one of the death drive's characteristics, that "something comes back because in some sense it was never properly there in the first place" (84). In *Supernatural*, this could apply as a motif of the whole structure of the show's episodic plotlines. However, what changes in this case is that death itself becomes the natural element, and the brothers are the ones disrupting the order of things meant-to-be. The recurrence of Tuesday's events create an uncanny situation where the familiar becomes hostile: Sam will catch the falling hot sauce bottle; he will come to know details about everyone's lives. He even makes a point about the waitress' archery skills, hinting, she too, has killed his brother during one of the past Tuesdays. For Freud and Royle, the death drive is about an innate death instinct, the unavoidable journey of a person from life to death. In "Mystery Spot," we see that Dean's death instinct is not necessarily innate, as the concept is originally articulated, but instead fulfilled by external actors. From the waitress to the "mystery spot" owner, to an elderly driver, the moving crew, even an otherwise harmless dog, everyone partakes in Dean's death, especially the deity that creatively orchestrates it every time.

For a show such as *Supernatural* discussing the fringe of life and death, it is more often than not that the protagonists deal with death in a stoic, impersonal manner. Even the procedural nature of the show has that quality. It usually introduces us to the weekly monster by showing a random minor character being (usually brutally) murdered. In the case of "Mystery Spot," the procedural nature is broken as the subject of demise is one of the cynics that treat death as another day at the office. If "the aim of all life is death" in psychoanalytic terms (Royle 84), then "for hunters there is no retirement," as the brothers often reiterate. Thus the death drive is part of the job description, no matter how many times the Winchesters will go to extreme means to avert it. Dean finds himself in his precarious position due to the deal he has made with a demon to save Sam's life. The contract cannot be broken, much like the unavoidable path from life to death. Dean's death drive is a de facto et de jure (even by demonic law standards) testament to his natural desire to die—even if the reason is noble.

The importance of the viewers' overexposure to a major character's death, especially in its repetitive nature, is important in understanding how the idea of the death drive is present in contemporary literature and culture, though its ramifications remain invisible. Benjamin Noys, in *Culture of Death,* notes how, when it comes to approaches we have concerning death, we often endeavor on a search of its "changing meanings" (148). Noys' arguments help illustrate the position of death "at the limit of culture" or "outside it" (148). It is the "fundamental absence" of death itself in discussions about death (Noys 148) that is addressed in "Mystery Spot" or rather the inversion of this cultural motif. The uncanny character of death is hyper-emphasized in this particular episode by not only its undeniable and commanding presence in Dean's varied endings, but also by the gradually resigned stance Sam seems to adopt.

Even though the discussion about déjà vu and the tricks of memory in the previous section covered the uncanniness of the déjà vu phenomenon, there is a pertinent question to be answered—one directly connected to the inescapable unconscious desire of humans to die: Why does Sam remember? Other than the didactic nature of the Trickster's presence, memory, repetition, and the concept of the death drive seem inextricably connected. Royle discusses the death drive as a manifestation of a "compulsion to repeat" (89), but not necessarily connected to the "object of repetition" (90). While the repetition in the traditional Freudian interpretation of the death drive is related to generational/familial recurrences of behaviors, here the repetition of death becomes uncanny because of its close temporal proximity, expanding the Freudian concept.

In the case of Sam and Dean, it is not simply Dean's death that makes the repetition unbearable for Sam; it is that he knows exactly what his brother will say, how to interact with his surroundings, and yet he still fails to save his brother. The "perpetual recurrence of the same thing" (Royle 90) as expressed in Freud's writings is eerie as a phrase on its own when used to describe the death drive. In "Mystery Spot," it is the lack of inwardly induced death drive that is also a catalyst that will push Sam onto a very dark path of grief and reconciliation of death. The Wednesday that Dean died transforms Sam from the " sensitive and poetic, 'thinker' younger brother" (227) as Blake (using Ralph Waldo Emerson's formulation) calls him, to a version of his deceased brother: a violent "fast-car-driving 'doer' of the present ... a modern-day manifestation of the figure of the frontiersman" (227). Ultimately, in the months after his brother's death, Sam becomes what he was trying to avoid his whole life: his father.

Sam's character seems to have changed on multiple levels after his brother's death. This includes his relationship with his father figure, Bobby Singer. As multiple voice messages indicate, Sam has not responded to Bobby's inquiries in months. Sam's silence toward Bobby, who served as a voice of reason for John Winchester as well, shows that he is also rejecting the voice of reason. The silence, as a trope itself, is also connected to the death drive: Sam does not respond to Bobby's messages because he is on a path that is fatally dangerous. Sam's exhibited behavior is what makes Bobby worry, as it signifies Sam's departure from logic toward a recklessness, symptomatic of a strongly inward disregard for the distinct possibility of death.

Sam's transformation into his father becomes more visible if we consider one of the death drive's archetypes, the loneliness also interwoven with the hunters' profession. The death drive is correlated to a "weird solitude" (93–94), which Sam embraces in many different ways: from canned food, to an extreme sense of cleanliness and tidiness that was unusual of both brothers, but characteristic of their father. The legendary Impala's trunk, usually full of weapons in scattered bags and chaos, has been radically transformed. The guns are in velvet cases; the hotel room is neat and tidy; and Sam has completed his transformation. He has become a cold, distant, independent—and quite skillful—hunter, much like his dad, John Winchester. Sam's solitude has become dangerous, too. From a random recorded phone message we learn that Bobby was concerned for Sam, as he had not contacted anyone in over three months. In an uncharacteristic fashion, Sam has embraced his own death drive and the solitude it results in; a solitude that seems very personal and, at the same time, alien, based on how viewers and other characters know Sam to be.

Paranoia and a Lesson Learned

In "Mystery Spot," the plot deliberately plays with the audience's minds. Freud says it is the authors' choice to create a "kind of uncertainty [...] by not letting us know, no doubt purposely, whether he is taking us into the real world or into a purely fantastic one of his own creation" (7), becomes a common literary trope to confuse audiences and keep them from guessing what comes next. At the same time, it succeeds in justifying the supernatural terror the characters feel. In Sam Winchester's case, he is not running away from the supernatural figure that destroyed his life and trapped him in experiencing Dean's last moments repeatedly. Sam's "death drive" is intrinsically connected to the "demonic and diabolical" elements Royle traces in the conception of the term (88), an outside force at play on a larger scale that Sam fights against.

Sam's desensitization to death leads him down a path that has the adverse effect to the Trickster's desires. Sam does not appreciate life as he ought to, and practically follows the same path his brother and father did. The lack of the Trickster's intervention in Sam's life after Dean's death is by no means accidental. Sam has the chance to become whomever he wants to be, in theory, without the influence of his role models. The deity offers Sam what he always wanted: the chance to live his life without any strings connecting him to his past. However, much like the way it happens with the death of familiars, the issue of legacy will consume Sam, leading him into following the same lifestyle he was rejecting.

The ultimate test for the person Sam has become will be not the murder of Bobby, though, even if Sam were sure at the time the Trickster was merely impersonating Bobby. Sam will nonetheless doubt himself and his sanity for a couple of seconds, showing how close to insanity he is, and how his death drive consumes him. His ruthless monster-hunting crusade is a symptom of his death drive, not the cause of it. The Trickster's final challenge is designed to directly test the limits of Sam's transformation. Sam has become a new kind of Gothic hero. Traditionally, the trope refers to a hero who will face supernatural adversaries in order to win the hand of the heroine, either prevailing or withering away in her absence; in this case, brotherly love replaces the heroine in distress. Sam will face the unthinkable—the restoration of the timeline and the revival of Dean. How does Sam return to their former life knowing where his life is headed without his brother? If the whole episode was based on the premise of the Trickster pulling a prank on the brothers, it has now evolved to a very tangible dilemma. Sam can pretend the whole experience never happened, especially since Dean remembers none of it, or he can start preparing for the inevitable life without his brother.

The Trickster himself puts the issue in very simple terms. For the deity, Sam's obsession to save Dean would be disastrous: "Nothing good comes out of it. Just blood and pain." For Sam, the Trickster's suggestion that "sometimes you gotta let people go" is unthinkable; the dead are with us so long as we remember them, and in this case, if there is a slim chance for death to be undone, the Winchesters will find it. Even if in later seasons the ramifications of that logic will be examined and criticized, the Trickster, here, expresses views about death that are prevalent in Western philosophy, which, with a didactic manner, explore the ethical dilemmas of the pursuit of immortality. Dollimore in discussing Schopenhauer's view on death and immortality argues that Schopenhauer sees the acceptance of death as a rational, ascetic choice (178). Sam's lifestyle in the months after his brother's death depict exactly that philosophical path of death's acceptance. However, Sam breaks away and relapses at the first opportunity he is presented, returning to the pursuit of undoing Dean's death that is ultimately, to paraphrase Schopenhauer, a perpetuation of an error forever.

The fragmented narrative, with its repetitions and continuously reset reality, is inextricably connected to a sense of hyperreality, an uncanny "double," which prevents both the conscious protagonist and the viewers from trusting their senses and their minds. Death, in other words, is the catalyst for the re-examination of reality, and the renegotiation of the self and the Other. The Trickster is an Othered presence that is impossible to defeat—a force of nature, simultaneously deadly and didactic. His perspective is not affected by the subjective experience, but has as its only goal the restoration of a natural order. Dean's death needs to occur for the natural order to be upheld, as he traded his soul for Sam's revival. Sam, on the other hand, has to learn to live with the loss of his brother, even if the loss is temporarily undone at the end of the episode. Sam, nonetheless, retains all the memories of the experience, all the lessons learned.

And Now...?

At the end of "Mystery Spot," the brothers will get into their black Impala and practically ride into the sunset with only one of them remembering what really happened. As my essay demonstrates, though, the educational nature of the challenge Sam faced was multifaceted and more complex. Rooted in the Gothic tradition, the continuous déjà vu Sam experienced is meant to be confusing and scary. But even after a hundred (or more) Tuesdays, the mundane routine loses its glamor and the act of the repetition itself is a torment. The Trickster's "lesson" is meant to alleviate any qualms Sam might have after Dean's death. And yet, once Sam gets the chance to live the aftermath of his experience, he blames the deity, and not Dean's choices for Dean's death. The grief process, which Sam was supposed to experience, is hindered by his devoted monster-hunting, a coping mechanism that makes his life a déjà vu of the one his father lived. The untidy bed that Sam looks at as they are leaving the hotel is a reminiscence of the alternative reality he lived in, when his cold order and efficiency was identical to that of John Winchester, a nod to a life Sam had wholeheartedly rejected.

Death in "Mystery Spot" is not a mere cause for emotional responses or the chance for a new life for any of the protagonists. Death in this episode becomes a finality; an eventual condition that no one can prevent, even a deity with reality-warping abilities. The Winchesters demonstrate how their demon hunting is a perpetual death drive, one that they will ironically do everything to avoid. Dean finds himself in a precarious position because of his sacrifice to save Sam, while Sam becomes the obsessed solitary figure he was fighting hard not to be, as a result of his failure to pay back the debt to Dean. However, as Sam will come to realize at the end of the episode, and to a certain extent throughout the whole season, death will come for Dean because it is what both Winchesters unconsciously chase in their adventures. Death might take many different forms, but as it is experienced in the form of déjà vu in "Mystery Spot" one thing becomes clear: death is a part of the same natural order the brothers fight daily as hunters to restore. At the end of the day, balance will be restored, through any (super)natural means necessary.

NOTE

1. See Susan Nylander's essay in this book "Death, American Style: Americana and a Cultural History of Death" for a discussion of photography and its affect on memory.

WORKS CITED

Asia. "Heat of the Moment." *Asia*, Geffen, 1982.
Botting, Fred. "In Gothic Darkly: Heterotopia, History, Culture." *A New Companion to the Gothic*, edited by David Punter. Wiley-Blackwell, 2015, pp. 13–24.
Dollimore, Jonathan. *Death, Desire, and Loss in Western Culture*. Routledge, New York, 2001.
Farnell, Gary. "Gothic's Death Drive." *Literature Compass*, vol. 8, no. 9, 2011, pp. 592.
Foresman, Galen A., editor. *Supernatural and Philosophy: Metaphysics and Monsters ... for Idjits*, Wiley-Blackwell, 2013.
Freud, Sigmund. *The Psychopathology of Everyday Life*. W.W. Norton, 1989.
_____. *The Uncanny*. Edited by Hugh Haughton, Penguin, 2003.
Groundhog Day. Written by Harold Ramis and Danny Rubin, directed by Ron Howard, performances by Bill Murray and Andie MacDowell, Columbia Pictures, 1993.
Jowett, Lorna, and Stacey Abbott. *TV Horror: Investigating the Dark Side of the Small Screen*. I.B. Tauris, 2013.
Kendrick, M. Gregory. *Villainy in Western Culture: Historical Archetypes of Danger, Disorder and Death*. McFarland, 2010.
Miles, Robert. "Ann Radcliffe and Matthew Lewis." *A New Companion to the Gothic*, edited by David Punter. Wiley-Blackwell, 2015, pp. 93–109.
"Mystery Spot." *Supernatural: The Complete Third Season*, story by Jeremy Carver and Emily McLaughlin, teleplay by Jeremy Carver, directed by Kim Manners, Warner Home Video, 2008.
Narvaìez, Peter. *Of Corpse: Death and Humor in Folklore and Popular Culture*. Utah State UP, 2003.
Noys, Benjamin. *The Culture of Death*. Berg, 2005.
Poe, Edgar Allan. "The Black Cat." *The Saturday Evening Post*, 1843.

_____. "The Tell-Tale Heart." *The Pioneer*, 1843.
Royle, Nicholas. *The Uncanny*. Manchester UP, 2003.
Rybinska, Krystyna. "The Marginalization of Death in Culture Based on Selected Examples of Modern Literature and Philosophy." *Forum for World Literature Studies*, vol. 5, no. 2, 2013, pp. 236–248.
Walker, Barbara. *Out of the Ordinary: Folklore and the Supernatural*. Utah State UP, 1995.

"In My Time of Dying"

Lessons on Grief in Supernatural

AMANDA TAYLOR

In the first five minutes of the pilot episode, *Supernatural* establishes itself as a case study in death, dying, and grief. From then on, we watch John, Dean, and Sam Winchester navigate their grief while trying to exact revenge for wife and mother Mary's death. Along the way, John gives his life for his sons, and each brother sacrifices himself for the other or the world at large. Sam and Dean also meet Death himself. We assume that the Winchesters grieve, but the grieving process is understated and often abbreviated in the series. However, *Supernatural* does hold lessons about grief in addition to its abundant lessons about death and dying.

What can *Supernatural* teach us of death, grief, and loss? By first examining what it means to grieve, we can then investigate how Bobby Singer, Sam Winchester, and Dean Winchester each come to terms with [their relationships to] death and grief. This investigation will show that *Supernatural* offers a way for viewers to both better understand the nature of grief and safely come to terms with both our own griefs and our eventual death.

The Necessity of Grief and Grieving

Contemplating our mortality is not (usually) a pleasant pastime. In current American culture, death is taboo, and most Americans are far removed from the processes of death. However, in her book *In the Presence of Grief*, Dorothy Becvar argues that "life could be enriched by wrestling with loss and grief and the fact of one's mortality" (vii). Optimistically, this struggle helps us discover who we are and what we may offer the world. Pessimistically, this struggle reinforces a nihilistic view that life is and always will be pain,

193

and there is nothing good to be found in it. Rather than make us choose sides in this, Becvar claims that "we can live with death. We can live—even have joy—in the presence of grief" (ix). In other words, we can find our way through the pain and find ways to enjoy life even though the pain never goes away. Rather, we make room for the grief and pain, acknowledge them, and carry on as best as we can.

As all of us have or will have experienced a loved one's death, this means we are, to use Becvar's terms, all already in the presence of grief. Because our loved ones have helped shape who we are, losing them creates a gap that no one else can fill. Once this happens, we must do "more than [pick] up the pieces and [move] on" according to Becvar (xii). Instead, we are "challenged to create an entirely new picture or story about ourselves, about our world, about what it means to live" (Becvar xii). This challenge is particularly evident in the ways Sam and Dean [do not] cope with the other's death. The brothers are so intertwined that neither functions well or wholly without the other. It doesn't help, either, that the Winchesters rarely have time to properly grieve.

Both Becvar and Elisabeth Kübler-Ross agree that grieving cannot be rushed, nor is there a specific formula to grief. Becvar is careful to note that

> the process of healing [from a loss] cannot be hurried. It may require a great deal of energy and attention. Nor is there any one right way that healing *should* be pursued or completed. There is no magic formula, and each person must be permitted to engage in the struggle to come to terms with death-related events in a manner that is unique and suitable for him or her [xii].

In other words, we should not, cannot, tell someone, or even ourselves, that it's time to be done grieving or that they are grieving the "wrong" way.

We see these clashing expectations and manifestations of grief in "Everybody Loves a Clown" (2.02). Standing in front of John's pyre, the brothers watch as their father's body burns to ash. Sam is visibly grieving, tears pooled in his eyes and sliding down his cheeks—all expected physical markers of grief. Dean is stoic, almost stonily so. Sam asks Dean about John's last words, searching for some kind of comfort.[1] However, Dean denies that John said anything, as his last words would, in fact, hurt Sam even more. It is only after this denial, with John's admonition that Dean must either save Sam or kill him in mind, that a single tear slips down Dean's cheek. This "single mantear" is often the extent of Dean's visible grief.

Later in the episode, Sam confronts Dean, upset that Dean doesn't seem to be grieving, or at least not grieving how Sam thinks Dean should. Sam, the more outwardly cerebral of the two, generally prefers to talk through his pain and grief. He is analytical and thoughtful by nature, prone to observation and articulation. In this specific scene, Sam comes to Dean as Dean works on the Impala and begins to confess how guilty he feels about John's death, about how much he and John argued. Now that John is gone, Sam is trying to do things John's way, a move Dean has called out and Sam acknowledges here as "too little, too late." Sam continues to verbalize his grief, with the hope that Dean may verbalize his own. However, Dean's silence about and reticence to "openly" grieve John's death disturbs Sam. "I miss him, man," Sam says, "and I feel guilty as hell. And I'm not all right. Not at all. But neither are you. That much I know. I'll let you get back to work."

Dean watches his brother leave, likely waiting until Sam is at least out of visual range, if not earshot, before he picks up a crowbar and bashes in the Impala's window. From there, he continues to beat the car, never truly verbalizing anything, unleashing his anger in a more primal, more visceral way that we might expect from Dean by now. The Impala (Baby) is a representation of John, among other things, and that it takes the brunt of Dean's outburst in this scene is no accident.

Dean gives Baby the beating he can't give John, venting the frustrations he always internalized and could never truly articulate. Dean's world is violent, and it is through violence he will find catharsis. Indeed, despite Sam's accusations that Dean is not grieving John's death, it is quite the opposite. Dean is clearly suffering, but is working it out in his own way. Usually the buffer between Sam and John during arguments, Dean is again the buffer for Sam's grief. Sam can and will verbalize his grief; Dean must take it and likely feels guilty that Sam is suffering. Dean cannot or will not admit weakness to Sam. He has, after all, been charged with caring for Sam, and he has no time for a chick-flick moment over their dad. Dean needs action, not words, to vent his anger, and violence is the only outlet he has at that moment.

The Five Stages

Anger is one of the stages of loss Kübler-Ross first identified in her 1969 book *On Death and Dying,* which focuses on the needs of the dying and how they approach their death. In this book, Kübler-Ross described five stages of loss: Denial, Anger, Bargaining, Depression, and Acceptance. This general model has prevailed with some criticism and tweaking since first posited. It is important to note that Kübler-Ross' book was undertaken as a way of "privileging the voice of the dying" (Kellehear) and was not a systematic study of death. As *Supernatural* depicts each stage of grief with various levels of intensity, allowing viewers to both name and experience each stage, Kübler-Ross' model merits exploration.

Often seen as linear, Kübler-Ross and David Kessler explain in the 2005 book *On Grief and Grieving* that the stages of loss "have been very misunderstood over the past three decades. They were never meant to help tuck messy emotions into neat packages" (7). Indeed, Kübler-Ross is careful in both texts to remind us that the stages are not linear, can overlap, can last a long time, and that not everyone may go through all of them. Both the dying and the bereaved can experience more than one stage at a time and may never fully move out of a stage. For Kübler-Ross and Kessler, that is acceptable, even if current American culture urges us to shut up, move on, and get over it and not linger "too long" in any one stage.

Denial

Denial is not necessarily saying that a loved one's death or other traumatic experience did not occur. The bereaved may be perfectly aware of the reality of the loss but still vehemently shake their head and murmur or cry out, "No!" or any other indication of denial. Kübler-Ross & Kessler claim that denial helps us to "survive the loss" (10) and "find a way to simply get through the day. Denial and shock help us to cope and make survival possible. Denial helps us to pace our feelings of grief. There is a grace in denial. It is nature's way of letting in only as much as we can handle" (10). Denial is a natural defense mechanism. To acknowledge the loss is to have to face the enormity of that loss and its consequences. The mind and body can only take so much—to try to grasp everything all at once would be too overwhelming, so denial steps in to help stop the pain until it can be processed.

Denial is fairly easy to see in *Supernatural*: each time a brother faces death and the other says, screams, or whispers, "No." Or, most recently, in one of the final scenes of the Season Twelve finale, Dean clearly cannot come to terms with Castiel's death or Mary's disappearance. Though unspoken, the denial is evident in his expression. However, he and Sam must yet again set aside their grief to deal with the task at hand, further exacerbating the boys' ability to mourn and, perhaps, causing them to languish in one of the stages. Dean, especially, seems to wallow in anger.

Anger

As seen in "Everybody Loves a Clown," (2.02), anger is usually one of the more difficult stages because it is "displaced in all directions and projected onto the environment at times almost at random" (*On Death* 63), making it hard to predict. Anger may not always manifest in "typical" ways such as yelling or physical altercations, either, making it difficult to pinpoint and acknowledge. The angry bereaved or dying may not want to admit their anger, either. Or, as Kübler-Ross suggests, we do not properly consider the reasons behind the anger, and we may take it personally when it has nothing to do with us and respond with our own anger. This can feed into a cycle of anger where no one can process or move on from their grief.

Rational or not, anger is an important and natural part of the grieving process. Kübler-Ross & Kessler argue that "anger is strength, and it can be an anchor, giving temporary structure to the nothingness of loss ... [becoming] a bridge" over the emptiness the bereaved feels (15–16). Whether or not the object of our anger deserves it, anger can bring people together, if only for a moment. We can see this in *Supernatural* where John and Sam clash over how to help Dean in "In My Time of Dying" (2.01). Sam accuses John of being more concerned about the Colt than Dean, while John is clearly frustrated with Sam's inability to see a bigger picture. The Colt is the key to saving Dean.

We also see anger later in the same episode when John is trying to make amends, but Sam is still clearly angry over his perception of John's actions. To Sam, John went to hunt Azazel, when, in reality, John made a deal *with* Azazel to save Dean's life, continuing the pattern of Winchester dealmaking that began with Mary ("In the Beginning").

Bargaining

Bargaining often entails a game of "If I give you X, then you do Y" between the bereaved and a higher power, be it a doctor or a deity. Typically, the "Y" in this equation is extended life, or a rescindment of the diagnosis, or anything that might mean the dying person's recovery. For those facing certain death, bargaining is natural.[2] Kübler-Ross explains that those facing certain death know "from past experiences that there is a slim chance that [they] may be ... granted a wish" (*On Death*) of either total recovery or the removal of pain, or at least a few more days to do the work they feel they still have to do. The unfinished business for either the dying or the bereaved makes it difficult to consider moving on.

Kübler-Ross & Kessler extend this discussion, calling bargaining "a way station that gives our psyche the time it may need to adjust" (*On Grief* 19) and explaining that it "allows us to believe that we can restore order to the chaos that has taken over" (*On Grief* 20). In essence, bargaining gives the illusion of action, the feeling that something can be done to forestall the coming loss. However, even if bargaining is successful, particularly in the case of the Winchesters' demon deals, there is always a catch. And, it rarely ends well.

There are numerous examples of bargaining in *Supernatural*. Three are particularly germane to my discussion. First is Dean's discussion with the reaper Tessa in "In My Time of Dying" (2.01). Tessa has come to take Dean to his fated afterlife, though she doesn't know exactly where he will go. He tries to reason with her, give her all of the reasons he shouldn't go. He tells her, "Look, I'm sure you've heard this before, but ... you've gotta make an exception. You've gotta cut me a break." Tessa simply replies, "Stage three:

bargaining." Here is explicit mention of Kübler-Ross' work and a direct call-out of Dean's stall tactics. There is no bargaining with Tessa, however, and Dean is "saved" from her only through Azazel's intervention.

Azazel's intervention comes at a cost, of course, and is the result of John Winchester's bargain, the second I wish to highlight here. John is a seasoned and fearsome hunter. He summons Azazel with the understanding that he will likely die, but that sacrifice is worth it if Dean lives. In the end, that's all that matters for John. If Dean lives, he can take care of Sam, who, to this point in the series, is unaware of the monstrous potential within him.[3] However, John does not fully count on the torment his death will cause his sons, even if, in the end, it was part of their salvation.

Indeed, John's bargain leads directly to Dean's bargain for Sam's life at the beginning of "All Hell Breaks Loose: Part 2" (2.22). This episode highlights the non-linear nature of grief, showing how Dean's simultaneous anger and depression lead to his demon deal. Unable to live with Sam's death, and still reeling from John's sacrifice and death, Dean does the only thing he knows he can do. He will give up his borrowed time. "At least this way," he tells Bobby, "something good could come out of it, you know. It's like my life could mean something." As Bobby tries to tell Dean that Dean's life already had meaning, Dean remains convinced that this is the best thing he could do for Sam. Dean can accept his own death now, but he will never accept Sam's death. Interestingly, though, Dean's bargain in Season Two and his time in Hell sets the Apocalypse in motion and directly leads to Sam's ultimate sacrifice in "Swan Song" (5.22). With nowhere else to go, Dean abides by Sam's last wish and goes to Lisa and Ben, one of the few safe places where he can slow down enough to face the depression stage of grief.

Depression

Kübler-Ross & Kessler remind us that depression, like the other stages, is normal and to be expected. It, too, has no set timeframe or manifestation. Some people may withdraw or go silent; other people may dive headfirst into activities they would usually shun or try to keep themselves busy so as not to dwell on the loss. Kübler-Ross & Kessler state that depression occurs when we finally start focusing on the moment—when denial, anger, and bargaining have eased for the time being. While the depressive stage seems to last forever, it is "not a sign of mental illness"[4] (*On Grief* 20). Rather, depression "is the appropriate response to great loss" (20). We need time to process our losses, and the inclination to retreat from daily life for a while allows us the time and space to do this important work.

The depression stage is difficult to see in *Supernatural*. This may be because depression is one of the more taboo stages of grief. Depression is also generally a taboo topic in American culture. It is perhaps most visible in "In My Time of Dying" (2.01) in John's silent brooding at Dean's bedside.[5] John's eventual bargain with Azazel is a direct result of his depression and inability to accept Dean's imminent death. We can also see depression in "Adventures in Babysitting" (7.11) as Sam and Dean struggle with the aftermath of Bobby Singer's death.

Acceptance

When it comes to death and grief, acceptance is a fraught concept. Kübler-Ross & Kessler argue that acceptance does not mean that the bereaved are "all right or okay with what has happened" (*On Grief* 24). Rather, this "stage is about accepting the reality that our loved one is physically gone and recognizing that this new reality is the permanent reality" (25). In other words, acceptance doesn't mean that everyone is happy or satisfied with the outcome. Even if death brings relief from suffering, it is still a loss and opens a void.

Kübler-Ross & Kessler continue, claiming that as we grieve and accept the death of a loved one or our own imminent death, we grow closer to our lost loved one or those we will leave behind. For the bereaved, "A new relationship begins. We learn to live with the loved one we lost. We start the process of reintegration, trying to put back the pieces that have been ripped away" (25). We will never be the same, and we may never "get over" the loss of a loved one, but we can move on. Arguably, the entirety of *Supernatural* is devoted to Sam and Dean coming to accept their losses. In fact, the only death they seem to accept is John's. This may be due to the moment in "All Hell Breaks Loose: Part 2" where John's spirit comes to his sons' aid as they fight and kill Azazel. Mission accomplished, John can move on, and the brothers can, too.

Understanding these stages helps us both come to terms with the death of loved ones and face our own mortality. Though the Winchesters consistently face and even parley with death, it is unlikely most viewers would have such a burden (or privilege). Bobby Singer, the Everyman in the series, represents the majority of viewers. He is a common man who leads a simple life and does what he can to make the world better. It is his death that gives us the most insight into what we might face when our time comes.

Bobby Singer

Bobby Singer is a complex simple man. By all appearances, he operates a self-serve salvage yard, but that is primarily a cover for his hunting work.

He is akin to a Watcher from *Buffy the Vampire Slayer*, holding a wealth of knowledge in his head and in the expanse of his home library. If he doesn't have it, he knows how to find it. But unlike a Watcher, Bobby is also a man of action and can easily dispatch a monster or two as needed. He "keeps a beautiful pantry" ("The French Mistake") and has experienced his share of grief and loss. As with most hunters, Bobby came to the life through losing a loved one, his wife, Karen. She was possessed by a demon, and Bobby stabbed her to death. It is unclear how he also rid her of the demon, as demons can occupy dead bodies.[6] Guided by partner and reluctant friend Rufus Turner, Bobby learns about the supernatural and the ways of hunting, leaving him well-acquainted with death. His relationship with death is best shown in two episodes from Season Seven, "Death's Door" (7.10) and "Survival of the Fittest" (7.23).

"Death's Door"

The bulk of Season Seven revolves around Sam, Dean, and Bobby fighting the newest villains, the Leviathan—an ancient evil from the first days of creation that has been locked in Purgatory almost since those first days. Led by Dick Roman, the Leviathan plan on turning humans into docile livestock that will feed the Leviathan for as long as they wish. In the midst of discovering the Leviathans' plans, Bobby is kidnapped and rescued in "How to Win Friends and Influence Monsters" (7.09). During the getaway, however, Dick Roman shoots Bobby in the head, leaving Bobby in a coma.[7]

"Death's Door" traces the path of Bobby's death, which is played out primarily in Bobby's mind. Viewers watch with Bobby as he relives specific memories in hopes of finding the door back to consciousness. In some measure, this episode mimics both Dickens' *A Christmas Carol* and Dante's *Inferno* where Bobby—guided by Rufus, a Virgil/Ghost of Christmas Past figure—must descend through levels of hellish memories before he can find his way out. Bobby cannot alter or influence these memories; instead, they are a means for him to learn and a vehicle for him to escape the prison of his mind.

It is important to remember that Bobby is aware of the fact that he is dying. His presence in his own mindscape is akin to lucid dreaming.[8] While he cannot alter the memories, he can look for specific memories. According to Rufus, Bobby must "go deep. Deep like ... crap you do not want to think about, so you bury it, you shove other crap over it, and you don't go there. Ever." Thus instructed, Bobby reveals that he has important information to give to Sam and Dean, potential unfinished business, that is his sole motivation to getting out of his own mindscape. Also, though it seems quick to Sam and Dean, Bobby's death can still be considered slow. Sam and Dean have some time to come to grips with the situation and exhibit classic signs of grief, particularly denial, anger, and depression. Sam verges on the brink of acceptance when he tries to get Dean to talk about the situation, but Dean categorically refuses to let Bobby go.

A similar struggle goes on in Bobby's mindscape. Confronted by his reaper, Bobby refuses to go quietly or gently. The reaper is implacable—Bobby's time is up, or will be very soon, and the reaper would prefer that Bobby come now. By running, Bobby is "prolonging the inevitable" and seemingly putting the reaper behind schedule, harkening back to the idea of a natural order: a time, place, and purpose for everything. When a person's time is up and their purpose fulfilled, their place may need to change. The reaper tries to bargain with Bobby, praising him for a good life despite having been dealt poor cards and offering the respite of death: "Bobby. You've helped. You got handed a small, unremarkable life, and you did something with it. Most men like you die of liver disease, watching *Barney Miller* re-runs. You've done enough. Believe me."

For hunters, though, there is no such thing as enough. There is always one more case, one more monster, one more person to save. Once drawn into the fight, it's hard to set the fight down, especially when fighting for loved ones. Until the last bit of work that he can do is done, Bobby will continue to search for a way out of his mindscape prison. Though he is eventually successful in momentarily escaping, he must still face his reaper, who allows him one last memory—fittingly of Sam and Dean—before demanding that Bobby decide whether he will move on as he "should" or stay as a ghost. This is an irrevocable choice, the same choice Tessa posed to Dean in "In My Time of Dying" (2.01) before Azazel interrupted them.

Bobby's struggle in this episode teaches us at least three things. First, the dying struggle with their death as much as the bereaved. Both must come to terms with the event, and both may come to terms in different timeframes. Bobby does not want to die, and it is in him to fight as long as he can. We can see the satisfaction on his face when he regains consciousness, and the loving, smiling benediction in his last word—Idjits—was both pleasing and heartbreaking. Like John Winchester, Bobby was not one to say "I love you" or show much physical affection; his love was in action and code words. For Bobby, idjit serves as both a term of endearment and (mostly) a rebuke for the Winchesters, which is part of the reason Dean objects so strenuously to Garth using it in "Southern Comfort" (8.06).

Second, Bobby's experience teaches us that pain of all kinds is integral in shaping who we are. We tend to think of pain as fundamentally unfair or as some kind of cosmic or divine punishment. Yet, it is often through pain that we learn our most significant lessons. A classic example is teaching a child about not touching a hot stove; one single touch of a hot burner is more instructive than a hundred lectures on why we shouldn't touch the stove. Pain can teach us what not to do, but it can also be a signal of growth. Long-unused muscles will protest after a workout, but once they have recovered, they are stronger than they were before. C. S. Lewis writes that "the evil of pain depends on degree, and pains below a certain intensity are not feared or resented at all" (24). It makes sense, then, that our deepest wounds are those we fear the most and those that have shaped us the most. That Bobby had to find and confront his deepest pain in order to regain consciousness, even if for a few moments, matters greatly. To come to a greater understanding of who we have been, who we are, and who we might become (or avoid becoming), we need to understand our deepest pain. We do not have to like them or revisit them often, but we do need to know our traumas so we can grieve them.

"Survival of the Fittest"

Third, Bobby's death reinforces the idea that, in *Supernatural*, spirits of the dead have a choice of moving on to Heaven or Hell or staying in the mortal realm as ghosts. We learn in "Party on, Garth" (7.18) that Bobby chose to not cross over and has become a ghost. By Survival of the Fittest" (7.23), Bobby has begun to cross the line from benevolent ghost to vengeful spirit, something that he thought he could avoid but seems to be the natural progression for disembodied, displaced spirits. Sam and Dean notice the signs but are hesitant to intervene because it is Bobby. Their reluctance mirrors Bobby's reluctance to "deal with" his late wife Karen's reappearance and imminent turn to darkness in "Dead Men Don't Wear Plaid" (5.15). Bobby has already had to kill her once, and he wanted to savor the time he had with her again, even though he knew it was unnatural and would likely end badly. Similarly, Dean and Sam want more time with Bobby, even though they know things can't end well.

Ultimately, Bobby has to ask them to help him cross over as he should have done in the first place. Sam and Dean prepare a fire to melt the flask Bobby is tied to, and, the father-figure, fellow Hunter, and friend that he is, Bobby offers some final advice. He warns the Winchesters that if they're going to kill Dick Roman, and by extension any other monster they encounter, they need to do so because "it's the job" and not because they *want* to kill. More importantly, though, he urges the boys to not fight their deaths. "When it's your time, go." He wants Sam and Dean to learn from his experience so they don't go down the same road. No strangers to killing, dying, death, or resurrection, helping Bobby cross over is still heartbreaking for the brothers. Sam and Dean know he stayed for them, and we see in their eyes that watching Bobby's spirit "die" is no easy task.[9] Yet, not for the first time, Sam and Dean do not have the luxury of grief. There is still a job to do, so mourning must wait. When they do have time, though, it is certain they will face it differently, calling on their various experiences with death, dying, and killing.

Sam Winchester

As any other hunter, Sam Winchester is no stranger to death. His entire life has been shaped by it, dogged by it. The more cerebral of the brothers, Sam is more prone to observation, reflection, and introspection than Dean. This directly affects his outlook on the hunter life and how he approaches all of their cases. He is the go-to man for research and tends to keep a lot of lore and trivia in his head. In the early seasons of the series, Sam often tries to persuade Dean to wait until they have more information or to find another way than just outright killing the monster. Sam prefers to save lives, even a monster's life, if he can. Thus, Sam is often tasked to get bystanders or potential victims to safety while Dean dispatches the monster. However, in "Heart" (2.17), Sam learns that sometimes, death is the only way to save someone.

"Heart" finds Sam and Dean tracking a werewolf in San Francisco. On the trail of the monster, they meet Madison, a co-worker of one of the victims. Dean leaves Madison in Sam's care while he investigates Madison's ex-boyfriend, Curt, Sam and Dean's prime suspect. Eventually, they determine that Madison is actually the werewolf, something she vehemently denies. In denial himself, despite the clear physical evidence of Madison's monstrosity, Sam throws himself into the task of finding a way to save her. His fervor is likely driven as much by his inability to protect or save his girlfriend Jessica[10] in the pilot episode (1.01) as his general desire to save people.

Sam's sexual relationship with Madison also complicates matters. Sam's intimate relationships tend to be extensions of an emotional connection, in contrast to the more physical connection of Dean's sexual encounters.[11] Sam and Madison could have had a fuller relationship, Sam's Hunter status notwithstanding, but her lycanthropy is untenable. Unlike Buffy and Angel in *Buffy the Vampire Slayer*, who carry on a relationship despite Angel's controlled vampirism (though they ultimately reap the consequences of consummating their relationship),[12] lycanthropy is much more difficult to control. Lycanthropy is more beastly, more carnal than vampirism, leaving Sam and Madison little recourse. The only solution other than Madison's death would be Sam's transformation.

All other avenues exhausted, it becomes clear that the only way to solve Madison's lycanthropy is her death. Sam continues to argue that he can find a way to save her while Dean offers condolences. Dean seems to appreciate the fact that Madison understands her situation as well as his and Sam's. It may even be that Dean doesn't want to kill her, even though he knows he needs to. Ultimately, though, Madison's agency prevails, and she appeals to Sam to help her, although it is an unfair burden she places on him.[13] Madison has quickly come to the acceptance stage while Sam is still cycling through anger, denial, and bargaining. He has yet to accept the fact that death is the only way here. His final exchange with Madison is particularly instructive.

SAM: I'm gonna save you.

MADISON: You tried. I know you tried. But this is all there is left. Help me, Sam. I want you to do it. I want it to be you.

SAM: I can't.

MADISON: I don't want to die. I don't. But I can't live like this. This is the way you can save me. Please. I'm asking you to save me.

Madison's deliberate choice of words leaves Sam no alternative, and the brothers adjourn so Sam can come to terms with killing a loved one.

The final scenes of the episode are set to Queensrÿche's "Silent Lucidity," which serves to underscore the emotion of Sam's task. A lullaby, or at least lullaby-esque, the song talks about how a child must come to terms with the loss of a loved one and can do this through lucid dreaming. The task in the song mirrors Sam's imminent actions, though Sam is clearly not dreaming. Dean tries to take the burden from Sam, but Sam refuses, citing Madison's dying wish. And, as Dean knows, dying wishes must be heeded when possible. Both brothers are crying as Sam turns to go to Madison one last time, but the camera focuses only on Dean as "Silent Lucidity" continues to play. The last lyrics we hear, meant to soothe the child in the song, are punctuated by a gunshot before the screen goes black. Sam has faced his fear and accepted his roles: as lover, he is to give comfort; as Hunter, he is to eradicate a monster.[14] He has learned that death can be salvation.

Sam's lessons in "Heart" come to fruition in "Swan Song" (5.22) and "Sacrifice" (8.23). In these episodes, though, it is Sam's death, that leads to global salvation. In "Swan Song," he chooses to become Lucifer's vessel (Samifer) in hopes of locking Lucifer back in his Cage in Hell, ultimately succeeding and spending an undisclosed amount of time in the Cage with both Lucifer and the archangel Michael, who were, to put it mildly, displeased by the new living arrangements. Similarly, in "Sacrifice," Sam undertakes three grueling Trials to close the gates of Hell. Full success will mean Sam's death, a final and true sacrifice. On the verge of completing the third trial and lacking only a final incantation, Dean intervenes and stops Sam, who collapses, clearly drained and unwell and still on the verge of death.

Self-Sacrifice: The Winchester Way

Hunters are well-versed in sacrifice, and the Winchesters are no exception. Ilona Pajari discusses the logic of sacrifice specific to soldiers' deaths. It is not a far stretch to liken American hunters to a regiment of specially trained—if not entirely disciplined—soldiers, perhaps akin to the Minutemen of the American Revolution.[15] Pajari argues that "the logic of sacrifice ...

promises to give meaning to every soldier's death as well as consolation to mourning families" (179). Soldiers fight for a cause or country (or another personal motivation) and, as such, "sacrificing oneself is presented as something natural" (Pajari 184) to those off the battlefield. Rarely discussed is the fear, the grief, the pain that soldiers face as most civilians do not want to know about those parts. When soldiers dare to vocalize their feelings, any narrative other than how much they love their country and were "happy" to fight is often dismissed.

Sometimes, too, surviving soldiers feel as if they did something wrong because they *didn't* die or give the ultimate sacrifice—a dilemma compellingly illustrated by Lieutenant Dan[16] in *Forrest Gump* as well as in the movie *Dunkirk* when surviving soldiers are greeted by an elderly blind man who tells them, "Well done, lads." One soldier objects, saying, "All we did was survive." The man simply replies that that is enough. Living to fight another day is, indeed, meritorious, but, perhaps, not sufficiently heroic. Pajari argues that the logic of sacrifice allows for a soldier's death in war to "wash away all sins, whether [this is] literally in a religious sense or more generally on the level of society" (186). A soldier's sacrifice is a heroic death, a good death, something we can applaud.[17] However, to receive these accolades, a soldier must die, not just be wounded. Pajari explains: "The fallen are easier to glorify; they only ask for a gravesite and a cross" (186) rather than medical services or for their stories to be heard. Or, in other words, only death is laudable.

Raised as warriors ("Pilot"), both Sam and Dean have a penchant for self-sacrifice, and neither are particularly adept at letting the other go. Both also suffer from survivor guilt. Dean has a harder time, though, as he has been tasked as Sam's caregiver for almost his entire life. Dean has been father, mother, and brother to Sam, and it is a constant battle for Dean to grant Sam any type of autonomy. Yet, he realizes that Sam is right, as much as he doesn't like it, and agrees to Sam's plan, much to Sam's surprise. Dean admits that it's "not on [him] to *let* [Sam] do anything," though it does go "against every fiber" Dean has to let Sam walk into the fray alone. Dean wants Sam to stay in the fight, or at least help him fight, but this is something Sam needs to do alone, and Dean must let him. It also seems that Dean can only let Sam go once, even though Sam has had to see Dean die many, many times.

Sibling Loss

Sibling loss is one of the least studied types of grief. When a child dies young and leaves behind siblings, the surviving siblings can be overlooked. Dorothy Becvar explains that the bond between siblings will affect the way the surviving sibling may grieve. For example, if a sibling relationship is strained, and "one of the siblings dies without a resolution of negative feelings and ill will, the [survivor] is faced with the task of coming to terms with the situation on his or her own" (127). The opposite can also happen—siblings may reconnect after another sibling dies. In either case, "whether embattled or beloved, the bond that is severed by the death of [a sibling] is likely to constitute an event of major proportions" (128), and siblings may overlook or push aside their own grief, especially as adults.

Becvar explains this tendency as a belief that "as adults, [surviving siblings] may believe that what is expected of them is the ability to carry on and to deal with the loss on their own" (131). Depending on the family dynamic, this very well may be the case. Grieving siblings may experience a range of emotions, and "the list of possible reactions is probably endless" (Becvar 135). Again, the reactions are dependent on family dynamics and the relationships between siblings, which can be more complicated as the size of the sibling group increases. No matter the size of the sibling group, though, each sibling must come to grips with the loss of a fellow family member, someone with whom they had a reasonable expectation of sharing old age and parallel life experiences such as college, intimate relationships, children, parental loss, etc. "Sibling loss is most likely to profoundly influence and precipitate changes in perception about oneself, one's career choices, and one's priorities in life" (Becvar 140).

While both Sam and Dean have seen each other die (more than once) and both are deeply affected by those deaths, it is, arguably, Sam who is more altered by Dean's deaths. We see this most keenly in "Mystery Spot" (3.11) where Sam must relive a countless string of Tuesdays where Dean dies in various ways, all for the sake of learning to live with Dean's death, something that Sam cannot ever accept.[18] When Dean dies again, this time on Wednesday, the death seems permanent, and Sam turns into a cold, efficient killing machine, shades of both John and Dean Winchester as well as a preview of Soulless Sam in Season Six. Dean could have mediated his brother's coldness, snapped him out if it, but in Dean's absence, Sam turns to what he knows. The Winchester way may be self-sacrifice, but it is also revenge. Sam is a capable hunter, both in research and in killing monsters. He will do what he feels he needs to in order to find a way to bring Dean back. He needs his brother.

Despite their differences and arguments, Sam still regularly defers to Dean's leadership as younger siblings usually do. This is particularly evident in "Devil's Trap" (1.22) where Dean, John, and Sam are running from Azazel and have the Colt at their disposal. Dean has used a bullet from the Colt, and John tells Dean how proud he is of Dean's actions. When Dean senses something off with John's behavior—sadly, John's praise is out of character—and turns the Colt on John, claiming John is possessed, Sam sides with Dean. As much as Sam lambasts Dean for being a good soldier and blindly following John, he knows Dean would not defy John without good reason. Dean has always had Sam's welfare at heart, even if some of the ways he tries to protect Sam are out of line.

We also see Sam's deference in "About A Boy" (10.12). While working a case, Dean is de-aged to his early teens and kidnapped. He escapes and makes his way back to the motel where Sam is trying to find clues about his brother's disappearance. When Sam answers a thunderous knock at the door, a teenage Dean greets him with a simple "Hiya, Sammy" and walks in the door. Visibly stunned, Sam watches as Dean combs through their arsenal and explains what he can of the case and his predicament. As they leave the motel to get in the car and go back to where Dean was kidnapped, Sam automatically walks to the passenger side of the Impala, although he has just been mistaken for Dean's father. As older brother—even in a younger body—Dean has specific expectations, one of those is that he is Baby's primary driver unless it is absolutely essential that Sam take over.

While Sam does take over occasionally, perhaps the most poignant and heartbreaking example is in "Regarding Dean" (12.11). Dean is hit with a memory spell that mimics Alzheimer's disease. Over the course of the episode, he forgets almost everything about himself and his way of life. Sam has to re-teach Dean almost everything, including small things like identifying a lamp as a lamp instead of a light-stick and big things like the fact that monsters are real and that Sam and Dean hunt them. Upon hearing this, Dean's face lights up in boyish glee as he pronounces the situation "Awesome" in a tone recognizable to any longtime *Supernatural* viewer.

As Dean's condition worsens, Sam calls on Rowena for help. As Dean stands in front of the hotel room's bathroom mirror reminding himself of who he is by murmuring, "My name is Dean Winchester" and other salient facts about himself, Sam and Rowena try to gauge the severity of the situation. Sam finally admits, "You know, I've seen my brother die. But watching him become … not him…. This might actually be worse." Such sentiment is in line with many of those who care for dementia patients—it is a living death. The body remains, but the mind, the personality diminishes or changes so that the person the patient was is no longer. Such a condition requires survivors to mourn their loved ones twice. And, as painful as it is seeing Dean metaphorically die in this episode, his death isn't surprising. Dean is a warrior, and warriors develop a special relationship with death, seeing death as friend, enemy, instructor, companion.

Dean and Death the Horseman

Dean's relationship with Death himself, then, should not be surprising, even though theirs is a complicated relationship. A personified Death gives

Dean a target; a warrior must always have a foe. Yet, Death commands both fear and respect from Dean, particularly during their first meeting in the pizzeria in "Two Minutes to Midnight" (5.21). Dean and Sam need Death's ring to complete the key to Lucifer's Cage. They have already dispatched War, Famine, and Pestilence, but Death is in a league all of his own. The other Horsemen and their blights could, theoretically, all be eliminated if humans could learn to coexist and take care of each other, but death has yet to be truly conquered.

Nevertheless, Dean approaches with a weapon, despite the carnage in the restaurant where Death waits. Death quickly disarms Dean and invites him to sit and eat. This foodsharing is significant, as explained by Hamburg, et al.: "Offering food to strangers ... may represent a strategy to establish initial contact" (5) and could be seen as an initial sign of peace. Where Dean came armed and ready to kill or threaten, Death offers food—nourishment and sustenance. Such an offering signifies Death's good manners and general civility, though he is cool and professional. Dean does sit and simply watches Death, visibly upset and scared—and very little scares Dean Winchester. Death eyes him dispassionately and, in reply to Dean's query if Death is going to kill him, puts Dean in his place:

> You have an inflated sense of your importance. To a thing like me, a thing like you, well.... Think how you'd feel if a bacterium sat at your table and started to get snarky. This is one little planet in one tiny solar system in a galaxy that's barely out of its diapers. I'm old Dean. Very old. So, I invite you to contemplate how insignificant I find you.

Clearly, Death is unimpressed. By his expression, Dean finally understands and then admits that he is in the presence of a being "above [his] pay grade." Death agrees, then commands Dean to eat as Dean has yet to partake of the pizza in front of him.

Dean takes only one bite, which is also significant. Hamburg, et al. claim that "the closer the relationship with someone, the larger the meal people ate in the presence of that person. People [tend] to have larger meals when eating with, for example, family members and close friends than when eating with classmates and colleagues" (2). Dean and Death do not have a close relationship here, and Dean is clearly worried for his life throughout the entire conversation. However, Death has a proposal for Dean. This is why he invited Dean to eat—the meal was a pretense, a way to, ideally, break the ice and allow them to confront the matter at hand in a more relaxed manner, though relaxed may not always apply to Dean's encounters with Death.

Relaxed or not, all of Dean's meetings with Death through Season Twelve are deliberate, involve food in some way, and serve to move *Supernatural's* narrative forward in a way only Death can.[19] Bobby tells Dean, and us, to "think of the bird's-eye view" Death must have on the world ("Two Minutes"). Where Dean, Sam, and Bobby see immediate moments, Death can and does see the ramifications of every action. He affects disinterest in the Winchesters, but he has some investment in them, as he does give them important information, and it is clear that he wants Dean to understand the natural order of things, particularly that interrupting this order has serious consequences.

Death deliberately sets out to teach Dean this lesson in "Appointment in Samarra" (6.11). In exchange for Death retrieving Sam's soul from the Cage and re-ensouling Sam, Dean must be Death for a full 24-hour period. In that time, Dean must kill everyone he is supposed to and cannot take Death's ring off. If he does, no deal. Dean agrees and sets out with Tessa, who will guide Dean to each person he must take. And while the first two are easy, Dean finds it difficult to kill a seemingly innocent girl, and sets off a chain of death and misery that didn't have to happen, resulting in Dean taking off the ring, seemingly losing the bet.

In a debrief with Death, complete with hot dogs "from a little stand in Los Angeles known for their bacon dogs," Dean ungraciously complains to Death about the situation. Death's expression barely changes, but it is evident in his tone that Dean has both crossed a line and failed to learn a lesson. Yes, being Death is not easy, but hunters make life and death decisions all the time, and never seem to think of the consequences. More importantly for Death, the Winchesters bandy their lives about as if they have more than one life to live:

> Wrecking the natural order's not quite such fun when you have to mop up the mess, is it? This is hard for you, Dean. You throw away your life because you've come to assume that it'll bounce right back into your lap. But the human soul is not a rubber ball. It's vulnerable, impermanent, but stronger than you know. And more valuable than you can imagine.

In other words, Dean, be careful with your life.

Conclusion

Death's message holds for us, too, though. If the soul is what makes us who we are, and *Supernatural* suggests that it is, then we, too, are stronger than we know and more valuable than we can imagine. The impermanence of the soul is why life matters so much; we only get one. What we do with it becomes our legacy, the permanent marker of the life we led. Sam and Dean ponder their legacy in "The Memory Remains" (12.18), inviting us to ponder ours along with them. They determine that though they'll "eventually fade away" when no one remembers them anymore, they will have "left the world better than [they] found it" which is really all anyone can ask. With all the death, dying, and grief that the Winchesters have suffered, they ultimately went about doing good in the ways they could.

Likewise, as we come to terms with our own griefs and losses, we can find ways to do good and to pick up the pieces and move on, knowing that while the pain will always be with us, we do not and must not let it hold us hostage. It is possible to live with grief, with death. By immersing us into a world of death, pain, grief, and loss from the very beginning, *Supernatural* offers ways for us to both see how people build lives after loss and consider how we might fit our pieces back together, even if the result isn't what we expected or wanted. Ultimately, even though our grief is individual, and we walk the path of our own sadness, *Supernatural* shows us that we are not alone, that we can make a life, perhaps even find joy, in the presence of grief and death.

NOTES

1. See Susan Nylander's essay "Death, American Style: Americana and a Cultural History of Death" in this collection for a fuller discussion of the importance of last words.

2. In *Supernatural*, this can be a literal face-to-face encounter with Death himself or a reaper as well as a more metaphorical encounter.

3. See Racheal Harris' essay "Wheelin' and Dealin': Crossroads Mythology, Deal-Making, and Death" in this collection for a more in-depth discussion of deal-making.

4. This in no way diminishes the reality of depressive disorders that require medical attention. Grief-related depression may require professional help. There is no shame in seeking this help, and if you need it, please seek it.

5. See Sarah Elaine Neill, Ph.D.'s essay "A Familiar Soundscape: Existentialism, Winchester Exceptionalism, and Death in *Supernatural*" for a discussion of the music that accompanies this scene and other emotionally-laden scenes in the series.

6. See "I Know What You Did Last Summer" (4.09) for more on this. Also, Crowley's meat suit is killed, reinhabited, and resurrected several times.

7. Or, as Bobby puts it, Dick Roman "Lincolned [him]" ("The Girl With the Dungeons and Dragons Tattoo").

8. Lucid dreaming entails having the dreamer be aware of the fact they are dreaming. If the dreamer is aware of this, then they may be able to control and/or alter the content of the dream. The dreamer is more of an observer than a participant. The *Nightmare on Elm Street* series plays with lucid dreaming. See also the discussion of Queensrÿche's "Silent Lucidity" later in this essay.

9. In *Supernatural*, the primary way to force vengeful spirits to cross over is to salt and burn bodily remains and/or any material object the spirit may be tied to. See Rebecca Stone Gordon's essay "Got Salt? Human Remains and Haunting in *Supernatural*" for more explication of human remains in the series.

10. Jessica dies in the pilot episode in a carbon-copy of Mary's death: pinned to the ceiling, a slash through the abdomen, and burned as Sam watches. Again, Dean rescues Sam to help him to safety. Also see Freddie Harris Rambsy's essay "'I prefer ladies with more experience': Virgins, Whores, and Post-Feminine Death in *Supernatural*" in this collection for a deeper exploration of the significance of Jessica's death.

11. Possible exceptions to this are Sam's tryst with Piper in "Baby" (11.04) and his time as Soulless Sam in Season Six.

12. See the following episodes of *Buffy the Vampire Slayer* for more details on Buffy and Angel's relationship: "Angel" (1.07); "Surprise" (2.13), "Innocence" (2.14), "Becoming (Part 2)" (2.22), and "Faith, Hope, and Trick" (3.03).

13. Madison's situation also raises question of euthanasia, death with dignity, and physician-assisted suicide. Her death could be seen as hunter-assisted suicide. It is Sam Win-

chester the hunter who pulls the trigger, not Sam the lover. It would be interesting to explore the ethics of/in *Supernatural* in another project.

14. Once we discover Purgatory in Season Six and that it is the final resting place of monsters, Madison's mercy killing takes on a new light. If Sam had known where he was sending her, would he have still pulled the trigger? Or, does Madison end up in Purgatory if she was made a monster against her will? The natures of Heaven, Hell, and Purgatory in *Supernatural* have yet to be fully delineated or explored.

15. The British Men of Letters had a particular disdain for the disorganization of the American hunters, particularly the fact that American hunters didn't and wouldn't take orders, worked on their own, and were not engaged in a systematic annihilation of all monsters.

16. In the movie, Lieutenant Dan (Gary Sinise) has had a family member die in every major American war since the Revolution. Lieutenant Dan thought it was his destiny to die in Vietnam, a fate he does not meet due to Forrest's bravery and ability to run. Dan is critically injured and loses his legs due to those injuries, and faces the specter of living after the war rather than dying a war hero.

17. See Susan Nylander's essay "Death, American Style: Americana and a Cultural History of Death" for a deeper explication of the heroic or "good" death.

18. See Michail-Chrysovalantis Markodimitrakis' essay for a more in-depth analysis of "Mystery Spot" (3.11) and the lessons therein.

19. Death as Dean and Sam knew him was killed at the end of Season Ten in "Brother's Keeper." We do not see a new incarnation of Death until Season Thirteen, though we do see reapers, usually Billie (see Season Eleven's "Form and Void," "Red Meat," and "Alpha and Omega," as well as Season Twelve's "Celebrating the Life of Asa Fox" and "First Blood"). Billie is introduced as the new incarnation of Death in Season Thirteen in "Advanced Thanatology." Billie and Dean do not (yet) have the same quasi-friendly relationship Dean and pre–Season Thirteen Death had.

WORKS CITED

"About a Boy." *Supernatural: The Complete Tenth Season*, written by Adam Glass, directed by Serge Ladouceur, Warner Home Video, 2015.

"All Along the Watchtower." *Supernatural: The Complete Twelfth Season*, written by Andrew Dabb, directed by Robert Singer, Warner Home Video, 2017.

"Angel." *Buffy the Vampire Slayer: The Complete First Season*, written by David Greenwalt, directed by Scott Brazil, 20th Century–Fox, 2002.

"Appointment in Samarra." *Supernatural: The Complete Sixth Season*, written by Sera Gamble & Robert Singer, directed by Mike Rohl, Warner Home Video, 2011.

"Baby." *Supernatural: The Complete Eleventh Season*, written by Robbie Thompson, directed by Thomas J. Wright, Warner Home Video, 2016.

"Becoming (Part 2)." *Buffy the Vampire Slayer: The Complete Second Season*, written and directed by Joss Whedon, 20th Century–Fox, 2002.

Becvar, Dorothy. *In the Presence of Grief: Helping Family Members Resolve Death, Dying, and Bereavement Issues*. Guilford, 2003.

Buffy the Vampire Slayer, created by Joss Whedon, performances by Sarah Michelle Gellar, David Boreanaz, and Anthony Stewart Head, WB and UPN, 1997–2003.

Dante Alighieri. "The Inferno." *The Divine Comedy*.

"Dead Men Don't Wear Plaid." *Supernatural: The Complete Fifth Season*, written by Jeremy Carver, directed by John Showalter, Warner Home Video, 2010.

"Death's Door." *Supernatural: The Complete Seventh Season,* written by Sera Gamble, directed by Robert Singer, Warner Home Video, 2012.

"Devil's Trap." *Supernatural: The Complete First Season*, written by Eric Kripke, directed by Kim Manners, Warner Home Video, 2006.

Dickens, Charles. *A Christmas Carol*. Chapman & Hall, 1843.

Dunkirk. Directed by Christopher Nolan, Warner Home Video Pictures, 2017.

"Everybody Loves a Clown." *Supernatural: The Complete Second Season*, written by John Shiban, directed by Phil Sgriccia, Warner Home Video, 2007.

"Faith, Hope, and Trick." *Buffy the Vampire Slayer: The Complete Third Season*, written by David Greenwalt, directed by James A. Contner, 20th Century–Fox, 2009.

Forrest Gump. Directed by Robert Zemeckis, performances by Tom Hanks, Sally Field, Robin Wright, and Gary Sinise, Paramount Pictures, 1994.

"The French Mistake." *Supernatural: The Complete Sixth Season*, written by Ben Edlund, directed by Charles Beeson, Warner Home Video, 2011.

"The Girl with the Dungeons and Dragons Tattoo." *Supernatural: The Complete Seventh Season*, written by Robbie Thompson, directed by John MacCarthy, Warner Home Video, 2012.

Hamburg, Myrte E., Catrin Finkenauer and Carlo Schuengel. "Food for Love: The Role of Food Offering in Empathic Emotion Regulation." *Frontiers in Psychology*, vol. 5, Jan. 2014, pp. 1–9. DOI: 10.3389/fpsyg.2014.00032.

"Heart." *Supernatural: The Complete Second Season*, written by Sera Gamble, directed by Kim Manners, Warner Home Video, 2007.

"How to Win Friends and Influence Monsters." *Supernatural: The Complete Seventh Season*, written by Ben Edlund, directed by Guy Bee, Warner Home Video, 2012.

"I Know What You Did Last Summer." *Supernatural: The Complete Fourth Season*, written by Sera Gamble, directed by Charles Beeson, Warner Home Video, 2009.

"In My Time of Dying." *Supernatural: The Complete Second Season*, written by Eric Kripke, directed by Kim Manners, Warner Home Video, 2007.

"Innocence." *Buffy the Vampire Slayer: The Complete Second Season*, written and directed by Joss Whedon, 20th Century–Fox, 2002.

Kellehear, Allen. "On Death and Dying Foreword." www.ekrfoundation.org, 2017.

Kübler-Ross, Elisabeth. *On Death and Dying: What the Dying Have to Teach Us Doctors, Nurses, Clergy and Their Own Families*. Scribner's, 1969.

Kübler-Ross, Elisabeth, and David Kessler. *On Grief and Grieving: Finding the Meaning of Grief Through the Five Stages of Loss*. Scribner's, 2005.

Lewis, C.S. *The Problem of Pain*. Centenary, 1940. HarperCollins ebook, 2009.

"The Memory Remains." *Supernatural: The Complete Twelfth Season*, written by John Bring, directed by Phil Sgriccia, Warner Home Video, 2017.

"Mystery Spot." *Supernatural: The Complete Third Season*, story by Jeremy Carver & Cathryn Humphris, teleplay by Jeremy Carver, directed by Kim Manners, Warner Home Video, 2008.

Pajari, Ilona. "Soldier's Death and the Logic of Sacrifice." *Death and Mortality—From Individual to Communal Perspectives*, editors Outi Hakola, Sara Heinamaa and Sami Pihistrom. *Studies Across Disciplines in the Humanities and Social Sciences*, 19. Helsinki Collegium for Advanced Studies, pp. 179–201.

"Party On, Garth." *Supernatural: The Complete Seventh Season*, written by Adam Glass, directed by Phil Sgriccia, Warner Home Video, 2012.

"Pilot." *Supernatural: The Complete First Season*, written by Eric Kripke, directed by David Nutter, Warner Home Video, 2006.

Queensrÿche. "Silent Lucidity." *Empire*, EMI USA, 1990.

"Regarding Dean." *Supernatural: The Complete Twelfth Season*, written by Meredith Glynn, directed by John Badham, Warner Home Video, 2017.

"Sacrifice." *Supernatural: The Complete Eighth Season*, written by Jeremy Carver, directed by Phil Sgriccia, Warner Home Video, 2013.

"Southern Comfort." *Supernatural: The Complete Eighth Season* written by Adam Glass, directed by Tim Andrew, Warner Home Video, 2013.

"Surprise." *Buffy the Vampire Slayer: The Complete Second Season*, written by Marti Noxon, directed by Michael Lange, 20th Century–Fox, 2002.

"Survival of the Fittest." *Supernatural: The Complete Seventh Season*, written by Sera Gamble, directed by Robert Singer, Warner Home Video, 2012.

"Swan Song." *Supernatural: The Complete Fifth Season*, story by Eric Gewitz, teleplay by Eric Kripke, directed by Steve Boyum, Warner Home Video, 2010.

"Two Minutes to Midnight." *Supernatural: The Complete Fifth Season*, written by Sera Gamble, directed by Phil Sgriccia, Warner Home Video, 2010.

"That's It? A Kansas Song?"

A Conclusion (?)

AMANDA TAYLOR *and* SUSAN NYLANDER

"Endings are hard."—Chuck Shurley, "Swan Song" (5.22)

Chuck is not wrong. But, if *Supernatural* has taught us anything, it's that nothing really ever ends. So, it stands to reason that we should struggle with a conclusion, right? And, yet here we are, trying to find some final words to make sense of what this all means.

Granted, it is a bit macabre and morbid to consider death so closely. Yet, in *Supernatural*, death is impossible to escape. The fact that the series personifies death—gives us faces instead of a nebulous, terrifying specter—makes death all the more personal and even harder to ignore. A single collection is not enough to discuss everything in the series. For example, the relationship between Dean and Death the Horseman deserves more attention, especially their shared love of junk food. Mary Winchester's resurrection and subsequent struggle to adjust to life on earth opens the door to questions of mortality, changing identities, and our place in the world.

Season Thirteen has introduced us to a new personification of Death as the reaper Billie has been "promoted," or as Dean notes, she "died to become Death" ("Advanced Thanatology"). The replacement of an older white man with a younger black woman has myriad implications for cultural, history, and literary studies of all kinds and seems incredibly timely in perhaps a manner of zeitgeist. Season Fourteen will undoubtedly open up more opportunities for further study.

Sam and Dean face their fate over and over throughout the series, yet as the years pass and aging is an inevitable consequence for both actors and characters, we will have to confront an ending that most of us do not want to contemplate. Theories about the series finale abound, and both Jared

Padalecki and Jensen Ackles have weighed in. Padalecki has changed his mind from a previously open fate for the brothers to saying that "I feel like I do either want the boys both to die or Sam to die" (Highfill). Ackles, on the other hand, has revealed that he has dreamt the final scene. In a wide open space, Dean silently exchanges the Impala for a one-seat motorcycle. "I don't need the extra seat anymore," Ackles says, and then Dean rides off, alone (Highfill). We are already verklempt at the thought.

Yes, endings are hard, but through shows such as *Supernatural* we can laugh, cry, yell, and scream at our inevitable end. Perhaps, we can even make peace with our own demons. Or, at least make a deal.

Afterword

LYNN S. ZUBERNIS

It may be hard to understand how a television show that deals so much with a topic we humans often try to avoid has become so popular, let alone to have that popularity endure over fourteen seasons. Yet, as every essay in this book makes clear, death is an integral part of *Supernatural*—just as it is an integral part of life.

For a television show on the youth-focused CW network, *Supernatural* has never been afraid to explore the darkness; in fact, the show has been fascinated with darkness from the start. Creator Eric Kripke wanted to tackle his own demons in the time-honored way that humans have always done, by writing them into existence and then moving heaven and earth to vanquish them. Thus, *Supernatural* begins and ends with darkness, and with death. From the first few minutes of the first episode, death defines the lives of the Winchester family. Mary, the mother who kept her knowledge of the dark side from her husband and sons to protect them from that darkness, meets an extraordinarily violent end, and with her gone all those things that go bump in the night become visible to her family. John—and later Sam and Dean— are defined by Mary's death in that moment, the rest of their lives devoted to keeping others safe and preventing their deaths the way they couldn't prevent Mary's.

Kripke's bold move in killing the family's matriarch at the onset telegraphs his subconscious and equally bold intention with *Supernatural*—sweep our built-in protection against too much knowledge of darkness and our own impending death aside, and force ourselves into the reality we often try to avoid. That reality includes violence and danger and ultimately, death. Like the Winchesters, we as viewers are confronted again and again throughout the series with uncomfortable and threatening truths—there are things out there to fear, things that might destroy us, things that will eventually kill us and those we love. In *Supernatural*, those things are monsters and spirits and ghosts and demons; in real life, they are brutal tyrants and dreaded diseases and nuclear holocaust. In both worlds, that thing is death.

Supernatural does not shy away from confronting its heroes with (almost) more than they can deal with, throwing powerful and terrifying creatures at them repeatedly with only brief moments of respite in between. The show also does not shy away from showing us the aftermath of those sort of confrontations—trauma, repression, grief, revenge, addiction. *Supernatural* does not shy away from exploring the ultimate human fear, that of death itself. In fact, the show personifies Death so we can look at both our fascination with and terror of death right in the eye. And, maybe buy it a pizza.

The show, and the essays in this collection, deal with every aspect of how we as humans struggle with awareness of our own mortality. The crushing burden of grief and loss is explored repeatedly, at times in ways so realistic that it's painful to watch. The desperation we feel to stop an impending loss is also portrayed in such a way that any one of us might feel that we too would go to those lengths to save someone we love. Mary's deal to save John, John's to save Dean, Dean's to save Sam, Sam's to save Dean—the theme of wanting to forestall death and keep those we love with us winds throughout the series, simultaneously inspiring us with the depths of the Winchesters' devotion and not sparing us the reality of the tragic consequences that result.

Supernatural also repeatedly tackles another deeply held human longing—for the ultimate denial of death, resurrection. It has become a joke that "nobody really dies on *Supernatural*" because the trope of resurrection has been used so often, but it remains a powerful one simply because it's a part of us as humans. Early season episodes echo the warning of "what's dead should stay dead," but the Winchesters have never heeded that warning when one of their loved ones has died. From re-animation to crossroads deals, on *Supernatural*, death is not necessarily forever. Even their beloved car has been resurrected repeatedly.

Perhaps the most creative way to flaunt death on the show has been the introduction of the Alternate Universe in Season Twelve. Some of the most beloved characters on the show (Charlie and Bobby, for example) were able to be brought back to life in the form of their AU counterparts. While that isn't technically a resurrection, it is a way for the Show to change its mind when the powers that be realize they may have made a mistake in killing off a character that the fans adore.

If death cannot be counteracted, humans have long found solace in a belief in some kind of afterlife. As several essays of this book make clear, the world that Kripke created mirrors both humanity's longing for an afterlife and its ambivalence about what that would be like. Angels and Heaven exist, but instead of the paradise we want to believe in, Heaven is (depending on the episode you're watching) a room where you relive your greatest hits or a place inhabited by a bunch of angels who are far from benevolent. In fact, instead of angels watching over us, they are often trying to destroy us—which isn't exactly the reassuring belief humans were hoping for.

Kripke's ambivalence about an afterlife is explored repeatedly, especially with the existence of ghosts, lost or angry and inevitably sliding toward the dark side because they can't move on. The show expresses our deep fear of the unknown, especially when it comes to who we will be once we die. The horror of not being ourselves is a deep fear, portrayed on the show with zombies who aren't truly alive, the lost and confused victims of necromancers, vampires who stay alive only at a great cost to self and others, and perhaps most vividly with demons who were once human and have lost their humanity and yet remain "alive." Even Sam, Dean and Castiel are not immune. Cas has been taken over by Leviathans, Sam has been possessed and rendered soulless, Dean has been "carved into a new animal" by Hell and then by the Mark of Cain, and has himself become a demon. This is the stuff of nightmares, intimately tied to our fear of death.

Supernatural leaves no stone unturned when it comes to exploring humanity's complicated feelings about death and how we deal with it. The Winchesters attempt to ease the sting of their own intimate awareness of mortality by leaving a legacy, symbolized by the carving of their initials—as children, into their first home, Baby, and as adults into the library table at the bunker. Their father attempts to leave behind his wisdom for his sons in the form of his journal, a ubiquitous part of the show from episode one. Even the Men of Letters, the library and the lore left behind by Sam and Dean's ancestors, is built around the wish to not be forgotten and to live on.

We also fear dying before being able to tell those we love how we feel about them, and that fear too is explored in the show. Castiel, when he believes he's on the verge of non-existence, struggles to express his feelings for the Winchesters before it's too late, his last breaths used to tell them he loves them, that they are his family. A dying (temporarily) Sam and Dean have done the same. Many episodes address our need for closure, whether through ghosts who can't move on or survivors who need to make sense of a loved one's death. Perhaps Sam and Dean's greatest fear, like many of us, is to die alone—even that fear is acknowledged in the show. In Season Thirteen as the Winchesters once again face almost certain death, Sam confides something to his brother: "And if we die? We'll do that together, too" ("Unfinished Business").

Ultimately, the Winchesters must come to terms with their fear of death and with its inevitability, as we all must—and yet, find a way to not be rendered inhuman by that awareness. As our culture has moved farther and farther from an open discussion and awareness of death, perhaps it is more important than ever to explore those fears and feelings, which nevertheless continue to define us. *Supernatural* externalizes those emotions, allowing us to project them onto beloved characters who stand in for both the self and humanity. Every time the Winchesters confront their fears and challenge death as they "always keep fighting," we are emboldened to keep fighting, too.

Lynn S. Zubernis, Ph.D., is a clinical psychologist and professor at West Chester University and the author/editor of six books on fandom and Supernatural. *She chairs the Stardom & Fandom area of Southwest Popular/American Culture Association and blogs at fangasmthebook.wordpress.com. Follow her on social media at @FangasmSPN.*

Appendix 1

Cast of Characters

Abaddon . . . . Alaina Huffman
Adam Milligan . . . . Jake Abel
Alastair . . . . Mark Rolston; Andrew
Wheeler; Christopher
Heyerdahl (all in Season 4)
Alicia Banes . . . . Kara Royster
Alpha Vampire . . . . Rick Worthy
Amara . . . . Emily Swallow
Amelia Richardson . . . . Liana Balaban
Amy Pond . . . . Jewel Staite
Anna Milton . . . . Julie McNiven
Arthur Ketch . . . . David Haydn-Jones
Asa Fox . . . . Shaine Jones
Ash . . . . Chad Lindburg
Asmodeus . . . . Jeffrey Vincent Parise
Azazel . . . . Fredric Lehne
Balthazar . . . . Sebastian Roché
Becky Rosen . . . . Emily Perkins
Bela Talbot . . . . Lauren Cohen
Ben Braeden . . . . Nicholas Elia
Benny Lafitte . . . . Ty Olsson
Billie/Death . . . . Lisa Berry
Bobby Singer . . . . Jim Beaver
Bobby's Reaper . . . . Henri Lubatti
Cain . . . . Timothy Omundson
Carver Edlund . . . . Rob Benedict
Castiel . . . . Misha Collins
Cesar Cuevas . . . . Hugo Ateo

Charlie Bradbury .... Felicia Day
Christian Campbell .... Corin Nemec
Chuck Shurley .... Rob Benedict
Claire Novak .... Kathryn Newton
Crowley .... Mark A. Sheppard
Dagon .... Ali Ahn
Dean Winchester .... Jensen Ackles
Dean Winchester (old) .... Chad Everett
Dean Winchester (young) .... Ridge Canipe (Seasons 1–3),
                             Brock Kelly (Season 3),
                             Dylan Everett (Seasons 9–11)
Death (Horseman) .... Julian Richings
Dick Roman .... James Patrick Stuart
Doc Benton .... Billy Drago
Donatello Redfield .... Keith Szarabajka
Donna Hanscum .... Briana Buckmaster
Dorothy Baum .... Kaniehtiio Horn
Doug Stover .... Brenden Taylor
Ellen Harvelle .... Samantha Ferris
Entity (the Empty) .... Misha Collins
Famine (Horseman) .... James Otis
Gabriel/Loki/Trickster .... Richard Speight, Jr.
Garth Fitzgerald, IV .... DJ Qualls
Gordon Walker .... Sterling K. Brown
Hannah .... Erica Carroll
Henry Winchester .... Gil McKinney
Jack .... Alexander Calvert
Jake Talley .... Aldis Hodge
Jesse Cuevas .... Lee Rumohr
Jessica (reaper) .... Kayla Stanton
Jessica Moore .... Adrianne Palicki
Jimmy Novak .... Misha Collins
Jo Harvelle .... Alona Tal
Jody Mills .... Kim Rhodes
John Winchester .... Jeffrey Dean Morgan
John Winchester (young) ..... Matt Cohen
Joshua (Angel) .... Roger Aaron Brown
Karen Singer .... Carrie Anne Fleming
Kelly Kline .... Courtney Ford
Kevin Tran .... Osric Chau
Kubrick .... Michael Massee
Len Fletcher .... Jared Gertner

Lisa Braeden	Cindy Sampson
Lucifer	Mark Pellegrino
Madison	Emmanuelle Vaugier
Mary Winchester	Samantha Smith
Mary Winchester (young)	Amy Gumenick
Max Banes	Kendrick Sampson
Meg Masters	Nicki Aycox; Rachel Miner
Metatron	Curtis Armstrong
Michael (Archangel)	Jake Abel (Season 5); Matt Cohen (Season 5)
Michael (Archangel/ Alt. Universe)	Christian Keyes (Season 13); Jensen Ackles (Seasons 13–14)
Missouri Moseley	Loretta Devine
Naomi	Amanda Tapping
Pamela Barnes	Traci Dinwiddie
Patience Turner (Moseley)	Clark Backo
Pestilence (Horseman)	Matt Frewer
Ramiel	Jerry Trimble
Raphael	Demore Barnes; Lanette Ware
Rowena MacLeod	Ruth Connell
Roy	Kerry van der Griend
Ruby	Katie Cassidy (Season 3); Genevieve Cortese (Season 4)
Rufus Turner	Steven Williams
Sam Winchester	Jared Padalecki
Sam Winchester (young)	Colin Ford
Sidney	Tess Atkins
Samuel Campbell	Mitch Pileggi
Tasha Banes	Alvina August
Tessa	Lindsay McKeon
Toni Bevell	Elizabeth Blackmore
Walt	Nels Lennarson
War (Horseman)	Titus Welliver
Zachariah	Kurt Fuller

Appendix 2
Episode List

Season 1 (2005–2006)

1. "Pilot"—*Directed by:* David Nutter; *Written by:* Eric Kripke; Sep. 13, 2005
2. "Wendigo"—*Directed by:* David Nutter; *Story by:* Ron Milbauer & Terri Hughes Burton; *Teleplay by:* Erick Kripke; Sep. 20, 2005
3. "Dead in the Water"—*Directed by:* Kim Manners; *Written by:* Sera Gamble and Raelle Tucker; Sep. 27, 2005
4. "Phantom Traveler"—*Directed by:* Robert Singer; *Written by:* Richard Hatem; Oct. 4, 2005
5. "Bloody Mary"—*Directed by:* Peter Ellis; *Story by:* Eric Kripke; *Teleplay by:* Ron Milbauer & Terri Hughes Burton; Oct. 11, 2005
6. "Skin"—*Directed by:* Robert Duncan McNeill; *Written by:* John Shiban; Oct. 18, 2005
7. "Hook Man"—*Directed by* David Jackson; *Written by:* John Shiban; Oct. 25, 2005
8. "Bugs"—*Directed by* Kim Manners; *Written by:* Rachel Nave & Bill Coakley; Nov. 8, 2005
9. "Home"—*Directed by:* Ken Girotti; *Written by:* Eric Kripke; Nov. 15, 2005
10. "Asylum"—*Directed by:* Guy Bee; *Written by:* Richard Hatem; Nov. 22, 2005
11. "Scarecrow"—*Directed by:* Kim Manners; *Story by:* Patrick Sean Smith; *Teleplay by:* John Shiban; Jan. 10, 2006
12. "Faith"—*Directed by:* Allen Kroaker; *Written by:* Sera Gamble & Raelle Tucker; Jan. 17, 2006
13. "Route 666"—*Directed by:* Paul Shapiro; *Written by:* Brad Buckner & Eugenie Ross-Leming; Jan. 31, 2006

14. "Nightmare"—*Directed by:* Phil Sgriccia; *Written by:* Sera Gamble & Raelle Tucker; Feb. 7, 2006
15. "The Benders"—*Directed by:* Peter Ellis; *Written by:* John Shiban; Feb. 14, 2006
16. "Shadow"—*Directed by:* Kim Manners; *Written by:* Eric Kripke; Feb. 28, 2006
17. "Hell House"—*Directed by:* Chris Long; *Written by:* Trey Callaway; Mar. 30, 2006
18. "Something Wicked"—*Directed by:* Whitney Ransick; *Written by:* Daniel Knauf; Apr. 6, 2006
19. "Provenance"—*Directed by:* Phil Sgriccia; *Written by:* David Ehrman; Apr. 13, 2006
20. "Dead Man's Blood"—*Directed by:* Tony Wharmy; *Written by:* Cathryn Humphris & John Shiban; Apr. 20, 2006
21. "Salvation"—*Directed by:* Robert Singer; *Written by:* Sera Gamble & Raelle Tucker; Apr. 27, 2006
22. "Devil's Trap"—*Directed by* Kim Manners; *Written by* Eric Kripke; May 4, 2006

Season 2 (2006–2007)

1. "In My Time of Dying"—*Directed by:* Kim Manners; *Written by:* Eric Kripke, Sep. 28, 2006
2. "Everybody Loves a Clown"—*Directed by:* Phil Sgriccia; *Written by:* John Shiban, Oct. 5, 2006
3. "Bloodlust"—*Directed by:* Robert Singer; *Written by:* Sera Gamble; Oct. 12, 2006
4. "Children Shouldn't Play with Dead Things"—*Directed by:* Kim Manners; *Written by:* Raelle Tucker; Oct. 19, 2006
5. "Simon Said"—*Directed by:* Tim Iacofano; *Written by:* Ben Edlund; Oct. 26, 2006
6. "No Exit"—*Directed by* Kim Manners; *Written by:* Matt Witten; Nov. 2, 2006
7. "The Usual Suspects"—*Directed by:* Mike Rohl; *Written by:* Cathryn Humphris; Nov. 9, 2006
8. "Crossroad Blues"—*Directed by:* Steve Boyum; *Written by:* Sera Gamble; Nov. 16, 2006
9. "Croatoan"—*Directed by:* Robert Singer; *Written by:* John Shiban; Dec. 7, 2006
10. "Hunted"—*Directed by:* Rachel Talalay; *Written by:* Raelle Tucker; Jan. 11, 2007
11. "Playthings"—*Directed by:* Charles Beeson; *Written by:* Matt Witten; Jan. 18, 2007

12. "Nightshifter"—*Directed by*: Phil Sgriccia; *Written by* Ben Edlund; Jan. 25, 2007

13. "Houses of the Holy"—*Directed by* Kim Manners; *Written by*: Sera Gamble; Feb. 1, 2007

14. "Born Under a Bad Sign"—*Directed by*: J. Miller Tobin; *Written by*: Cathryn Humphris, Feb. 8, 2007

15. "Tall Tales"—*Directed by*: Bradford May; *Written by*: John Shiban; Feb. 15, 2007

16. "Roadkill"—*Directed by*: Charles Beeson; *Written by*: Raelle Tucker; Mar. 15, 2007

17. "Heart"—*Directed by*: Kim Manners; *Written by*: Sera Gamble; Mar. 22, 2007

18. "Hollywood Babylon"—*Directed by*: Phil Sgriccia; *Written by*: Ben Edlund; Apr. 19, 2007

19. "Folsom Prison Blues"—*Directed by*: Mike Rohl; *Written by*: John Shiban; Apr. 26, 2007

20. "What Is and What Should Never Be"—*Directed by*: Eric Kripke; *Written by*: Raelle Tucker; May 3, 2007

21. "All Hell Breaks Loose: Part 1"—*Directed by*: Robert Singer; *Written by*: Sera Gamble, May 10, 2007

22. "All Hell Breaks Loose: Part 2"—*Directed by* Kim Manners; *Story by*: Eric Kripke & Michael T. Moore; *Teleplay by*: Eric Kripke; May 17, 2007

Season 3 (2007–2008)

1. "The Magnificent Seven"—*Directed by*: Kim Manners; *Written by*: Eric Kripke, Oct. 4, 2007

2. "The Kids are Alright"—*Directed by*: Phil Sgriccia; *Written by*: Sera Gamble; Oct. 11, 2007

3. "Bad Day at Black Rock"—*Directed by*: Robert Singer; *Written by*: Ben Edlund; Oct. 18, 2007

4. "Sin City"—*Directed by*: Charles Beeson; *Written by*: Robert Singer & Jeremy Carver; Oct. 25, 2007

5. "Bedtime Stories"—*Directed by*: Mike Rohl; *Written by*: Cathryn Humphris; Nov. 1, 2007

6. "Red Sky at Morning"—*Directed by* Cliff Bole; *Written by*: Laurence Andries; Nov. 8, 2007

7. "Fresh Blood"—*Directed by*: Kim Manners; *Written by*: Sera Gamble; Nov. 15, 2007

8. "A Very Supernatural Christmas"—*Directed by*: J. Miller Tobin; *Written by*: Jeremy Carver; Dec. 13, 2007

9. "Malleus Maleficarum"—*Directed by:* Robert Singer; *Written by:* Ben Edlund; Jan. 31, 2008

10. "Dream a Little Dream of Me"—*Directed by:* Steve Boyum; *Story by:* Sera Gamble & Cathryn Humphris; *Teleplay by:* Cathryn Humphris; Feb. 7, 2008

11. "Mystery Spot"—*Directed by:* Kim Manners; *Story by:* Jeremy Carver & Emily McLaughlin; *Teleplay by:* Jeremy Carver; Feb. 14, 2008

12. "Jus in Bello"—*Directed by:* Phil Sgriccia; *Written by:* Sera Gamble; Feb. 21, 2008

13. "Ghostfacers"—*Directed by:* Phil Sgriccia; *Written by:* Ben Edlund; Apr. 24, 2008

14. "Long Distance Call"—*Directed by:* Robert Singer; *Written by:* Jeremy Carver; May 1, 2008

15. "Time Is on My Side"—*Directed by:* Charles Beeson; *Written by:* Sera Gamble; May 8, 2008

16. "No Rest for the Wicked"—*Directed by:* Kim Manners; *Written by:* Eric Kripke; May 15, 2008

Season 4 (2008–2009)

1. "Lazarus Rising"—*Directed by:* Kim Manners; *Written by:* Eric Kripke; Sep. 18, 2008

2. "Are You There, God? It's Me, Dean Winchester"—*Directed by:* Phil Sgriccia; *Story by:* Sera Gamble & Lou Bollo; *Teleplay by:* Sera Gamble; Sep. 25, 2008

3. "In the Beginning"—*Directed by:* Steve Boyum; *Written by:* Jeremy Carver; Oct. 2, 2008

4. "Metamorphosis"—*Directed by:* Kim Manners; *Written by:* Cathryn Humphris; Oct. 9, 2008

5. "Monster Movie"—*Directed by:* Robert Singer; Written by: Ben Edlund; Oct. 16, 2008

6. "Yellow Fever"—*Directed by:* Phil Sgriccia; *Written by:* Andrew Dabb & Daniel Loflin; Oct. 23, 2008

7. "It's the Great Pumpkin, Sam Winchester"—*Directed by:* Charles Beeson; *Written by:* Julie Siege; Oct. 30, 2008

8. "Wishful Thinking"—*Directed by:* Robert Singer; *Story by:* Ben Edlund & Lou Bollo; *Teleplay by:* Ben Edlund; Nov. 6, 2008

9. "I Know What You Did Last Summer"—*Directed by:* Charles Beeson; *Written by:* Sera Gamble; Nov. 13, 2008

10. "Heaven and Hell"—*Directed by:* J. Miller Tobin; *Story by:* Trevor Sands; *Teleplay by:* Eric Kripke; Nov. 20, 2008

11. "Family Remains"—*Directed by:* Phil Sgriccia; *Written by:* Jeremy Carver; Jan. 15, 2009

12. "Criss Angel is a Douchebag"—*Directed by:* Robert Singer; *Written by:* Julie Siege; Jan. 22, 2009

13. "After School Special"—*Directed by:* Adam Kane; *Written by:* Andrew Dabb & Daniel Loflin; Jan. 29, 2009

14. "Sex and Violence"—*Directed by:* Charles Beeson; *Written by:* Cathryn Humphris; Feb. 5, 2009

15. "Death Takes a Holiday"—*Directed by:* Steve Boyum; *Written by:* Jeremy Carver; Mar. 12, 2009

16. "On the Head of a Pin"—*Directed by:* Mike Rohl; *Written by:* Ben Edlund; Mar. 19, 2009

17. "It's a Terrible Life"—*Directed by:* James L. Conway; *Written by:* Sera Gamble; Mar. 26, 2009

18. "The Monster at the End of This Book"—*Directed by:* Mike Rohl; *Story by:* Julie Siege & Nancy Weiner; *Teleplay by:* Julie Siege; Apr. 2, 2009

19. "Jump the Shark"—*Directed by:* Phil Sgriccia; *Written by:* Andrew Dabb & Daniel Loflin; Apr. 23, 2009

20. "The Rapture"—*Directed by:* Charles Beeson; *Written by:* Jeremy Carver; Apr. 30, 2009

21. "When the Levee Breaks"—*Directed by:* Robert Singer; *Written by:* Sera Gamble; May 7, 2009

22. "Lucifer Rising"—*Directed by:* Eric Kripke; *Written by:* Eric Kripke; May 14, 2009

Season 5 (2009–2010)

1. "Sympathy for the Devil"—*Directed by:* Robert Singer; *Written by:* Eric Kripke; Sep. 10, 2009

2. "Good God, Y'all!"—*Directed by:* Phil Sgriccia; *Written by:* Sera Gamble; Sep. 17, 2009

3. "Free to Be You and Me"—*Directed by:* J. Miller Tobin; *Written by:* Jeremy Carver; Sep. 24, 2009

4. "The End"—*Directed by:* Steve Boyum; *Written by:* Ben Edlund; Oct. 1, 2009

5. "Fallen Idols"—*Directed by:* James L. Conway; *Written by:* Julie Siege; Oct. 8, 2009

6. "I Believe the Children Are Our Future"—*Directed by:* Charles Beeson; *Written by:* Andrew Dabb & Daniel Loflin; Oct. 15, 2009

7. "The Curious Case of Dean Winchester"—*Directed by:* Robert Singer; *Story by:* Sera Gamble & Jenny Klein; *Teleplay by:* Sera Gamble; Oct. 29, 2009

8. "Changing Channels"—*Directed by:* Charles Beeson; *Written by:* Jeremy Carver; Nov. 5, 2009

9. "The Real Ghostbusters"—*Directed by:* James L. Conway; *Story by:* Nancy Weiner; *Teleplay by:* Eric Kripke; Nov. 12, 2009

10. "Abandon All Hope..."—*Directed by:* Phil Sgriccia; *Written by:* Ben Edlund; Nov. 19, 2009

11. "Sam, Interrupted"—*Directed by:* James L. Conway; *Written by:* Andrew Dabb & Daniel Loflin; Jan. 21, 2010

12. "Swap Meat"—*Directed by:* Robert Singer; *Story by:* Julie Siege & Rebecca Dessertine & Harvey Fedor; *Teleplay by* Julie Siege; Jan. 28, 2010

13. "The Song Remains the Same"—*Directed by:* Steve Boyum; *Written by:* Sera Gamble & Nancy Weiner; Feb. 4, 2010

14. "My Bloody Valentine"—*Directed by:* Mike Rohl; *Written by:* Ben Edlund; Feb. 11, 2010

15. "Dead Men Don't Wear Plaid"—*Directed by:* John Showalter; *Written by:* Jeremy Carver; Mar. 25, 2010

16. "Dark Side of the Moon"—*Directed by* Jeff Woolnough; *Written by:* Andrew Dabb & Daniel Loflin; Apr. 1, 2010

17. "99 Problems"—*Directed by* Charles Beeson; *Written by:* Julie Siege; Apr. 8, 2010

18. "Point of No Return"—*Directed by:* Phil Sgriccia; *Written by:* Jeremy Carver; Apr. 15, 2010

19. "Hammer of the Gods"—*Directed by:* Rick Bota; *Story by:* David Reed; *Teleplay by:* Andrew Dabb & Daniel Loflin; Apr. 22, 2010

20. "The Devil You Know"—*Directed by:* Robert Singer; *Written by:* Ben Edlund; Apr. 29, 2010

21. "Two Minutes to Midnight"—*Directed by:* Phil Sgriccia; *Written by:* Sera Gamble; May 6, 2010

22. "Swan Song"—*Directed by* Steve Boyum; *Story by:* Eric Gewitz; *Teleplay by:* Eric Kripke; May 13, 2010

Season 6 (2010–2011)

1. "Exile on Main St."—*Directed by:* Phil Sgriccia; *Written by:* Sera Gamble; Sep. 24, 2010

2. "Two and a Half Men"—*Directed by:* John Showalter; *Written by:* Adam Glass; Oct. 1, 2010

3. "The Third Man"—*Directed by:* Robert Singer; *Written by:* Ben Edlund; Oct. 8, 2010

4. "Weekend at Bobby's"—*Directed by:* Jensen Ackles; *Written by:* Andrew Dabb & Daniel Loflin; Oct. 15, 2010

5. "Live Free or Twihard"—*Directed by:* Rod Hardy; *Written by:* Brett Matthews; Oct. 22, 2010

6. "You Can't Handle the Truth"—*Directed by:* Jan Eliasberg; *Story by:* David Reed & Eric Charmelo & Nicole Snyder; *Teleplay by:* Eric Charmelo & Nicole Snyder; Oct. 29, 2010

7. "Family Matters"—*Directed by:* Guy Bee; *Written by:* Andrew Dabb & Daniel Loflin; Nov. 5, 2010

8. "All Dogs Go to Heaven"—*Directed by:* Phil Sgriccia; *Written by:* Adam Glass; Nov. 12, 2010

9. "Clap Your Hands If You Believe…"—*Directed by:* John Showalter; *Written by:* Ben Edlund; Nov. 19, 2010

10. "Caged Heat"—*Directed by:* Robert Singer; *Written by:* Brett Matthews & Jenny Klein; Dec. 3, 2010

11. "Appointment in Samarra"—*Directed by:* Mike Rohl; *Written by:* Sera Gamble & Robert Singer; Dec. 10, 2010

12. "Like a Virgin"—*Directed by:* Phil Sgriccia; *Written by:* Adam Glass; Feb. 4, 2011

13. "Unforgiven"—*Directed by:* David Barrett; *Written by:* Andrew Dabb & Daniel Loflin; Feb. 11, 2011

14. "Mannequin 3: The Reckoning"—*Directed by:* Jeannot Szwarc; *Written by:* Eric Charmelo & Nicole Snyder; Feb. 18, 2011

15. "The French Mistake"—*Directed by:* Charles Beeson; *Written by:* Ben Edlund; Feb. 25, 2011

16. "…And Then There Were None"—*Directed by:* Mike Rohl; *Written by:* Brett Matthews; Mar. 4, 2011

17. "My Heart Will Go On"—*Directed by:* Phil Sgriccia; *Written by:* Eric Charmelo & Nicole Snyder, Apr. 15, 2011

18. "Frontierland"—*Directed by:* Guy Bee; *Story by:* Andrew Dabb & Daniel Loflin & Jackson Stewart; *Teleplay by:* Andrew Dabb & Daniel Loflin; Apr. 22, 2011

19. "Mommy Dearest"—*Directed by:* John Showalter; *Written by:* Adam Glass; Apr. 29, 2011

20. "The Man Who Would Be King"—*Directed by:* Ben Edlund; *Written by:* Ben Edlund; May 6, 2011

21. "Let It Bleed"—*Directed by:* John Showalter; *Written by:* Sera Gamble; May 20, 2011

22. "The Man Who Knew Too Much"—*Directed by:* Robert Singer; *Written by:* Eric Kripke; May 20, 2011

Season 7 (2011–2012)

1. "Meet the New Boss"—*Directed by:* Phil Sgriccia; *Written by:* Sera Gamble; Sep. 23, 2011

2. "Hello, Cruel World"—*Directed by:* Guy Bee; *Written by:* Ben Edlund; Sep. 30, 2011

3. "The Girl Next Door"—*Directed by:* Jensen Ackles; *Written by:* Andrew Dabb & Daniel Loflin; Oct. 7, 2011

4. "Defending Your Life"—*Directed by:* Robert Singer; *Written by:* Adam Glass; Oct. 14, 2011

5. "Shut Up, Dr. Phil"—*Directed by:* Phil Sgriccia; *Written by:* Brad Buckner & Eugenie Ross-Leming; Oct. 21, 2011

6. "Slash Fiction"—*Directed by:* John Showalter; *Written by:* Robbie Thompson; Oct. 28, 2011

7. "The Mentalists"—*Directed by:* Mike Rohl; *Written by:* Ben Acker & Ben Blacker; Nov. 4, 2011

8. "Season Seven, Time for a Wedding!"—*Directed by:* Tim Andrew; *Written by:* Andrew Dabb & Daniel Loflin; Nov. 11, 2011

9. "How to Win Friends and Influence Monsters"—*Directed by:* Guy Bee; *Written by:* Ben Edlund; Nov. 18, 2011

10. "Death's Door"—*Directed by:* Robert Singer; *Written by:* Sera Gamble; Dec. 2, 2011

11. "Adventures in Babysitting"—*Directed by:* Jeannot Szwarc; *Written by:* Adam Glass; Jan. 6, 2012

12. "Time After Time"—*Directed by:* Phil Sgriccia; *Written by:* Robbie Thompson; Jan. 13, 2012

13. "The Slice Girls"—*Directed by:* Jerry Wanek; *Written by:* Brad Buckner & Eugenie Ross-Leming; Feb. 3, 2012

14. "Plucky Pennywhistle's Magical Menagerie"—*Directed by:* Mike Rohl; *Written by:* Andrew Dabb & Daniel Loflin; Feb. 10, 2012

15. "Repo Man"—*Directed by:* Thomas J. Wright; *Written by:* Ben Edlund; Feb. 17, 2012

16. "Out with the Old"—*Directed by:* John Showalter; *Written by:* Robert Singer & Jenny Klein; Mar. 16, 2012

17. "The Born-Again Identity"—*Directed by:* Robert Singer; *Written by:* Sera Gamble; Mar. 23, 2012

18. "Party on, Garth"—*Directed by:* Phil Sgriccia; *Written by:* Adam Glass; Mar. 30, 2012

19. "Of Grave Importance"—*Directed by:* Tim Andrew; *Written by:* Brad Buckner & Eugenie Ross-Leming; Apr. 20, 2012

20. "The Girl with the Dungeons and Dragons Tattoo"—*Directed by* John MacCarthy; *Written by:* Robbie Thompson; Apr. 27, 2012

21. "Reading is Fundamental"—*Directed by:* Ben Edlund; *Written by:* Ben Edlund; May 4, 2012

22. "There Will Be Blood"—*Directed by:* Guy Bee; *Written by:* Andrew Dabb & Daniel Loflin; May 11, 2012

23. "Survival of the Fittest"—*Directed by:* Robert Singer; *Written by:* Sera Gamble; May 18, 2012

Season 8 (2012–2013)

    1. "We Need to Talk About Kevin"—*Directed by:* Robert Singer; *Written by:* Jeremy Carver; Oct. 3, 2012

    2. "What's Up, Tiger Mommy?"—*Directed by:* John Showalter; *Written by:* Andrew Dabb & Daniel Loflin; Oct. 10, 2012

    3. "Heartache"—*Directed by:* Jensen Ackles; *Written by:* Brad Buckner & Eugenie Ross-Leming; Oct. 17, 2012

    4. "Bitten"—*Directed by:* Thomas J. Wright; *Written by:* Robbie Thompson; Oct. 24, 2012

    5. "Blood Brother"—*Directed by:* Guy Bee; *Written by:* Ben Edlund; Oct. 31, 2012

    6. "Southern Comfort"—*Directed by:* Tim Andrew; *Written by:* Adam Glass; Nov. 7, 2012

    7. "A Little Slice of Kevin"—*Directed by:* Charlie Carner; *Written by:* Brad Buckner & Eugenie Ross-Leming; Nov. 14, 2012

    8. "Hunteri Heroici"—*Directed by:* Paul Edwards; *Written by:* Andrew Dabb; Nov. 28, 2012

    9. "Citizen Fang"—*Directed by:* Nick Copus; *Written by:* Daniel Loflin; Dec. 5, 2012

    10. "Torn and Frayed"—*Directed by* Robert Singer; *Written by:* Jenny Klein; Jan. 16, 2013

    11. "LARP and the Real Girl"—*Directed by:* Jeannot Szwarc; *Written by:* Robbie Thompson; Jan. 23, 2013

    12. "As Times Goes By"—*Directed by:* Serge Ladouceur; *Written by:* Adam Glass; Jan. 30, 2013

    13. "Everybody Hates Hitler"—*Directed by:* Phil Sgriccia; *Written by:* Ben Edlund; Feb. 6, 2013

    14. "Trial and Error"—*Directed by:* Kevin Parks; *Written by:* Andrew Dabb; Feb. 13, 2013

    15. "Man's Best Friend with Benefits"—*Directed by:* John Showalter: *Written by:* Brad Buckner & Eugenie Ross-Leming; Feb. 20, 2013

    16. "Remember the Titans"—*Directed by:* Steve Boyum; *Written by:* Daniel Loflin; Feb. 27, 2013

    17. "Goodbye, Stranger"—*Directed by:* Thomas J. Wright; *Written by:* Robbie Thompson; Mar. 20, 2013

    18. "Freaks and Geeks"—*Directed by:* John Showalter; *Written by:* Adam Glass; Mar. 27, 2013

    19. "Taxi Driver"—*Directed by:* Guy Bee; *Written by:* Brad Buckner & Eugenie Ross-Leming; Apr. 3, 2013

    20. "Pac-Man Fever"—*Directed by:* Robert Singer; *Written by:* Robbie Thompson; Apr. 24, 2013

21. "The Great Escapist"—*Directed by*: Robert Duncan McNeill; *Written by*: Ben Edlund; May 1, 2013
22. "Clip Show"—*Directed by*: Thomas J. Wright; *Written by*: Andrew Dabb; May 8, 2013
23. "Sacrifice"—*Directed by*: Phil Sgriccia; *Written by*: Jeremy Carver; May 15, 2013

Season 9 (2013–2014)

1. "I Think I'm Gonna Like It Here"—*Directed by*: John Showalter; *Written by*: Jeremy Carver; Oct. 8, 2013
2. "Devil May Care"—*Directed by*: Guy Bee; *Written by*: Andrew Dabb; Oct. 15, 2013
3. "I'm No Angel"—*Directed by*: Kevin Hooks; *Written by*: Brad Buckner & Eugenie Ross-Leming; Oct. 22, 2013
4. "Slumber Party"—*Directed by*: Robert Singer; *Written by*: Robbie Thompson; Oct. 29, 2013
5. "Dog Dean Afternoon"—*Directed by*: Tim Andrew; *Written by*: Eric Charmelo & Nicole Snyder; Nov. 5, 2013
6. "Heaven Can't Wait"—*Directed by*: Rob Spera; *Written by*: Robert Berens; Nov. 12, 2013
7. "Bad Boys"—*Directed by*: Kevin Parks; *Written by*: Adam Glass; Nov. 19, 2013
8. "Rock and a Hard Place"—*Directed by*: John MacCarthy; *Written by*: Jenny Klein; Nov. 26, 2013
9. "Holy Terror"—*Directed by*: Thomas J. Wright; *Written by*: Brad Buckner & Eugenie Ross-Leming; Dec. 3, 2013
10. "Road Trip"—*Directed by*: Robert Singer; *Written by*: Andrew Dabb; Jan. 14, 2014
11. "First Born"—*Directed by*: John Badham; *Written by*: Robbie Thompson; Jan. 21, 2014
12. "Sharp Teeth"—*Directed by*: John Showalter; *Written by*: Adam Glass; Jan. 28, 2014
13. "The Purge"—*Directed by*: Phil Sgriccia; *Written by*: Eric Charmelo & Nicole Snyder; Feb. 4, 2014
14. "Captives"—*Directed by*: Jerry Wanek; *Written by*: Robert Berens; Feb. 25, 2014
15. "#THINMAN"—*Directed by*: Jeannot Szwarc; *Written by*: Jenny Klein; Mar. 4, 2014
16. "Blade Runners"—*Directed by*: Serge Ladouceur; *Written by*: Brad Buckner & Eugenie Ross-Leming; Mar. 18, 2014
17. "Mother's Little Helper"—*Directed by*: Misha Collins; *Written by*: Adam Glass; Mar. 25, 2014

18. "Meta Fiction"—*Directed by:* Thomas J. Wright; *Written by:* Robbie Thompson; Apr. 15, 2014

19. "Alex Annie Alexis Ann"—*Directed by:* Stefan Pleszczynski; *Written by:* Robert Berens; Apr. 22, 2014

20. "Bloodlines"—*Directed by:* Robert Singer; *Written by:* Andrew Dabb; Apr. 29, 2014

21. "King of the Damned"—*Directed by:* P. J. Pesce; *Written by:* Brad Buckner & Eugenie Ross-Leming; May 6, 2014

22. "Stairway to Heaven"—*Directed by:* Guy Bee; *Written by:* Andrew Dabb; May 13, 2014

23. "Do You Believe in Miracles?"—*Directed by:* Thomas J. Wright; *Written by:* Jeremy Carver; May 20, 2014

Season 10 (2014–2015)

1. "Black"—*Directed by:* Robert Singer; *Written by:* Jeremy Carver; Oct. 7, 2014

2. "Reichenbach"—*Directed by:* Thomas J. Wright; *Written by:* Andrew Dabb; Oct. 14, 2014

3. "Soul Survivor"—*Directed by:* Jensen Ackles; *Written by:* Brad Buckner & Eugenie Ross-Leming; Oct. 21, 2014

4. "Paper Moon"—*Directed by:* Jeannot Szwarc; *Written by:* Adam Glass; Oct. 28, 2014

5. "Fan Fiction"—*Directed by:* Phil Sgriccia; *Written by:* Robbie Thompson; Nov. 11, 2014

6. "Ask Jeeves"—*Directed by:* John MacCarthy; *Written by:* Eric Charmelo & Nicole Snyder; Nov. 18, 2014

7. "Girls, Girls, Girls"—*Directed by:* Robert Singer; *Written by:* Robert Berens; Nov. 25, 2014

8. "Hibbing 911"—*Directed by:* Tim Andrew; *Story by:* Jenny Klein & Phil Sgriccia; *Teleplay by:* Jenny Klein; Dec. 2, 2014

9. "The Things We Left Behind"—*Directed by:* Guy Bee; *Written by:* Andrew Dabb; Dec. 9, 2014

10. "The Hunter Games"—*Directed by:* John Badham; *Written by:* Eugenie Ross-Leming & Brad Buckner; Jan. 20, 2015

11. "There's No Place Like Home"—*Directed by:* Phil Sgriccia; *Written by:* Robbie Thompson; Jan. 27, 2015

12. "About a Boy"—*Directed by:* Serge Ladouceur; *Written by:* Adam Glass; Feb. 3, 2015

13. "Halt & Catch Fire"—*Directed by:* John Showalter; *Written by:* Eric Charmelo & Nicole Snyder; Feb. 10, 2015

14. "The Executioner's Song"—*Directed by:* Phil Sgriccia; *Written by:* Robert Berens; Feb. 17, 2015

15. "The Things They Carried"—*Directed by:* John Badham; *Written by:* Jenny Klein; Mar. 18, 2015

16. "Paint It Black"—*Directed by:* John Showalter; *Written by:* Brad Buckner & Eugenie Ross-Leming; Mar. 25, 2015

17. "Inside Man"—*Directed by:* Rashaad Ernesto Green; *Written by:* Andrew Dabb; Apr. 1, 2015

18. "Book of the Damned"—*Directed by:* P. J. Pesce; *Written by:* Robbie Thompson; Apr. 15, 2015

19. "The Werther Project"—*Directed by:* Stefan Pleszczynski; *Written by:* Robert Berens; Apr. 22, 2015

20. "Angel Heart"—*Directed by:* Steve Boyum; *Written by:* Robbie Thompson; Apr. 29, 2015

21. "Dark Dynasty"—*Directed by:* Robert Singer; *Written by:* Eugenie Ross-Leming & Brad Buckner; May 6, 2015

22. "The Prisoner"—*Directed by:* Thomas J. Wright; *Written by:* Andrew Dabb; May 13, 2015

23. "Brother's Keeper"—*Directed by:* Phil Sgriccia; *Written by:* Jeremy Carver; May 20, 2015

Season 11 (2015–2016)

1. "Out of the Darkness, Into the Fire"—*Directed by:* Robert Singer; *Written by:* Jeremy Carver; Oct. 7, 2015

2. "Form and Void"—*Directed by:* Phil Sgriccia; *Written by:* Andrew Dabb; Oct. 14, 2015

3. "The Bad Seed"—*Directed by:* Jensen Ackles; *Written by:* Brad Buckner & Eugenie Ross-Leming; Oct. 21, 2015

4. "Baby"—*Directed by:* Thomas J. Wright; *Written by:* Robbie Thompson; Oct. 28, 2015

5. "Thin Lizzie"—*Directed by:* Rashaad Ernesto Green; *Written by:* Nancy Won; Nov. 4, 2015

6. "Our Little World"—*Directed by:* John Showalter; *Written by:* Robert Berens; Nov. 11, 2015

7. "Plush"—*Directed by:* Tim Andrew; *Written by:* Eric Charmelo & Nicole Snyder; Nov. 18, 2015

8. "Just My Imagination"—*Directed by:* Richard Speight, Jr.; *Written by:* Jenny Klein; Dec. 2, 2015

9. "O Brother, Where Art Thou?"—*Directed by:* Robert Singer; *Written by:* Eugenie Ross-Leming & Brad Buckner; Dec. 9, 2015

10. "The Devil in the Details"—*Directed by:* Thomas J. Wright; *Written by:* Andrew Dabb; Jan. 20, 2016

11. "Into the Mystic"—*Directed by:* John Badham; *Written by:* Robbie Thompson; Jan. 27, 2016

12. "Don't You Forget About Me"—*Directed by:* Stefan Pleszczynski; *Written by:* Nancy Won; Feb. 3, 2016

13. "Love Hurts"—*Directed by:* Phil Sgriccia; *Written by:* Eric Charmelo & Nicole Snyder; Feb. 10, 2016

14. "The Vessel"—*Directed by:* John Badham; *Written by:* Robert Berens; Feb. 17, 2016

15. "Beyond the Mat"—*Directed by:* Jerry Wanek; *Written by:* John Bring and Andrew Dabb; Feb. 24, 2016

16. "Safe House"—*Directed by:* Stefan Pleszczynski; *Written by:* Robbie Thompson; Mar. 23, 2016

17. "Red Meat"—*Directed by:* Nina Lopez-Corrado; *Written by:* Robert Berens & Andrew Dabb; Mar. 30, 2016

18. "Hell's Angel"—*Directed by:* Phil Sgriccia; *Written by:* Brad Buckner & Eugenie Ross-Leming; Apr. 6, 2016

19. "The Chitters"—*Directed by:* Eduardo Sánchez; *Written by:* Nancy Won; Apr. 27, 2016

20. "Don't Call Me Shurley"—*Directed by:* Robert Singer; *Written by:* Robbie Thompson; May 4, 2016

21. "All in the Family"—*Directed by:* Thomas J. Wright; *Written by:* Eugenie Ross-Leming & Brad Buckner; May 11, 2016

22. "We Happy Few"—*Directed by:* John Badham; *Written by:* Robert Berens; May 18, 2016

23. "Alpha and Omega"—*Directed by:* Phil Sgriccia; *Written by:* Andrew Dabb; May 25, 2016

Season 12 (2016–2017)

1. "Keep Calm and Carry On"—*Directed by:* Phil Sgriccia; *Written by:* Andrew Dabb; Oct. 13, 2016

2. "Mamma Mia"—*Directed by:* Thomas J. Wright; *Written by:* Brad Buckner & Eugenie Ross-Leming; Oct. 20, 2016

3. "The Foundry"—*Directed by:* Robert Singer; *Written by:* Robert Berens; Oct. 27, 2016.

4. "American Nightmare"—*Directed by:* John Showalter; *Written by:* Davy Perez; Nov. 3, 2016

5. "The One You've Been Waiting For"—*Directed by:* Nina Lopez-Corrado; *Written by:* Meredith Glynn; Nov. 10, 2016

6. "Celebrating the Life of Asa Fox"—*Directed by:* John Badham; *Written by:* Steve Yockey; Nov. 17, 2016

7. "Rock Never Dies"—*Directed by:* Eduardo Sánchez; *Written by:* Robert Berens; Dec. 1, 2016

8. "LOTUS"—*Directed by:* Phil Sgriccia; *Written by:* Eugenie Ross-Leming & Brad Buckner; Dec. 8, 2016

9. "First Blood"—*Directed by:* Robert Singer; *Written by:* Andrew Dabb; Jan. 26, 2017

10. "Lily Sunder Has Some Regrets"—*Directed by:* Thomas J. Wright; *Written by:* Steve Yockey; Feb. 2, 2017

11. "Regarding Dean"—*Directed by:* John Badham; *Written by:* Meredith Glynn; Feb. 9, 2017

12. "Stuck in the Middle (With You)"—*Directed by:* Richard Speight, Jr.; *Written by:* Davy Perez; Feb. 16, 2017

13. "Family Feud"—*Directed by:* P. J. Pesce; *Written by:* Brad Buckner & Eugenie Ross-Leming; Feb. 23, 2017

14. "The Raid"—*Directed by:* John MacCarthy; *Written by* Robert Berens; Mar. 2, 2017

15. "Somewhere Between Heaven and Hell"—*Directed by:* Nina Lopez- Corrado; *Written by:* Davy Perez; Mar. 9, 2017

16. "Ladies Drink Free"—*Directed by:* Amyn Kaderali; *Written by:* Meredith Glynn; Mar. 30, 2017

17. "The British Invasion"—*Directed by:* John Showalter; *Written by:* Eugenie Ross-Leming & Brad Buckner; Apr. 6, 2017

18. "The Memory Remains"—*Directed by:* Phil Sgriccia; *Written by:* John Bring; Apr. 13, 2017

19. "The Future"—*Directed by:* Amanda Tapping; *Written by:* Robert Berens & Meredith Glynn; Apr. 27, 2017

20. "Twigs & Twine & Tasha Banes"—*Directed by:* Richard Speight, Jr.; *Written by:* Steve Yockey; May 4, 2017

21. "There's Something About Mary"—*Directed by:* P. J. Pesce; *Written by:* Brad Buckner & Eugenie Ross-Leming; May 11, 2017

22. "Who We Are"—*Directed by:* John Showalter; *Written by:* Robert Berens; May 18, 2017

23. "All Along the Watchtower"—*Directed by:* Robert Singer; *Written by:* Andrew Dabb; May 18, 2017

Season 13 (2017–2018)

1. "Lost and Found"—*Directed by:* Phil Sgriccia; *Written by:* Andrew Dabb; Oct. 12, 2017

2. "The Rising Son"—*Directed by:* Thomas J. Wright; *Written by:* Eugenie Ross-Leming & Brad Buckner; Oct. 19, 2017

3. "Patience"—*Directed by:* Robert Singer; *Written by:* Robert Berens; Oct. 26, 2017

4. "The Big Empty"—*Directed by:* John Badham; *Written by:* Meredith Glynn; Nov. 2, 2017

5. "Advanced Thanatology"—*Directed by:* John Showalter; *Written by:* Steve Yockey; Nov. 9, 2017

6. "Tombstone"—*Directed by:* Nina Lopez-Corrado; *Written by:* Davy Perez; Nov. 16, 2017

7. "War of the Worlds"—*Directed by:* Richard Speight, Jr.; *Written by:* Eugene Ross-Leming & Brad Buckner; Nov. 23, 2017

8. "The Scorpion and the Frog"—*Directed by:* Robert Singer; *Written by:* Meredith Glynn; Nov. 30, 2017

9. "The Bad Place"—*Directed by:* Phil Sgriccia; *Written by:* Robert Berens; Dec. 7, 2017

10. "Wayward Sisters"—*Directed by:* Phil Sgriccia; *Written by:* Robert Berens & Andrew Dabb; Jan. 18, 2018

11. "Breakdown"—*Directed by:* Amyn Kaderali; *Written by:* Davy Perez; Jan. 25, 2018.

12. "Various & Sundry Villains"—*Directed by:* Amanda Tapping; *Written by:* Steve Yockey; Feb. 1, 2018

13. "Devil's Bargain"—*Directed by:* Eduardo Sánchez; *Written by:* Eugenie Ross-Leming & Brad Buckner; Feb. 8, 2018

14. "Good Intentions"—*Directed by:* P. J. Pesce; *Written by:* Meredith Glynn; Mar. 1, 2018

15. "A Most Holy Man"—*Directed by:* Amanda Tapping; *Written by:* Andrew Dabb & Robert Singer; Mar. 8, 2018

16. "Scoobynatural"—*Directed by:* Robert Singer; *Written by:* Jim Krieg & Jeremy Adams; Mar. 29, 2018

17. "The Thing"—*Directed by:* John Showalter; *Written by:* Davy Perez; Apr. 5, 2018

18. "Bring 'em Back Alive"—*Directed by:* Amyn Kaderali; *Written by:* Brad Buckner & Eugenie Ross-Leming; Apr. 12, 2018

19. "Funeralia"—*Directed by:* Nina Lopez-Corrado; *Written by:* Steve Yockey; Feb. 1, 2018

20. "Unfinished Business"—*Directed by:* Richard Speight, Jr.; *Written by:* Meredith Glynn; Apr. 26, 2018

21. "Beat the Devil"—*Directed by:* Phil Sgriccia; *Written by:* Robert Berens; May 3, 2018

22. "Exodus"—*Directed by:* Thomas J. Wright; *Written by:* Eugenie Ross-Leming & Brad Buckner; May 10, 2018

23. "Let the Good Times Roll"—*Directed by:* Robert Singer; *Written by:* Andrew Dabb; May 17, 2018

Season 14

Season 14 premiered on Thursday, Oct. 11, 2018, and had 20 episodes.

Season 15

The final season of the series premieres on Oct. 10, 2019.

About the Contributors

Jessica **George** received her Ph.D. from Cardiff University (Wales) in 2014 and is an independent scholar interested in evolutionary theory and the weird tale, Gothic and horror studies, and contemporary Welsh writing in English. She is also an author of weird tales and completed her first novel under the Literature Wales mentoring scheme in 2017.

Erin M. **Giannini**, Ph.D., is an independent scholar in television studies whose work has focused on portrayals of industrial contexts around corporate culture on television, including a monograph on corporate culture in the works of Joss Whedon. She has published and presented work on religion, socioeconomics, and technology in series such as *Supernatural*, *Dollhouse*, *iZombie*, and *Mystery Science Theater 3000*, and is a contributor at PopMatters.

Racheal **Harris** is undertaking her Ph.D. at Deakin University in Geelong, Victoria, Australia. She has contributed essays to several edited collections and is working on a monograph for the Emerald Death and Culture series. She also has a forthcoming title on the Syfy series *12 Monkeys*, to be published by McFarland.

Freddie [Fiona] **Harris Ramsby** is an assistant professor of rhetoric and writing at Bloomfield College, New Jersey. Her research focuses on the intersection of rhetoric, performance, and discourse in popular culture. She is also the producing artistic director for The Company @ Bloomfield College, a theater company that is dedicated to producing new plays by emerging and underrepresented playwrights.

Rebecca M. **Lush** holds a Ph.D. in early American literature from the University of Maryland and is an associate professor and chair of the literature and writing studies department at CSU San Marcos. Her research focuses on horror works and their intersections with the American West and frontier as well as the representation of Native peoples. She has published work on a variety of topics, including James Fenimore Cooper, Lady Gaga, *The Vampire Diaries*, and Stephen Graham Jones.

Michail-Chrysovalantis **Markodimitrakis** is a doctoral student of American studies at Bowling Green State University. He studies the Gothic and horror in literature and media. His research focuses on the effect of horror narratives in both political discourses and popular culture. He also teaches courses in composition and in ethnic studies.

Sarah Elaine **Neill** holds a Ph.D. in musicology from Duke University and has taught at the UNC School of the Arts, Duke University, and Duke Kunshan University. Her research interests include modernism, reception history, music as cultural currency, orchestral history in the American Midwest and South, the intersection of popular culture and art music, and the role of music in memory and cognition. Her research has been supported by the Beinecke Foundation and Newberry Library's Rudolph Ganz Fellowship.

Susan **Nylander** has earned degrees in English and history. Prior to her academic pursuits, she spent fifteen years (pseudonym Susan Landers) working full-time, and another twenty part-time, in broadcast radio as an air talent and music director. Now a full-time professor of English composition and literature at Barstow College, she still rocks the radio on occasion at legendary SoCal rock station 96.7 KCAL-FM. A passionate *Supernatural* fan and scholar, she plans to continue working with her "partner-in-crime" Amanda (Mandy) Taylor on *Supernatural* studies.

Anastasia **Salter** is an associate professor of digital media at the University of Central Florida. Her publications include *Toxic Geek Masculinity in Media* (2017, coauthored with Bridget Blodgett), *Jane Jensen: Gabriel Knight, Adventure Games, Hidden Objects* (2017), and *What Is Your Quest? From Adventure Games to Interactive Books* (2014). She is collaborating with the editorial team of the Electronic Literature Collection, Volume 3 (2016) and is coediting the "Comics as Scholarship" experimental issue for *Digital Humanities Quarterly* (2015).

Rebecca **Stone Gordon** is working on an MA in public anthropology at American University in Washington, D.C. Her research areas include feminist theory, disability studies, the history of anatomy, archaeology, and horror in film and literature. She specializes in representations of anthropology, archaeology, and mummies in Anglo-American feature films. She is the director of volunteer management for the Museum of Science Fiction and also holds an interdisciplinary MS in audio technology and visual media from American University.

Amanda [Mandy] **Taylor** has an MA in English composition and literature and is a lecturer at CSU San Bernardino. In addition to *Supernatural*, her research interests include zombies, *Firefly*, *Futurama*, poet John Keats, science fiction, the cultural studies of science, and posthuman theory. Her publications include work on *The Walking Dead*, *Supernatural*, the Apollo space program, and a forthcoming title (from McFarland) on *Futurama*. She plans to continue working with "partner-in-crime" Susan Nylander on more *Supernatural* projects.

Index